321. 4104
CRO

Britain and Europe

This textbook provides a comprehensive account of Britain's uneasy relation-ship with continental Europe from 1918 to the present day.

Unlike other books on the subject, the author considers 'Europe' in its broadest sense and examines a wider history than just Britain's relations with the European Union (EU). This includes pre-war history and the role of key political institutions outside the EU such as the Council of Europe and the Western European Union.

Subjects covered include:

- How the experience of the inter-war years and the Second World War helped shape attitudes towards the EU.
- European perspectives on Britain as well as the other way round.
- Key theories on European integration.
- The changing nature of Britain's global role.
- Issues of sovereignty and legitimacy.
- The role of political parties and the Europeanisation of national government.
- The rise of Euroscepticism in British politics and how 'Europe' has become entwined in the ideological battles of the main political parties.

Exploring the political, diplomatic and military relationship between Britain and Europe, this accessible and wide-ranging textbook is essential core reading for students of British and European history and politics.

N. J. Crowson is Reader in Contemporary British History at the University of Birmingham, UK.

Britain and Europe

A political history since 1918

N. J. Crowson

Routledge
Taylor & Francis Group

LONDON AND NEW YORK

First published 2011 by Routledge
2 Park Square, Milton Park, Abingdon, Oxon, OX14 4RN

Simultaneously published in the USA and Canada
by Routledge
270 Madison Avenue, New York, NY 10016

Routledge is an imprint of the Taylor & Francis Group, an informa business

Typeset in Times New Roman by Taylor & Francis Books
Printed and bound in Great Britain by TJ International, Padstow, Cornwall

British Library Cataloguing in Publication Data
A catalogue record for this book is available from the British Library

Library of Congress Cataloging in Publication Data
Crowson, N. J.
Britain and Europe : a political history since 1918 / N. J. Crowson.
 p. cm.
Includes bibliographical references.
1. Great Britain–Foreign relations–Europe. 2. Europe–Foreign relations–
Great Britain. 3. Great Britain–Politics and government–20th century.
4. Great Britain–Politics and government–1997. 5. Europe–Politics and
government–20th century. 6. Europe–Politics and government–1989. I. Title.
D34.G7C76 2010
327.4104–dc22   2010017481

ISBN: 978-0-415-40018-3 (hbk)
ISBN: 978-0-415-40020-6 (pbk)
ISBN: 978-0-203-84049-8 (ebk)

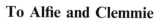

To Alfie and Clemmie

Contents

Abbreviations

ACML	Anti-Common Market League
BEF	British Expeditionary Force
BIE	Britain in Europe group
BNP	British National Party
BSE	Bovine spongiform encephalopathy
CAP	Common Agricultural Policy
CBI	Confederation of British Industries
CFSP	Common Foreign and Security Policy
CID	Committee of Imperial Defence
CJD	Creutzfeldt–Jakob Disease
CRG	European Conservative and Reformist Groups, European Parliament
EC	European Community
ECJ	European Court of Justice
ECSC	European Coal and Steel Community
ECU	European currency unit
EDC	European Defence Community
EEC	European Economic Community
EFTA	European Free Trade Association
EMS	European monetary system
EMU	European Monetary Union
EPC	European Political Co-operation
EPP-ED	European Peoples' Party and European Democrats
EPU	European Payment Union
ERDF	European Regional Development Fund
ERM	European Exchange Rate Mechanism
EU	European Union
Euratom	European Atomic Energy Community
FTA	Free trade area
GDP	Gross domestic product
I-FOR	NATO-led Implementation Force, Bosnia 1995–96
IGC	Inter-governmental conference
IMF	International Monetary Fund

INF	Intermediate nuclear forces
LNU	League of Nations Union
MAC	Mutual Aid Committee
MEP	Member of European Parliament, Strasbourg
MP	Member of Parliament, Westminster
NAFTA	North Atlantic Free Trade Area
NATO	North Atlantic Treaty Organisation
NRC	National Referendum Committee
OECD	Organisation for Economic Co-operation and Development
OEEC	Organisation for European Economic Co-operation
OMC	Open method of co-ordination
OPEC	Organization of Petroleum Exporting Countries
PR	Proportional representation
QMV	Qualified majority voting
SALT	Strategic Arms Limitation Talks
SEA	Single European Act
SNP	Scottish National Party
TUC	Trades Union Congress
UDI	Unilateral declaration of independence
UKIP	United Kingdom Independence Party
VAT	Value Added Tax
WEU	Western European Union
WTO	World Trade Organization

Introduction

Concept: organisations and meaning

The organisational concept of 'Europe' for much of the period of this book was only in the process of being 'defined'.[1] In the inter-war years after 1918 it was a geographical expression sustained by a series of nation-states, many of whom to the eastern periphery were relatively new cartographically determined entities, arising out of the Versailles settlements, loosely generated on the principle of self-determination. By the 1940s and 1950s the geopolitical realities of the Cold War meant that territorially 'Europe' was divided between communist and capitalist blocs, and was being articulated through these nation-states combining militarily, economically and ultimately politically. Organisationally for western Europe this meant that there were a whole raft of Europes: the Council of Europe (from 1948); the Organisation for European Economic Co-operation (from 1947); the European Coal and Steel Community (from 1951); the Western European Union (from 1954); the European Atomic Energy Community (from 1957); the European Economic Community (from 1957) and the European Free Trade Association (from 1958). Only with the collapse of the Soviet Union's empire after 1989 would the perspective open up once more to include the fledgling democracies of eastern Europe. In Britain, and particularly in populist terms since the 1960s, the European Economic Community (EEC) has become the organisation synonymous with 'Europe', and of all the 'Europes' it has most disproportionately absorbed the energies of British politicians, the media and public opinion. The EEC has through a succession of treaty arrangements and enlargements since 1957 expanded from being an organisation of six member states to one embracing twenty-seven nations, with the prospect of still further expansion. Until Britain joined in 1973 it was commonly referred to as either the Six or the Common Market, the latter of which remained in use into the early 1980s. As the organisation has evolved so has its formal name changed from EEC to European Community (from 1993) to European Union (from 2007): a reflection of its widening remit and developmental metamorphism.

What does 'Europe' mean in British usage? At its most basic level it is used interchangeably with 'continental' to imply a geographical area across the

English Channel that does not include Britain. This sense of European, Euro or continental difference from Britain can be used both positively and negatively, but always ultimately to denote difference. Its complexities and divergences are often emphasised, particularly by those warning of the dangers of trying to constrain Europe into an organisational structure. As Conservative shadow foreign secretary Michael Ancram suggested in 2002, the

> multiplicity of descriptions of Europe also hides a massive diversity of languages, peoples, cultures, economics and histories. Some aspects are shared. Many more are different. One has but to look at the patchwork quilt of the history of Europe. It underlines the infinite diversity in our continent which cannot be straight jacketed by simplistic definition.[2]

There might be a common denominator in terms of Christian faith, but then the prevalence of Catholicism on the continent is taken as reason for suspicion.[3] It was not uncommon in the 1960s to hear suggestions that the moves towards European integration were part of a 'papal' plot. In this the appellation 'Treaty of *Rome*', which created the EEC, was perhaps unfortunate.[4] There is a changing sense of influence of the continent on the British public. The impact of European culture from the Ancient Greeks to Italian opera to the paintings of the French impressionists have in one way or another permeated into the educational and cultural psyche of Britain.[5] The centrality of Latin and Ancient Greek in the education system until the mid-20th century implied a desire of British educationalists to associate with a European tradition that stretches back to classical antiquity. However, Latin and Greek are now rare beasts on the curriculum, pushed aside by a belief that dead languages have only limited 'skills' and 'employability' value, despite occasional rallying calls from politicians and the media.[6] The crisis of modern languages teaching experienced in the past thirty years, reinforced by a national curriculum that does not consider the skills of a second language an essential necessity, has emphasised Britain's isolation. This is typified by the media self-congratulation should a British politician address an overseas gathering in the mother tongue of the host nation, and yet there is an inverse presumption that continental politicians will always address us in the 'universal' English language. In terms of history 'British' historians have been prominent in studying and writing the history of many European countries, yet this is under threat from an education system that has seen the 'Hitlerisation' of the curriculum and produced a generation of sixth formers arriving at university unwilling, or unaware, of the breadth of history outside the narrow parameters of the mid-twentieth century and the rise of the European dictators and world war.[7] The cultural heritage of Europe has been widely enjoyed. The great composers like Bach, Beethoven, Mendelssohn, Verdi or Vivaldi hailed from continental lineage, and remind British audiences that perhaps with the exception of a few individuals like Elgar, Britain lacks its own populist classical composing tradition. Something that Gillian Shepherd, as education minister, discovered with her failed patriotic appeal to the BBC to adopt a 'rousing' English work for its theme tune for the coverage of the football Euro '96 competition instead of Beethoven's 'Ode to Joy'.[8] The celebration of British artists such as Damien Hurst, Tracey Emin and Banksey pales into insignificance to the 'blockbuster' appeal of exhibitions of works of the French impressionists or Van Gogh. The mid-nineteenth century had witnessed the growing popularity of German romantic literature and the influence of German methods on the disciplines of science and history. Significantly during World War II there was no attempt to purge the Henry Wood promenade concerts of their German influences, unlike during the First World War.[9] Travel to Europe during the inter-war period may have largely been the preserve of middle and upper classes, but represented a changing pattern of British and European relations. The British elites would decamp en masse to the French Riviera, whilst businessmen were frequent visitors to the continent. These visits did have the tendency to enforce the sense of difference. As one Warwickshire businessman wrote in early 1937 after visiting Germany: 'they are a queer lot over there, they look at things from an entirely different viewpoint to ours and they appear to see no difficulty in holding opinions which on the face of them are mutually contradictory'.[10] At the same time in 1937 Clement Attlee, the Labour leader, commented upon the 'consciousness of insularity' amongst the British left which made it 'difficult for British socialists to understand completely their continental comrades'.[11] Similar views were still being expressed after 1945. Studies that have considered the educational and personal background of foreign policy makers after the Second World War have observed the profound sense of detachment from the continent amongst these individuals.[12] But in fact this insularity was widespread. *Socialist Commentary* bemoaned in 1957 that the 'ordinary worker' had little reason for contact with the continent: 'For him Italians and Belgiums are "foreigners" representing a threat to his carefully cultivated world.'[13] During the first EEC application phase Conservative party officials were reporting amongst their membership a 'deep-seated insularity' and observing a feeling that 'Wogs start at the Channel.'[14] However, a changing of the guard in Whitehall during the 1960s saw a new generation of civil servants move into positions of prominence who were considerably more sympathetic and who saw Europe as a strategy. But it was also a group that increasingly sought to constrain European policy making within a Whitehall cliché. Nevertheless the advent of mass tourism, and the package holiday from the mid-1960s, has meant thousands of British tourists annually now flock to Greece, Spain, Italy and France and this has gone some way to challenging this insularity, whilst spawning new national stereotypes about Germans, towels and sunloungers and the like. The advent of the budget airline and the internet have opened up new opportunities for British interaction, whether purchasing second homes or taking weekend city breaks, whilst British sports fans have become accustomed to their teams, or favoured sports personalities, competing in European competitions, whether in football or rugby, swimming, athletics or motor-racing. Ultimately what this has achieved is to enhance the perception of Europe's closeness yet to reinforce its difference. In political terms, Europe has served as a tool to legitimise political visions, which have in turn reinforced notions of British national identity as both threat and opportunity. That message, and construction, has changed with time and circumstances. Until Britain actually joined the EEC in 1973 'Europe' was a matter of 'external' policy; upon entry European policy became inter-related with domestic policy issues, as European rules and regulations impinged on national planning. There are dangers in over-simplifying, but as Milward has noted, politically Europe is:

> two opposed constructs neither closer to reality. Either it was an entity which, if Britain led it, would restore the country's prosperity and increase its security, or it was an entity which would weaken Britain's economy, reduce its security, curb its freedom of action, and perhaps even bring to an end the very long history of an independent British state.[15]

Terms and phrases

But just as 'Europe' has a multitude of connotations and applications, problems arise too with much of the nomenclature. It is evident that many of the phrases associated with the 'political' integration of Europe have a multi-plicity of meanings amongst the nations involved, within generations and across history and often without agreed unanimity. In British eyes plans for European 'union' are too committal, implying a tight, formal organisational structure, whereas 'unity' is perceived as a more accommodating term that allows for changing circumstances. Confusion can arise in translation. In the articles of the Council of Europe the English text uses the phrase 'closer unity', the French 'une union plus étroite'.[16] The terms 'federalism' and 'appeasement' are two such terms that have changed with time. Winston Churchill in the late 1940s appeared to be quite free to use the word 'federalism', a word that since the 1990s has become a bogey word for those of a Eurosceptic persuasion. There was a tendency to use words like 'unity' and 'federation' without defining their meaning.[17] Yet to Churchill's audiences 'federalism' would have meant conceptions of trust and equality between partners. This was being actively promoted by organisations such as the Federal Union and 'one should not underestimate the influence of the European federalists in setting up different ideas, concepts and programmes on European integration'.[18] Parliament witnessed a number of all-party early day motions (EDMs) in 1948–49 that called for a long-term federal Europe; in more contemporary terms it is negatively perceived as a demand for greater centralised and collective institutional control, at the expense of national decision making processes. This negativity is not recognised by all and these individuals fear that the 'federalist' threat is a smokescreen.[19] Likewise 'appeasement' has largely since 1939 been used synonymously with surrender and concession to threats of force, and has been wielded as a political club to tarnish the reputation of contemporary politicians. In the 1930s it was a realistic strategic option borne out of flaws within the Versailles treaty that obliged its protagonists to seek 'just solutions by negotiation in the light of higher reason instead of by the resort to force'.[20] The changing definition is confirmed by comparing old versions of the *Oxford English Dictionary*.[21] Consequently appeasement as a term is one that some academics have suggested should be dispensed with, something that is suggested too for the term 'sovereignty'.[22] Academics appear unable to reach unanimity about what sovereignty is; yet it is one of the most potent of terms in the debates about Britain's organisational relationship with Europe.[23] For some it is concerned with national autonomy, whether in political, economic, legal or military decision making. For others it equates with notional rights that risk being signed away by acts of European integration. In foreign policy terms it is often portrayed as an issue of Britain exercising influence and power on the international stage without excessive external interference. It can also be portrayed as an ever-evolving concept, and in the sense of European integration has been likened by Geoffrey Howe, British foreign secretary in the late 1980s, to that of a rope with different strands representing the sovereignty of individual nation-states that are intertwining together to strengthen the bond and to which additional rope can be spliced.[24] Being aware of the shifting, and contested, nature of the phrases in the debate about Britain and European relations is important, not least because it is crucial to understand what the politicians and diplomats who employ them are thinking. Politicians are what they speak and publish.

The process of integration has also created a new language to explain the development and institutional procedures. Functionalism, neo-functionalism, and intergovernmentalism have emerged as theoretical frameworks to explain the moves towards closer unity. Over time each has fallen out of favour and been then rediscovered and redeployed. Since the 1990s the theoretical approaches have begun to shy away from seeking to explain the process of integration and have instead tried to capture more specialised elements of the governing and policy process. The challenge for these theoretical approaches has been to establish the empirical basis to sustain the theory. Neo-functionalism, which rose to prominence with Haas' 1958 study of the ECSC,[25] saw in the founding fathers a willingness to adopt technocratic processes which aimed at the transfer of functions from the nation-state to supranational bodies. This transfer of functions, or spillover, was used to explain how the expectations of key players shifted towards advocating greater integration. The argument that those Conservatives who served on the Council of Europe, earning the nickname Tory Strasbourgers, returned to British politics willing advocates of closer integration, appears to sustain this, and yet studies of former MEPs who subsequently took seats at Westminster, show they quickly abandoned their European credentials.[26] Events have also weakened neo-functionalism. The 'empty chair' crisis provoked by De Gaulle and the subsequent stagnation of EEC development in the 1970s appeared to render it unviable. Although neo-functionalism enjoyed a brief revival in the mid-1980s its approach is largely dismissed, although some leading theorists caution against dismissing 'its conceptual repertoire entirely'.[27] Much of the work of Alan Milward has similarly challenged neo-functionalism and presented the case that the EU is about national policy choices. This idea of intergovernmentalism, as epitomised by Stanley Hoffman's influential 1966 study,[28] sees the nation-state as the dominant actor in the EU. States engage in collective bargaining in order to protect their executive autonomy and sovereignty, but will concede some matters of sovereignty to supranational bodies with limited autonomy if they are able to achieve shared collective interests. Alongside these, concepts such as constitutionalism and governance have emerged. Constitutionalism sees integration as an evolving process that gains its constitutional authority through a succession of gradual expansions of its areas of competence and legal interest; whilst governance is less of a theory than a methodology that recognises that the EU is a complex structure in which national governments play significant roles in the 'defining' elements of treaty reform, but that community institutions and interests play an important role refining the remit of the EU at the lower orders. In recent decades newer strands of theoretical explanation have arisen, whether institutionalism, rational choice or multi-level governance. Rational choice theory would appear to overlook the relevance of a government's electoral self-interest whilst institutionalist theory has a premise about the long-term positions of actions and the gradual development of attitudes – does this really mean that Britain's European policy can be explained in terms of a strategic project? Some have suggested that institutionalism should be viewed on a theory spectrum ranging from rational choice institutionalism to new institutionalism to historical institutionalism. What links them is the assumption that with the presence of institutions, actors pursue their preferences around them. Therefore if treaty rules are amended the actors are obliged to reconsider the manner in which they will act in order to secure their preferences.[29] Multi-level governance advocates that different patterns of policy making occur in different areas of EU activity and that governance is being redirected away from national government towards a variety of public and private agents. In explaining the development of the theoretical approaches to European integration it is clear that these are as much bound up in social science fashion as they are in the desire to evolve concepts of what the EU is.[30]

Chronology and traditions

The chronology of Britain and European unity is important too. The overwhelming majority of the literature published on this subject is concerned with the issue from a post-1945 perspective. The 1945 start-point is understandable, both in the convenience that the ending of the Second World War appears to herald a new chronological beginning and because of the processes of organisational integration beginning in the immediate years after. Yet in doing so, this overlooks how the war experience itself was vitally important in shaping attitudes, especially amongst those under Fascist subjugation or in exile in London and Washington.[31] It overlooks too, the nascent discussions about European unity that occurred in the aftermath of the First World War and during the 1930s.[32] But furthermore by ignoring the British response to the continent during the 1920s and 1930s it fails to offer a longitudinal narrative that may explain why Britain appeared to be a reluctant participant in the European project after 1945. Such an approach allows for an appreciation of the fact that the problems facing British policy makers in the years after 1945 were recognisable to the policy makers at the dawn of the twentieth century: how does a nation manage an overextended empire and provide social cohesion and promote economic competitiveness in the face of growing global competition especially from the USA? The questions may have been universally recognised but the solutions were disputed. It appears that two strategic narrative traditions emerge, which have variously found favour with decision makers, but neither has secured continued exclusivity of application. On the one side there is a continental commitment that has demonstrated recognition that Britain should participate in a concert of Europe and that she could have a leadership role of play. Association with Europe economically, as the USA increasingly imposed itself upon the world trading order after 1918, would increase Britain's potential to assert her independence over the USA. In contrast a limited liability tradition saw that prestige in economic and military terms gave Britain a world power, and allowed it to operate either independently, or increasingly as an equal of the USA. A strong British economy based upon empire and world trade were paramount, and the avoidance of continental entanglements would enable Britain to act as the arbiter of the European balance of power either by leading or controlling allies. There is perhaps a danger in adopting such a structuralist framework for it risks robbing the narrative of its historical specificity, of losing the nuance and the detail. The age of Blair and Brown was different from that of Baldwin and MacDonald and these differences should not be ignored. What the long-term view does is offer a perspective on how successive British governments have handled European policy. The individual variable may be circumstanced by particular periods, but the patterns remain remarkably consistent in their broader outline.

The presence of the Second World War, and the descent towards that event, perhaps unbalances the structural approach. Yet there is a psychological hurdle that needs jumping – namely the assumption of guilt associated with the foreign policy events of the Chamberlain administration 1937–39. Although revisionist historians for more than thirty years have striven to rehabilitate Chamberlain's diplomatic travails, the legacy of Munich and appeasement resonates into the post-war political and historical psyche.[33] It is perhaps too convenient to dismiss this foreign policy as something specific to the Chamberlain years, or perhaps of the inter-war period, as does Martin Gilbert when he suggests 'appeasement was born' on 4 August 1914 and until 1937 was a noble policy aimed at reaching an understanding with Germany.[34] In fact it has been suggested that appeasement was a 'positive' policy that can be seen as 'traditional' British foreign policy since the death of Palmerston in 1865. This traditional foreign policy, which rested upon an assumption of man's inherent reasonableness, mixed morality with calculated national interest (economic aspirations, global considerations and domestic concerns). This obliged Britain to consider only the Low Countries and France as being spheres of direct interest and to diplomatically retain a freedom of action that allowed her to manipulate the European balance of power by either leading or controlling allies and having the ability to avoid others' quarrels. War was expensive to fight, so the preservation of peace was crucial, and in doing so it was necessary to cap defence costs to ensure sound finance and a strong economy, and in so doing had to prioritise home and naval defence over a continental field force. The growing prevalence of the theory that the economy was the 'fourth arm of defence' recognised Britain's increased reliance on the 'invisibles' of world trade and that these were vulnerable to disruptions and if the economy slowed down then it was harder to pay for economic and social reforms, the so-called 'guns versus butter' argument. But appeasement had a global dimension to it too. Britain's dealings with America demonstrated appeasement at work, whether granting Washington the right to intervene in the Venezuela/British Guiana dispute, or failing to support Canada over the Alaskan boundary quarrel. Of course, there were exceptions: the Anglo–South African wars, the reconquest of Sudan and the naval races against France, Russia and later Germany in the Edwardian era. But the frequent attempts at conciliation with Wilhelminean Germany bear comparison too with the 1930s. The Hague conferences tried to decrease international armaments and when this failed bilateral arms reductions were proposed, such as Churchill's 'naval holiday', the colonial concessions in the Middle East and Africa and Haldane's 1912 mission to Berlin. Although the size of the German fleet and the threat to the Low Countries could not be ignored, there was a natural hope that rationale negotiation would avoid the need for war. This tradition would only end in March 1939 with the guarantee to Poland, by which point the term appeasement had been sullied forever.[35] The idea that 1939/1940 somehow marks a new departure carries some weight. Maurice Cowling sensed that from May 1940, Britain realised that she could only achieve victory by allying with the USA and on her terms. This ultimately led to the loss of the British empire and an economic subservience. Post-war decision makers would consequently look to European integration as a means of alternative interdependence.[36] This thesis downplays the economic domination that the USA had already exerted over Europe, and Britain, during the inter-war years, and the realisation within Whitehall that choices were faced about whether Britain could continue to compete.

Britain's concerns for Europe have been dual throughout: security and commercial. As Baldwin declared in November 1923, the interests of the British Empire in foreign countries are first of all economic and commercial. When we speak of peace being the greatest British interest, we mean British trade and commerce, which are essential to the life of our people, who flourish best in conditions of peace.[37]

What this meant in practice was preventing one power from dominating Europe, and thereby protecting Britain's own security such as the guaranteeing of the Low Countries, or having an interest in affairs of the Mediterranean in order to protect routes to the Far East. The means by which this could be achieved have been contested. Some turned this argument back on itself and proposed that mediating the balance of power was the reason Britain needed to participate in the moves towards unity. Austen Chamberlain in 1925 told the king 'I am working not for today or tomorrow but for some date like 1960 or 1970' by which point a revived Germany would exist. And unless Britain was prepared to mediate between Germany and France 'I say without hesitation that the chance of permanent peace is gone.'[38] As Harold Macmillan told the cabinet in December 1951 in ten years 'there would be a European Community, which would dominate Europe and would be roughly equal to Hitler's Europe of 1940. If we stay out, we risk that German domination of Europe which we have fought two world wars to prevent.'[39] The pedigree of this had longer antecedents stretching into the nineteenth century. In 1897 Lord Salisbury observed

the federated action of Europe ... is our hope of escaping the constant terror and calamity of war, the constant pressure of the burdens of armed peace, which weigh down the spirits and darken the prospect of every nation in this part of the world. The Federation of Europe is the only hope we have.[40]

But was this involvement one of mediation from across the Channel or actual physical commitment? Security demands have variously seen British military forces stationed in Germany in peacetime, whether as occupation forces in the Ruhr in the 1920s or as the British Army on the Rhine during the Cold War, yet when the French sought a military commitment in the 1930s there was considerable reluctance. Consequently an impression emerges of Britain's role with respect to European integration as having been one of piecemeal progress and grudging concession. Yet Britain's perceptions of where her interest lay were broader than just her formal borders. Baldwin speaking to the House of Commons in 1934 observed 'when you think of the defence of England you no longer think of the chalk cliffs of Dover: you think of the Rhine. That is where our frontier lies.'[41] The development of air technology meant this was a view frequently articulated in the 1930s. The division of Europe after 1945, and the presence of British armed forces on the Rhine, meant that, militarily at least, many continued to conceive this as Britain's natural border. With the collapse of communism after 1989, the defence became one supporting 'democracy' such that William Hague could declare 'Our Europe today should not end at the banks of the Oder and the Danube.'[42]

History, democracy and empire

Despite the earlier observation on the importance of European culture to British education, it has also had a negative impact, in the sense of how British policy makers have been liable to interpret recent European history in a manner that betrays both a sense of British superiority and uniqueness. There is a distinctive willingness to dismiss the stability of Europe and its democratic credentials: 'on the continent between 1940 and 1945 it was recognised that the nation state had contained the seeds of its own destruction; in Britain it had achieved its apotheosis.'[43] Anthony Nutting thought he could attribute the Six's desire to sign the Treaty of Rome because they no longer believed in national sovereignty 'as we do' because it had let them down in two world wars. Similarly Derek Walker Smith thought the 'continental and collective' political development of Europe was incompatible with Britain's 'insular and imperial' past. A similar view was expressed by Enoch Powell in 1971: 'the sovereignty of our Parliament is something other for us than what your assemblies are for you', whilst Thatcher considered that for Britain 'European democracy is remote resting on very different traditions.'[44] These sentiments undoubtedly persist today, and manifest themselves in the attacks on the EU's undemocratic structures and repeated questioning of MEPs' and commissioners' integrity and freedom from corruption. The arrogance of the British position is the presumption that Germany and France have willingly hitched their national interest to the European juggernaut without appreciating that perhaps these nations perceive involvement as being in their best interests, and even to the enhancement of their own national interest. For those supporting British involvement these prejudices were frustrating, as one Labour MP bemoaned:

> If we, as a nation, insist that, the Channel being God-given, it is blasphemy to leap it and participate in some form of political union with our friends in Europe, then in the end, we have no place in the Community which, whatever its shortcomings now, is based on a less parochial vision.[45]

However, the sense that European integration was for losers, not winners, has proved hard to shake.

Although contemporary memories of the British empire are long diminished, for much of this period under consideration Britain was an imperial power. Its presence has repeatedly been held up as an explanation for Britain's apparent reluctance to commit to Europe. The very presence of the empire meant that Britain had evolved into a long-term maritime global power as opposed to regional European power. This led to a vast empire of which Britain was the economic and political centre. Her defence system was entwined with imperial possessions. From this arose the prioritised objectives: (a) defence of homeland, (b) defence of trade routes and lines of communication, and (c) defence and development of empire. Powerful forces, at one time or another, would advocate Britain economically allying with her empire through trading preferences. Thus it appeared that due to the need to concentrate on empire, Europe was of less relevance, provided Europe was experiencing relative peace and stability which then left Britain free to pursue her global ambitions. But it needs to be remembered that having an empire was not unique to Britain. In 1957 on signing the Treaty of Rome, both Belgium and France still possessed sizeable empires. Similarly, the notion that Britain has been alone in having other policy models to consider is to disregard the Italian's inter-war view of the Mediterranean as *Mare Nostrum* and the Scandinavian states' recurring interest in Nordic unity. The difference has been that these 'alternatives' have not prevented these nations from considering European integration. They have either been ditched in favour of participating in European co-operation or been incorporated into that country's European strategy.[46]

Lost opportunities and the historiography

Avi Shlaim, writing in the late 1970s, characterised Britain's European policy as 'negative in character and as such was rarely susceptible to precise definition.' Anne Deighton has a slightly more positive perspective, suggesting that contrary to the perceptions of insularity British views of the balance of power required involvement in Europe.[47] Yet a persistent, and almost orthodox, theme of the historiography of Britain's European relations has been one of missed opportunities.[48] Whether a criticism made by key actors from Edward Heath to Denis Healey to Leon Brittan to Douglas Hurd, the idea that somehow Britain has at one point or another chosen a course of non-participation, which explains the contemporary difficulties in the British-European relationship, has taken hold amongst elements of the political establishment.[49] Although some would dismiss this as the politicisation of history by 'self-styled Europeans',[50] the 'missed opportunity' thesis retains a powerful rhetorical hold. Tony Blair used his Ghent speech, 23 February 2000, to lament Britain's response to the 1955 Messina conference as 'one of my country's greatest miscalculations during the post-war years'.[51] It is also a premise based upon the assumption that the means by which the EU has achieved its current format was a more natural route than the alternative offered by Britain at various points. This has presented historians with the challenge of explaining how, and why, Britain's relationship with Europe has evolved as it has, and thereby disentangling the political myth from reality. Consequently diplomatic historians have succeeded in demonstrating how 'Europe' represented one strand of a wider global strategy used by British governments to bolster her international position, and that the presence of extra-European commitments (certainly until the late 1960s) goes a considerable way to explaining the reluctance to join the European project.[52] But this would be to ignore the economic imperatives that underpinned Britain's external economic policy. The need to preserve the pound sterling as an international currency, the problems of sterling-dollar convertibility, appeared to be contradicted by the European project's concern for equality amongst member nations.[53] Historians are also increasingly recognising the importance of domestic pressures on the formulation of Britain's external policies, or what political scientists have termed 'statecraft'.[54] It is evident that party politics, electoral concerns and fears about public opinion have all helped shape the evolution of Britain's European policies.[55] Ultimately what this body of literature demonstrates is that external European policy is not made in a vacuum and that it responds to a web of different, often complex, pressures, whether financial, military, strategic or domestic. The policy makers will prioritise some aspects over others, but the emphasis is in constant flux. The process of governmental administration has essentially been the emphasis of the overwhelming majority of studies on Britain and Europe, with relatively little on the popular or cultural aspects of the relationship. From the earliest near-contemporary accounts of the 1961 EEC application the complexities of balancing the economic, political, domestic and strategic differences between Britain and Europe have been brought out to explain the reluctance of British policy makers to embrace the European vision.[56]

Observation needs to be made too about the credentials of many of the early writers, who, it has been observed, 'possessed multiple identities: political activists, journalists, broadcasters and contemporary historians'.[57] Individuals like Miriam Camps: an American, she served with the US State Department 1939–54 and again in the 1960s where she specialised in problems relating to the European economic co-operation, alongside spending a period as an editor on the *Economist* 1954–56, one of the early media champions of integration. Broadly sympathetic to the concept of European integration, she authored the seminal study *Britain and the EEC* (1964), in which she demonstrated how the economic, political and strategic differences between Britain and Europe explained the reluctance of British policy makers to embrace the supranational project. Her privileged access to policy makers, even briefing the Conservative party on a number of occasions, gave her work an authority that would not be challenged until the opening up of the archives in the 1980s.[58] Another would be the Oxford don Uwe Kitzinger, who served as the first British economist at the Council of Europe 1951–56, followed by a period in the early 1970s as advisor to Christopher Soames, the first British vice-president of the European Commission. Kitzinger founded the *Journal of Common Market Studies* in 1961 and wrote key books on the 1970s negotiations and referendum processes.[59] Other examples would include John Pinder of the Federal Trust and Political and Economic Planning (PEP) and author of numerous books on European integration.[60] Also, Roger

Broad, Labour party apparatchik in the 1960s who established the Young European Left and edited the monthly *Newsbrief* for the Labour Common Market Committee, and subsequently become the European Parliament's press officer in London 1964–73 and founding member of the British section of the Association of European Journalists in 1969.[61]

Early portrayals of Labour's relationship with Europe suggested that the party and their government of 1945–51 desired greater European integration and only differed over the means of achieving it: by federalist or functionalist methods? This is a verdict now overturned by historians.[62] Understanding the British decision to seek EEC membership has drawn considerable academic attention. Some see the process as being driven by economic factors, whether globalisation, balance of payments issues, the industrial structure of the UK, or the growing stagnation of imperial markets for Britain.[63] Others sense a political rationale. The failure of détente at the 1960 Paris summit demonstrated to Macmillan that Britain's diplomatic clout was diminishing and the importance of sustaining Anglo-US relations was paramount.[64] Alan Milward has suggested that the global strategy of Britain was that of seeking to maximise her position by whatever means, whether imperial preference, an independent nuclear deterrent, or if necessary EEC membership. A sense had arisen that exclusion risked weakening Britain's influence with the USA (which appeared to be turning towards West Germany) and further damaging the economy.[65] For Milward the July 1962 summit with the Six was the point at which Britain realised that EEC membership had to be a central objective of British strategy.[66] That may have been the case for the leadership of the Conservative party, but it's not clear that Labour thought similarly. Gaitskell and Wilson had strongly opposed Macmillan's entry bid, and it seemed that despite their return to government in 1964 little had changed. Indeed, near-contemporary analysis characterised Labour as taking office with outdated assumptions about Britain's world power which obliged them to undertake a rapid re-evaluation, one that left them realising that EEC entry was Britain's only choice. This was a situation that American political scientist Robert Leiber characterised as 'collapsing alternatives'.[67] In seeking to explain the failures of the first two applications, a range of views is offered. Prominent is the role of the French, and their leader De Gaulle. His ability to act independently was enhanced by his resolution of the Algerian uprising and having secured his own political position.[68] Some suggest that Britain's acceptance of the deal on Polaris nuclear technology at Nassau in December 1962 was the final straw for De Gaulle and his vision of a 'European Europe'.[69] Likewise, should Britain shoulder the burden of failure? Were the terms outlined by Macmillan squandering the opportunity, making it too much for the Six to accept, or did domestic pressures prevent Britain from offering concessions?[70] The internal dynamics of the EEC (as with the CAP negotiations or the Empty Chair crisis) also added to complexities of the negotiations – it was not solely the case of negotiating with one entity: before the EEC could even come to the table with Britain agreement had first to be reached amongst the Six. It has also been shown that the British first application forced the Six to consider precisely where, and by what means, they wished to evolve. Thereafter Britain was trying to join a club on terms and conditions that were very much skewed against it.[71] Also, would Britain's position have been stronger if she had been more active in courting Adenaur and West Germany?[72] Explaining Wilson's reversal of position has proved more complex. Parr has argued that by the mid-1960s Wilson had accepted that membership had to happen whether now or at a later point, but that he failed (and indeed made no effort) to secure a consensus for the terms on which Britain would enter and as a result this was 'a contributory factor to later distaste towards the terms of Community membership'.[73] It has been a criticism that Whitehall has deliberately sought to restrict the debate and policy formation.[74]

Political science has recognised the centrality of electoral/domestic interests in the policy making of EU nation-states, likening it to 'domestic statecraft'.[75] In the British sphere the EU policy has been 'just another Zimmerframe' that allowed governments to subvert foreign policy to domestic concerns.[76] This has concerned historians too and carries echoes of Maurice Cowling's conclusions about the association between 1930s foreign policy and domestic party politics.[77] Although the Conservative party since 1997 has been a Eurosceptic party, its position has been anything but consistent on the matter. At various times it has been damning of concepts of European unity, at others indifferent, and for much of the 1960s and 1970s its leadership vigorously promoted entry into the EEC. Since the 1990s 'Euroscepticism' has become an 'article of faith'[78] and ideology has crept into the formula. The party's civil war from Maastricht onwards has been well documented, as has the parliamentary party's Commons rebellions.[79] The issue has proved just as toxic for the Labour party, contributing to the party's split in 1981, and has long been an ideological battleground for the varying interpretations of socialism, social democracy and political economy.[80] Furthermore, the Maastricht legislation provoked the most instances of Labour rebellion in the 1992–97 parliament.[81]

One feature of the debate about Britain and Europe has been the relatively unhindered application of the 'pro' and 'anti' European tags to key participants. Yet, just as scholarship has shown that the late 1930s 'anti-appeaser' label is no more than a mirage that has been abused and obscured a wide divergence of perspectives on foreign policy, the same is proving of the post-war 'European' protagonists.[82] Robins suggests a direct correlation between Labour left wing views and opposition to EEC entry, although a less obvious association between the Labour right and support for entry. What is suggested is that, in fact, the party should be viewed from the perspective of a fundamentalist left, a revisionist right and a 'solid' non-aligned centre.[83] Others have noticed similar divisions with the Conservative party, with a large 'agnostic' rump supported on the extremes by minorities of either enthusiastic champions of European entry or implacable opponents.[84] Studies of 1990s parliamentarians demonstrated that individual positions on Europe indicated that these failed to conform to neat ideological left/right divisions.[85] It is largely accepted that to talk of 'pro' and 'anti' as groups is to attribute to them an artificial cohesion and consistency that has never been the case. Individuals over time, even short periods, have reversed their stances, such as Peter Walker and Richard Body. The reality is that when a politician appeared to take a stance on Europe that was in contradiction to their basic conceptions of political economy it would be because considerations such as nationalism, idealism and sovereignty overrode. The year 1975, with the EEC referendum, provides an obvious separation point. Prior to the referendum the debates revolved around whether UK membership, or an alternative form of closer political and economic association, was necessary. After 1975 membership was a reality and the questions now were how Britain would work in Europe and how Europe would work for Britain.

Much of the political science writing on EU affairs has less been concerned with Britain and Europe, than explaining and interpreting the evolution of EU institutional processes. For example, Garrett and Tsebelis have sensed a strengthening of the EU Council as a result of the co-decision process whilst contradictory explanations are offered for the roles of the Commission and the European Courts of Justice.[86] Wincott has argued that these institutions have demonstrated creativity in developing and extending the remit of the EU's founding fathers, whilst Pollock has attributed this to the preparedness of the member states to delegate tasks to these supranational institutions.[87] Analysis of the Single European Act has seen neo-functionalists finding evidence of spillover in the moves towards greater social policy co-ordination and monetary union; whilst inter-governmentalists would portray it as an obvious case of treaty reform arising from the convergence of mutual interests in Britain, France and Germany. The SEA was the subject of Jim Buller's 'Europeanisation' thesis in which he argued that Thatcher and Major saw domestic advantages in linking the British economy with Europe, but that the consequences (greater integration and increased Euroscepticism) were unintended.[88] In doing so this goes someway to explaining why some appeared to favour an international monetarism, over domestic monetarism, as a more credible counter-inflation measure in the mid-1980s. Yet given the turmoil over the ERM in the 1980s, the suddenness of Thatcher's sanctioning entry into the system in October 1990 is perhaps surprising.[89]

Over the next five chapters this book will offer a survey of Britain's political relationship with Europe since 1918. Such a study cannot expect to explain every detail of the process, but in taking a survey approach it hopes to explain how and why the British response to Europe ensued and in doing so to consider whether Britain should be characterised as an 'ace-setter', 'foot-dragger' or 'fence-sitter'?[90] Chapter 1 illustrates how during the inter-war years, despite wishing to withdraw eventually from the continent, economic and diplomatic necessities and the growing impact of the USA obliged the British policy makers to observe a limited liability brief over the continent. Chapter 2 shows how a multitude of 'Europes' emerged in the immediate years after 1945, some of which were perceived as being compatible with British interests, and others less palatable. Throughout these early initiatives British policy makers maintained the perspective of limited liability, believing that Britain should be a sponsor rather than a participant in continental affairs. This position was reversed during the 1960s, as Chapter 3 demonstrates. Although a declineist narrative undercurrent is at work, there was a growing sense amongst the decision making elites that joining Europe was a positive strategy. The difficulty was that they found themselves joining a club that had already determined the rules in its own interests, some of which were detrimental to British interests. Confirmation of entry in 1975 meant that henceforth successive governments had the challenge of making Britain in Europe work. Chapter 4 illustrates how Thatcher used Europe as a tool in her domestic statecraft, but that the process of 'Europeanisation' meant the entwining of domestic policy with European. For much of the 1980s Conservatives were prepared to set aside their concerns in the belief that the wider Conservative project was still being enhanced. However, from the late 1980s that belief began to dissipate and the issue of Europe became a toxic cocktail as it linked together domestic and international policies. The result was electoral catastrophe for the Conservatives, and thirteen years of Labour rule from 1997 under Blair and Brown. In the final chapter the contradictions inherent in New Labour's Europeanism become apparent as first it appears to offer to re-embrace the European project and then reverts to a more typical grudging attitude. The refusal to sanction membership of the euro zone, and the scepticism about the European constitution, appear to suggest a schizophrenia. Behind all of this lay an apparent 'negativity' amongst 'public opinion' towards Europe which seems to have persuaded successive governments that it remains in their domestic interest to avoid becoming European positivists.

1   Inter-war years 1918–39

With European war imminent, the British foreign secretary, Edward Grey, observed 'The lamps are going out all over Europe; we shall not see them lit again in our lifetime.'[1] Even so, the scale and magnitude of the war could not have been envisaged. When the guns finally fell silent on 11 November 1918 the casualties suffered by the British empire alone were 908,000 killed and 2,090,000 wounded. Overall the British and their allies lost 5 million killed, 13 million wounded, and 4 million either prisoners of war or missing; whilst Germany and her allies (Austria, Turkey and Bulgaria) had 3.3 million killed, 8.3 million wounded and 3.6 million as POWs. The material damaged inflicted upon western Europe was intensive, but confined to a relatively narrow geographical strip. Although a global war, the scale of the destruction caused some to consider it a European civil war, and then the uncertainty of the new world scene owing to the Russian Revolution and the growing economic pre-eminence of America led to questions about the merit of the European order. The absence of any 'European institutional' form during the inter-war years would mean that 'Europe', what it was, what it meant and where it should go, shifted over time with each of the problems and proposals that emerged.

Negotiating the peace: Versailles and the new international order

Although the armistice took effect from 11 a.m. on 11 November 1918, in the eyes of some, European civilisation was still under threat from revolutions and diseases – flu pandemic, cholera and typhoid – and small-scale conflicts in central and eastern Europe, such as in Poland, threatened the stability. The speed at which hostilities were concluded found the Allies unprepared for negotiating peace. The British had a special inquiry in 1917, but its conclusions had little impact on Prime Minister Lloyd George. Furthermore, events were unfolding at a pace that the Allied victors had little control over. Poland was recreated, whilst Finland and the Baltic states were moving towards independence and Czechoslovakia had merged itself; likewise in the Balkans Serbia appeared to be linking up with Croatia and Slovenia. The fragility of the European economies was a serious concern, and it would take until 1925 till Europe was back to its pre-war levels of production. The absence of

Bolshevik Russia from the Paris conference, who had taken the 'cowards' peace' and signed the Treaty of Brest-Litovsk, meant that this dimension of the peace deal would not be satisfactorily resolved. The subjects of Finland, Poland, Estonia, Latvia amongst others all were issues for the peace conference, but their borders could not be finally confirmed until the future shape and status of Russia was established. For Clemenceau, the French president, this was inconsequential: Russia had betrayed the Allied cause in prematurely suing for peace and leaving France to the mercy of the Germans.[2]

The late entry of the USA into the First World War meant that when the peace came to be negotiated the old tripartite relationship of Germany, Britain and France, was broken open and a new more complex dimension added. Both Britain and France initially vied for 'most preferred' status with the USA, and it took both quite some time to appreciate that America intended to pursue its own aims and objectives.[3] President Wilson had expounded his views in a speech on 8 January 1918 in which he explained his fourteen points and added four principles and five particulars. Neither the French nor the British had been asked for their views on Wilson's points.[4] The Germans had already successfully offended the British and French by secretly approaching the Americans to discuss armistice terms, and Wilson compounded the offence by conducting two weeks of negotiations before the Allies found out, and the Supreme War Council stepped into the fray.[5] In a sense both Britain and France had similar objectives from the peace negotiations, namely a desire for security. The difference was that Britain hoped it could turn its back on Europe once this threat was neutralised (and the scuttling of the German fleet at Scapa Flow gifted them this) and seek safety in an imperial vision, whilst France continued to crave continental security against Germany. The prospect of a reinvigorated British empire appeared a possibility given that Dominion troops had fought in both large numbers and with success in Europe. The mother country and the Dominions had cooperated with one another in the Imperial War Cabinet, and the Dominions were all to be represented at the peace conference, and the empire would be swollen by the accession of the mandated territories (the imperial possessions of the defeated nations, put under the authority of the League of Nations and passed on around the victorious powers to hold in mandate). France had no such luxury, despite a significant empire; geographical location meant she was next door to Germany, and the war had effectively removed many of her traditional allies: Tsarist Russia was now Bolshevik, and eastern Europe had been broken up into various small nations, none of whom could offer realistic defence against Germany. The problem was that the means by which security could be achieved provoked very different responses and strained the Allies' relationship. The opening up of the French archives in the 1970s has led some historians to revise their verdict of French inflexibility during the peace negotiations – not that this meant that France was not trying to enhance her diplomatic position.[6] Clemenceau had tried to insist that French alone be the language of the Versailles conference documents, as for long periods French had been the official language of diplomacy and international congresses, but was forced to back down and accept it jointly with English – a precursor of the EEC debate in 1970. Furthermore within the Council of Four English was the working language.[7] Fortunately for Clemenceau he possessed a good competency with English. At the end of the First World War, the leaders of Europe were faced with the possibilities of trying to re-establish a global order based either on a regional format or a global one. This was certainly captured in the title of an influential book by Giovanni Agnelli (the founder of Italian car manufacturer Fiat) and Attilio Cabiati (an economist), *European Federation or League of Nations?* (1918). Their answer was 'a federation of European states under a central power which governs them. Any other milder version is an illusion.'[8] They broadly argued that a League of Nations could not expect to prevent war due to its absolute sovereignty whereas federation, in which sovereignty was pooled, could because it would work better in an age of economic interdependence. In developing these ideas they were deeply influenced by writers of the liberal tradition, and drew upon the American constitutional experience as evidence for their thesis. Certainly this work, and others by the likes of Luigi Einaudi and Coudenhove-Kalergi, influenced a generation of continental politicians, but it is unclear what impact it had in Britain.[9] The political establishment was swept up in the rhetoric of American president Woodrow Wilson and opted for his global vision of a League of Nations, but also because many in Europe were looking to America for aid and protection. The French for guarantees against a resurgent Germany, and the Germans for protection from a vengeful France. From January 1919 until August 1920 a series of peace conferences were conducted in Paris, with neither Russia nor Germany invited, during which not just the problems of Germany but also those of central Europe and the Balkans were thrashed out. Consequently, in addition to the Versailles treaty (28 June 1919) a further four treaties, complete with clauses on disarmament, reparations and 'war guilt', were initialised: the Treaty of St Germain with Austria (10 September 1919), the Treaty of Trianon with Hungary (4 June 1920), the Treaty of Neuilly with Bulgaria (27 November 1919) and the Treaty of Sèvres with Turkey (10 August 1920).

Under the terms of the Versailles settlement Germany was stripped of some territories (Alsace-Lorraine to France, the Saar region placed under League of Nations control, Danzig made a free city, Posen and elements of West Prussia given to Poland) as well as her colonial empire, her overseas investments and her merchant shipping fleet. She was denied a navy and an air force and granted only a small army. The Anschluss (union between Germany and Austria) was prohibited under the terms of the Treaty of St Germain, whilst the Sudetenland was redrawn into the borders of Czechoslovakia. The Allies inserted two clauses into the Treaty of Versailles, which would have a lasting significance. Article 231 obliged Germany and her allies to accept responsibility for the outbreak of war and became known as the 'war guilt' clause. Article 232 called upon Germany to compensate for specific civilian damages but recognised that Germany did not have adequate resources. This clause, although used to justify the settlement of reparations, actually carried a degree of moderation within its wording because it sought to protect Germany from the cost of the entire war. However, the settlement of reparations was to cause the most difficulty for the Allies. Lloyd George, concerned that the British electorate might not accept a relatively moderate settlement, insisted on tacking the pensions for all servicemen into the total of the UK reparations bill. Contrary to subsequent impressions the French were initially moderate in their demands, even proposing to tie up with the German iron and steel industry to mitigate the impact. The choice facing the French was ultimately one of ruining themselves or ruining their former foe. In settling on an interim reparations bill of 20 billion gold marks payable by May 1921, they chose the latter option. But in doing so the outcome of 1918 was that France risked being economically ruined by reconstruction, leaving Germany, who had experienced less material damage, with the potential to become economically dominant.[10]

The critics of the settlements emerged almost immediately from the British and American delegations to the Peace Conference. Maynard Keynes saw the settlement as both vindictive and disastrous whilst Harold Nicolson blamed the flawed peace on the conference's chaotic organisation. The American, Ray Stannard Baker, who had acted as Wilson's press secretary at the conference, criticised the European powers' vindictiveness for the punitive peace.[11] Historians have subsequently reapportioned the blame. Marc Trachtenberg is critical of Wilson's moralism which insisted upon Germany paying reparations, rather than agreeing a package that would have bundled debts, reparations and reconstruction together, and which would have seen the US cancellation of war debts and a contribution to reconstruction being made in a manner comparable to the 1947 Marshall Plan.[12] The manner in which the German delegation was obliged to unconditionally accept the terms in June 1919 also caused disquiet. It would fuel Germany's intense sense of injustice and hatred of the terms, which helped perpetuate many of the myths that would sustain the Nazi regime in the 1930s.

Britain did not regard Versailles as a definitive settlement; rather it was a flawed peace that required renegotiation in favour of Germany. Still, it would enable Britain to refocus her attentions. As Maurice Hankey, secretary to the Cabinet, penned in 1920 'we should as far as possible avoid military responsibilities in Europe, and devote our main attention to development of our overseas trade'.[13] Reviving Britain's economy after the dislocation was paramount. The League of Nations appeared to help with Hankey's first recommendation, as it enabled Britain to avoid specific commitments and instead shelter behind the vaguer provisions of the League's covenant. By the 1930s British politicians would repeatedly stress that Britain had no commitments to Europe beyond those entailed in the covenant of the League of Nations.[14] Consequently she wished to reduce her European role to that of impartial mediator. For now though it at least allowed Britain to physically withdraw from the continent – if one overlooks the involvement of British forces in the Russian civil war on behalf of the Whites, and the presence of an occupation force in the German Ruhr.

The League of Nations was drafted into the first chapter of each of the peace treaties. It was largely an Anglo–American work; Wilson was the intellectual force, British Conservative minister Lord Robert Cecil and General Jan Smuts of South Africa the detailed draftsmen. Consequently it carried that whiff of 'Anglo-Saxonism' that usually riled the French. Further, they were doubtful that it would provide the degree of security that they craved. It aspired to promote open diplomacy through a managed great power format that would oblige signatories to accept the rule of international law, to reduce armaments and to recognise and sustain the independence and integrity of member states. All of this would be co-ordinated through a council and permanent secretariat based in Geneva, which would seek to provide international arbitration to diplomatic disputes and through the threat of collective action hope to dissuade covenant breakers and avoid a repeat of the events of 1914. Disillusionment with the League of Nations order did emerge in Europe, especially once America retreated back into isolation and refused to join the organisation its president had helped create. Some recognised that by being a voluntary association of member states it was already weakened. Others sensed the contradiction between the insistences upon the equality of members in an organisation that operated on terms dictated by the great powers. There was a danger too that the Versailles settlement had actually fragmented Europe and sown the seeds for future problems. The break-up of the old multinational empires of Turkey and Austria–Hungary now meant myriad nation states 'created by woolly headed nationalists' in east and central Europe which whilst proud of their nationalist roots contained substantial minority populations.[15] The challenge had been to cauterise the localised wars in the region and prevent the spread of Bolshevism whilst satisfying expectations of subject nationalities that may have been promised enhanced post-war autonomy. That was one of the oddities of the several different peace treaties negotiated over eighteen months: that Germany as the principal defeated power survived largely intact (losing only 13.5 per cent of her 1914 territory, mostly to Poland) whereas Germany's main allies, Austria–Hungary and the Ottoman empire, ceased to exist.[16] Furthermore, the Versailles settlements had mixed idealism with revenge, and consequently failed to resolve the Franco–German problem.

Within the British establishment views of Europe there were two schools of thought. There were those who sensed that the Anglo–German rivalries of 1904–18 were an anomaly and were therefore more wary of France's intentions in the post-war world than of Germany; and those, like Austen Chamberlain, who sensed that Britain owed more to the *entente cordiale* with France. Added to this was a perception that Britain remained an imperial rather than continental power. Britain repeatedly refused to commit itself to the French network of alliances in eastern Europe. There was clearly a sense immediately after Versailles that France was the dominant continental power, but suspicion of France's interchangeable use of terms like security and hegemony persisted. A contradiction wryly observed by foreign secretary Arthur Balfour that the French 'were so dreadfully afraid of being swallowed up by the tiger, but would spend their time poking it'.[17] Yet the British failed to appreciate that with France now acting as arbiter to the European balance of power, her presence on the continent was required to nurture a Franco–German rapprochement. But withdrawal from continental commitments was the British intention. The French had failed to notice that during the Versailles negotiation Lloyd George had duplicitously downgraded the scale of commitment that Britain would offer France under the Agreement of Assistance. He inserted a clause that would 'only' make this valid if the USA ratified the Treaty of Versailles and the appended Agreement of Assistance. So when on 19 March 1920 the Americans failed to do so, the commitment to France was null and void in British eyes.

The reparations problem

Whilst Versailles had agreed that a payment of reparations was necessary it did not define the sum Germany should pay, rather this was left to a series of reparations conferences in the early 1920s. The problem was that without a settlement there was little hope of developing a lasting European peace, but also it meant that economics, foreign policy and politics were intimately entwined.[18] By now Britain was suffering an economic recession. The Treasury sought to pursue a policy that would ensure Germany was forced to pay equitable sums that would not damage her purchasing power for British goods whilst seeking to ensure American resources continued to be inwardly invested in Europe at a time when the Americans were insisting on the repayment of war debts. Entwined in this complex web of negotiation was the need of the British to appear unified with the French whilst trying to pacify the French desire for revenge and the need to understand the complexities of the German economy as it teetered on the verge of hyperinflation and collapse. Matters were further complicated by the intra-Whitehall rivalries between the Foreign Office and the Treasury over whether this was a matter for diplomacy or commercial policy. The Foreign Office's abilities in the economic sphere were hindered by the Treasury controlling expenditure, the Board of Trade overseeing trade policy and the Bank of England regulating fiscal policy. As for commercial policy, this was distasteful to the professional diplomats of the Foreign Office. It would not be until 1931 that the Foreign Office created an economic intelligence unit, but even then it only afforded it one desk officer.[19] During the 1920 negotiations, the British foreign secretary, Curzon, had been seeking to encourage the Germans to resist the agreeing of a final fixed total in preference for a flexible scheme that would take account of Germany's ability to pay reparations in light of her economic position. It appears that in the December 1920 Brussels conference this position was undermined by D'Abernon, the British ambassador to Berlin, and then exacerbated by subsequent disagreements between himself and Sir John Bradbury, who had the ear of the Treasury, and was Britain's representative on the Reparations Commission.[20] On 27 April 1921 revised reparation payment terms were established at 132 billion gold marks. Although all sides made considerable political mileage from this notional figure, it conveniently ignored the real total of reparations being 50 billion gold marks over a 36-year period that was hidden away in the technical appendixes of the agreement. Although this was still a significant figure it is probable that it fell within the abilities of Germany to pay. The protracted negotiations during 1921 were aggravated when Lloyd George agreed to British and French troops extending their occupation of German territory by moving troops into three Ruhr cities (Dusseldorf, Duisburg and Ruhrort) and establishing a customs barrier between these and the remainder of Germany. What this succession of international European reparations conferences showed was the growing recognition that economics was a vital component of foreign diplomacy. They suggested too that Lloyd George, conscious of informed opinion in Britain, was trying to claw back on the reparations terms it had felt unable to moderate at Versailles. Since the publication of Keynes' *The Economic Consequences of the Peace* in December 1919 there had been a steady stream of revulsion against the economic clauses of the peace treaties, and a growing sense that further German instability could have very profound effects. There was a considerable degree of double standards in British public opinion's position. Britain received 1,653,000 tons of German merchant shipping in reparations in kind without any objection, yet the French claims (which were still to be met) in the form of coal or coke were unjust or unworkable.[21] But matters soon deteriorated still further.

Lloyd George, motivated by increased concerns about German fiscal and monetary policy, convened a conference on security, economic reconstruction and reparations in Genoa during April 1922. The conference accepted the principle that Germany should only be made to pay what the nation could afford and that a loan of 4 billion marks should be given, although ultimately the conference was a failure. The USA refused to attend, as did the French, whilst the Russian and German delegations departed early to conclude the terms of their own bilateral deal: Rapallo, which was announced on Easter Sunday. This restored diplomatic relations between the two countries, and revoked claims of war debt whilst promising one another future economic assistance. It was the first official agreement to recognise the Bolsheviks as the new 'legitimate' rulers of Russia. Weimar's diplomats hoped this defiant act would drive a wedge between Britain and France and oblige both to face up to realities of treaty enforcement. The British were caught unawares by this development and feared that it suggested Germany was moving away from the Allies, and indeed it witnessed a rapid deterioration in relations. It was a 'gratuitous insult', fumed the British foreign secretary.[22] From the perspective of the Foreign Office, by being based upon an ideology the Bolsheviks defined rational calculation, but they presented a significant headache because communist activities (or perceived activities) were a significant threat to the British empire, particularly along the frontiers of Persia, Afghanistan and China, forcing London to keep a tight observation on Russia's actions. British forces had assisted the Whites during the Russian civil war. The overarching problem that faced Britain was her inability to understand how ideology applied to the actions of Moscow. As such a new phenomenon from 1917 Britain continued to seek to evaluate it within a traditional rational international relations framework, the outcome of which was usually a response that either sought to smoother with kindness or veered to diplomatic ostracism in the hope of bringing Moscow to its senses. These mistakes would be repeated with the rise of Nazi Germany.[23]

Since 1917 observers had waited to see whether the Bolsheviks would succeed in transforming the Soviet economy into an 'industrial' giant. The New Economic Policy of 1921 and the first five-year plan in 1928 appeared as potential signs of this intent. The danger was that if Russia succeeded in becoming an organised industrial nation no one in Europe would be able to match her economic might; Europe therefore needed to reorganise itself quickly after the end of the First World War. Coudenhove, one of the leading proponents of European unity, advocated a series of pacts between Europe and Russia in order to guarantee the borders of eastern Europe and thereby reduce the likelihood of Russian intervention in European affairs. Yet the British concluded, and then held this belief for much of the 1920s and early 1930s, that the Soviet Union and Weimar Germany were not strong enough to embark upon aggressive actions against their European neighbours, let alone offer assistance to one another, and consequently determined that Rapallo did not merit serious concern.[24] Although officials were generally dismissive of Russian's strengths, they were not averse to using the 'potential' threat in arguments with the French over the revision of Versailles, suggesting on a number of occasions after Rapallo, that the Allies needed to prevent Germany from slipping further into the Soviet orbit. Anglo–French relations were stretched still further by the Chanak crisis in September 1922, which contributed to the fall of Lloyd George's coalition. British and French troops were threatened with attack by Turkish forces, leading Lloyd George (without due consultation of either his foreign secretary, the French or the leadership of the Dominions) to threaten war upon Turkey. This outraged Poincaré, the French prime minister, and aroused considerable criticism from Lloyd George's Conservative coalition partners.[25] It ultimately cost Lloyd George the premiership.

From 1922 Germany was in the grip of a hyperinflation crisis, and by the autumn the German government was seeking a moratorium on reparations payments, but this was declined and in December the Reparations Commission reported that Germany had now defaulted on payments in kind. When a similar statement was issued relating to coal payments in January 1923, the French and Belgian governments determined upon their own solution and their troops entered the Ruhr, only agreeing to withdraw after the London conference of July–August 1924 which accepted the Dawes Plan. French coal and steel interests had been arguing since the war that a resurgent post-war Germany threatened France. This factored into the French attempts to territorially, and economically, fragment Germany during the peace treaties settlements and to subsequently insist on punitive reparations. The Ruhr occupation would collapse in the face of German opposition, British concerns about French ambitions and America's need for a prosperous Germany. But the crisis exposed the fragility of relations between Britain and France, and indicated that Europe had failed to provide a 'European' solution to its problems. Furthermore it sealed the fate of the beleaguered German mark. The response of the British was ambiguous. Whilst privately foreign office officials despaired at the action, they stopped short of public denouncement. Bonar Law's government feared a 'grave and even disastrous result upon the economic situation in Europe'.[26] It ultimately adopted a policy of 'wait and see'. The British were concerned that should the Allies fail to appear united it would make enforcement of the Treaty of Versailles impossible. As the crisis dragged on British public and elite opinion began to harden against the French: it all smacked of Bonapartist hegemonic ambitions. It was recognised too that the crisis was harming Anglo–German commercial relations and threatening Britain's ability to meet the repayments on its American war debts.[27] There was a sense too that this was recognised as a *European* problem – it highlighted the interdependence of the European economies. The consequences were profound nevertheless. Inflation took off in Germany and the French franc lost considerable value on the currency markets. Consequently Poincaré turned to the Americans to rescue the European currencies.

Dawes Plan

The creation of the Dawes and McKenna committees guaranteed American financial assistance in Europe, and ensured that a framework for the payment of future reparations was now in place, enabling Europe to return to matters of security. Suspicion existed about American motives for becoming involved in Europe, certainly some perceived that American commercial interests recognised an opportunity to exploit new markets, whilst also American self-interest meant that if it expected to have the European war debts paid back then the financial stability of Europe was paramount. Tension existed in Anglo–American relations not just because of the war debts issue, but also because of America's failure to ratify the Treaty of Versailles and its refusal to join the League of Nations. Their respective world power visions brought them into diplomatic conflict. London still believed that Britain had the mandate to be the world's dominant maritime power, whilst the Americas believed that they at least deserved equality in this sphere. The Washington Naval Conference of 1921–22, which sought to limit the tonnage and nature of military shipping, went some way towards diffusing this issue, but tensions persisted. Some anxiety existed in London over whether American financial assistance to Germany, and the restoration of diplomatic relations in February 1922, would undermine Britain's relations with the defeated power.

The Dawes Plan was the Allied attempt to resolve the Ruhr occupation and to increase the likelihood that Germany would be able to resume reparation payments. In exchange for the evacuation of Allied occupation forces from the Ruhr, Germany accepted that reparations payments would begin at 1 billion marks increasing to 2.5 billion over the next four years and the Reichbank would be reorganised. Reparations could now include 'in kind' payments such as transportation and custom taxes. In return the Germans were entitled to seek American loans whilst American and British loans to France were made conditional on the acceptance of the plan and withdrawal from the Rhine. This meant that America superseded Britain as the banker of the world's economies, and it made the German economy a matter of world concern, rather than exclusively European. Longer term, it meant that the German economy was tied to the fortunes of the American dollar. It also suggested that unilateral treaty enforcement was not a viable option. The extent of US interest still only remained financial. The fate of European security was still a matter expecting a European solution.

Locarno

The European security solution took a significant step forward when in October 1925 representatives from Britain, France, Germany and Italy met in Locarno, to sign a series of multilateral and bilateral treaties, the principal agreement of which was a Rhineland Security treaty concluded between Gustav Stresemann of Germany, Aristide Briand of France, Louis de Brouckère of Belgium and Austen Chamberlain of Britain. Germany agreed to accept the permanence of her western borders with France and Belgium as outlined at Versailles and the demilitarisation of the Rhineland.[28] A series of arbitration and guarantee treaties also helped resolve Germany's northern frontiers, but nothing was secured for eastern Europe.[29] This emphasis on the west demonstrated France's immediate concerns about Germany, but the failing was to prove costly in the 1930s. Britain joined Belgium and Italy in guaranteeing France and Germany from unprovoked aggression by the other power. Yet, the devil is in the detail, and the guarantee to the French provided Britain with plenty of room for manoeuvre. The guarantee was confined to matters of 'flagrant breach' and 'unprovoked aggression', conditions for which the British were to judge. It was little more than an empty (although hugely symbolic) gesture, in which it was hoped Britain was contributing to an atmosphere that would promote Franco–German reconciliation.

Throughout the early 1920s, Britain's response to the various European crises could be characterised as one of limited liability. The commitments that Britain might be drawn into were weighed against a multitude of imperial, domestic, political and economic considerations, which usually provoked the conclusion that Britain risked becoming committed to continental affairs in areas that carried little relation to British interests. As a consequence the British strategy towards Europe revolved around sheltering behind the League of Nations and seeking to maintain the illusion of the *entente cordiale* with France, although the Ruhr crisis had seriously tested this relationship. Consequently the British decision to guarantee the Locarno treaty appeared as a major break with the limited liability tradition – or was it? As recently as March 1923 and the winter of 1924 Stanley Baldwin had rejected proposals for a security pact between Britain, Germany and France. Yet Locarno also fits with a perception amongst the British foreign policy elites that saw the 1919 Versailles agreement as the beginning of a process of renegotiation, it was not a permanent peace akin to 1815, and consequently Locarno was another stepping stone in that attempt to find a permanent European settlement. Locarno was attractive to Britain because it allowed them to rectify a flaw of Versailles whilst confirming its security obligations to western Europe. Yet these security arrangements (or guarantees) were never formalised into concrete military preparations, and subsequently when they were challenged in March 1936 with Germany's reoccupation of the Rhineland, Britain, France and Italy stood aside.[30]

Lord D'Abernon, the British ambassador in Berlin, has been credited with being the force whom persuaded Stresemann and Briand that they should meet and for being the inspiration of the draft protocol that brought the two men together. The Germans dispatched their proposal for a security pact in January 1925, sending separate dispatches to London and Paris a month apart. Although recent scholarship has challenged D'Abernon's role, suggesting that his influence within the German government was considerably less than has been presumed and that he was excluded from major discussions about strategy and policy, additionally he was experiencing a strained relationship with the British Foreign Office.[31] Whether D'Abernon was Locarno's architect or not, Austen Chamberlain the foreign secretary was certainly convinced that he was.[32] Chamberlain's initial response to the proposals was sceptical; he had certain pro-French sentiments and had been entertaining ideas of a bilateral agreement with France. He had not envisaged that Germany would be the proponent of a new security pact and was therefore wary and wondered whether it was a German attempt to drive a wedge between Britain and France. Austen Chamberlain's biographer firmly takes the view that Locarno marks the continued limitation of British involvement in the affairs of western Europe.[33] Others see Locarno within a framework whereby Britain was trying to pull the main continental powers together into a security framework that promoted conciliation between France and Germany and thereby diminished the likelihood that Britain would again have to fight to maintain the European balance of power.[34] In Britain it was hoped that the integration of Germany into the League of Nations from 1926 would reinforce the influence of mainstream liberal middle-class politicians, diminish Germany's territorial and military revisionism and consolidate the post-war settlement. League membership for Germany offered two opportunities: it presented the possibility to deal with the Allies on an equal basis when renegotiating the terms relating to Germany's security and borders, whilst the desire for a permanent seat on the League Council suggested that Stresemann saw this as an opportunity for promoting German nationalist goals. Ultimately he was balancing the various conflicting influences in German politics. He was aiming, as Jonathan Wright has shown, at peaceful change in Europe whilst establishing a broad nationalist domestic front that would exclude the political extremes from German politics.[35] Britain had been pressing for German membership of the League since 1920, not least to help dispel the idea that the League was merely a tool of French diplomacy. When Germany finally secured membership in September 1926, Britain had achieved her aim, but at what cost? Gaynor Johnson has argued that 'by 1926, it is debatable whether Britain's role in European affairs was more clearly defined than it had been eight years earlier at the signing of the Armistice'.[36] This was because Britain was uncertain where to place her loyalties: was she an imperial power? The primary ally of the French? And if that was the case then indecision remained about the extent to which British policy should be guided by French sensibilities. And was she still an international player, especially given her declining global economic influence? Yet the Foreign Office was confident: 'we have got all that we want – and perhaps more. Our sole object is to keep what we have and live in peace.'[37] Yet almost immediately it appeared that Stresemann and the Germans were making excessive demands for the complete evacuation of the Rhineland as well as expressing some domestic political opposition to Locarno. What the British, and particularly Austen Chamberlain, were unable to rationalise was the extent to which Stresemann was having to appear to be defending German interests in order to garner the support of nationalist, right-wing politicians in the Reichstag in order to secure ratification of Locarno. The symbolism, and expectation, of Locarno was captured in the awarding of the Nobel peace prize to Chamberlain, Briand and Stresemann.

Early Europeanism

The 1920s saw the 'first wave' of Europeanism. Coudenhove-Kalergi's Pan-European Union was one of a proliferation of pro-unity organisations. Each of these groups wrestled with the concept of what Europe was, whom it should include and what ideological composition it should adopt. It was both a cultural, political and an economic movement. Some felt that given the descent to the First World War this responsibility could not left to politicians and instead looked to business, and there was a wave of cartel formations in the mid-1920s, most notably the International Steel Cartel in 1926. Historians, like Robert Boyce, suggest that the idea of European unity 'acquired a compelling quality during the 1920s' for many in the British business world.[38]

It was not so much that they were better informed, but rather that the hostile business atmosphere many operated in during the 1920s gave them a better sense of the global economic changes afoot. To consider Britain and European unity in the inter-war years from solely formal diplomatic and strategic perspectives misses the dense and often complex interaction at every level in the business, financial and commercial worlds that characterises Anglo–European relations in this period.[39] Many of the Scandinavian and Baltic nations were very dependent upon British economic markets. They were part of an informal sterling area after the collapse of the gold standard and all signed trade agreements with Britain between 1933 and 1934. The Bank of England and the Scandinavian banks established strong relationships and Montagu Norman, the Bank of England's governor, succeeded in creating the Bank for International Settlements at Basle. British business had also been at the fore of developing multinational investments such as Royal Dutch Shell and Unilever. So whilst British governments until 1931 undertook an international economic strategy aimed at maintaining the status quo and promoting prosperity, many in the British business world sought to promote greater trade liberalisation. Indeed, many businessmen were concerned that Britain would find itself squeezed by a burgeoning American economy and a countervailing European bloc. What gave greater British interest in coordinating the European economics was the stabilisation of European currencies after 1925, and this took shape through the League of Nations and the World Economic Conference. Free traders warned the British government against reaching 'preference' arrangements with the British empire, fearing the opportunity to reduce the Balkanisation of the European economies would be lost. On the other hand European protectionism appealed too. The British coal and steel industries were prepared to enter (or sometimes be pushed into by government) cartels with European counterparts, such as coal agreements with Poland in 1934 and Germany in 1939 and the 1935 agreement between the British Iron and Steel Federation and the International Steel Cartel – cartels that in hindsight could be seen as precursors of the 1950 European Coal and Steel Community. As Peter Stirk has observed, 'how people thought of their nation and its interest determined how they thought of Europe and the European interest, or whether they thought of Europe at all'.[40]

These economic notions fed into a political framework when on 5 September 1929 Aristide Briand, the French foreign minister, made an offer of European Union to the Assembly of the League of Nations. He expanded this further with a memorandum, on 17 May 1930, which argued for a 'federative organisation' of Europe in order to maintain peace and secure Europe's economic and social well-being. Not intending to detract from Article 21 of the League's covenant, it sought to assure too that there was no challenge to the national sovereignty of states. And the memorandum outlined the economic rationale for undertaking such a union, and proposed that it could be administered by a series of regular European conferences serviced by a permanent political committee and a secretariat. Both the British Foreign Office and the Labour government displayed 'cordial caution' to the suggestion, and ultimately responded by rejecting the plan, believing it would damage empire ties as well as the prestige and authority of the League of Nations.[41] Some were unclear precisely what Briand was seeking; a complaint common of the Frenchman, whose use of language could often leave his audience confused. According to Alexander Cadogan of the Foreign Office, it was 'really a terrible document, so overloaded with verbiage that it is clear that the author has been at great pains either to conceal his meaning or to screen his complete lack of ideas'.[42] Some in Britain suspected that whilst Briand may have been motivated by a desire for securing peace, it was a peace that aimed to benefit France and one that wished to organise European security on the basis of the status quo. This sort of argument, showing scepticism about any proposal that was not British in origin and suspecting that the originating country was only seeking to consolidate or enhance their own national self-interest, has punctuated the British debates about relations with the continent ever since. Yet, within the British foreign policy establishment Briand's reputation carried considerable respect, and it was precisely because he was the author of this proposal, that some in Britain were prepared to consider the plan in a less pejorative manner, as one of genuine international need rather than cynical French self-interest.[43] Economically, it did not appear to be in Britain's interests where a preference for free trade overrode interest in regional pacts. Much of Britain's exports were heavy industrial and there was only a limited European market for these products; furthermore during the inter-war years Britain's trade with Europe actually declined by 13 per cent. But Briand was an economic project, packaged as a political one in order not to offend America. It was an extension of the 1926 steel cartel between France, Germany, Luxembourg and Belgium and thereby an extension of tariff protection. Its novelty rested in the fact that it was prepared to sacrifice sovereignty to secure the national goals of European peace using economic policy rather than resorting to military might. Britain was not alone in its lukewarm response to Briand; consequently what emerged was a 'study group on European Union' under the auspices of the League of Nations which dissolved itself after only a short number of meetings. 'In this strange episode of the Briand Plan', suggests historian P.M. Bell, 'it is as though there was a gap in the curtain of time and we see a glimpse of the future.'[44] Whilst Horace Rumbold, the British ambassador in Berlin, may have formed the view that had Britain joined the Plan then Germany would have been compelled too, with the benefit of hindsight in rejecting Briand Britain was only acting to character, just as she would over Schuman and Messina in the 1950s.[45] Some historians see an irony in the rejection of a European form of protectionism by Britain only for it to then develop its own scheme of (imperial) protectionism, in the aftermath of the 1931 financial crisis.[46]

Not everyone in Britain was opposed to the ideas of a united Europe. It was an issue that attracted some Liberals and elements of the left, with a few individual Conservatives added in.[47] However, one of the difficulties for those in Britain who were attracted to the ideas of Briand and Count Coudenhove-Kalergi was how European Union could be squared with the British empire. In other words, did Britain's unique position make it possible for her to fit into models of European unity? Coudenhove himself originally did not envisage Britain as part of his pan-Europa idea, only revising his views in 1938. In the Edwardian era, some like Winston Churchill and Austen Chamberlain had been drawn to the federal ideas of Lionel Curtis. Chamberlain wondered whether federalism might be the answer to solving the Irish question.[48] For many federalists 1914–18 demonstrated that the nation-state was not the natural and final form of political organisation. It was a flawed concept because wars seemed to be the natural outcome of nations pursuing their own agendas, and with the proliferation of new states emerging after 1918 the risk of war had been multiplied. War also had increased the power of the state, increasing centralisation and weakening the individual. Federalism therefore offered a dual level of protection: peace and freedom for the individual.

Both Churchill and Chamberlain were to pen articles on the matter of European unity in the 1930s.[49] Ideas of European unity were closely entwined with inter-war discourses on decline. Western culture was under threat from a variety of directions: Islamic, Slavic or eastern. A unified Europe would offer the potential to reverse this diminution. Stresemann was dismissive of the notion of building a Europe based on anthropological claims, but sensed that economic and political necessities could be a way forward. Here emerged the concern that the economic might of Europe was now being challenged by the USA and Japan, but proponents argued that Europe could provide a credible challenge if crude indices of population destiny, raw material and so forth were brought together. In hindsight these might offer a potential lineage to the post-1945 thinking on European unity, but there would be a danger of overstating this significance. Nevertheless, a theme that carried over was the idea that because of Britain's uniqueness as a colonial power she should be a sponsor of European unity rather than a direct participant. As Churchill wrote in 1930, 'we have our own dream and our own task. We are with Europe, but not of it. We are linked but not comprised. We are interested and associated but not absorbed.'[50] For those favourable to greater imperial ties there was a distinct tendency to emphasise the inevitability of European economic unity and the challenges from American economic might in order to justify their cause. As Lord Beaverbrook told readers of the *Daily Express* in July 1929,

> The United States of Europe will become the reality of the twentieth century, not from reasons of sentiment, but as the only way of equalising the odds against transatlantic competition. [For Britain] it is the choice between (1) Europe and deterioration; (2) America and subservience; (3) the British Empire made once and everlastingly prosperous by the unbreakable link of free trade between all its parts.[51]

Amongst the left there was ambiguity over the ideas of European union. Kier Hardie had declared on eve of the First World War that 'the rulers and statesmen could, had they the will ... have a United States of Europe in one generation'.[52] Traditionally Labour has been much more internationalistic in outlook than the political right in the Britain, yet despite this Attlee observed in 1937 that his party suffered from an insularity which 'has always made it difficult for British Socialists to understand completely their Continental comrades. Continental Socialists are often puzzled by the attitudes of British Labour representatives.'[53]

Within the professional foreign policy establishment in London, the ideas of Coudenhove-Kalergi found little sympathy; not only had the Foreign Office library not stocked any of his published works by 1930, but also he was dismissed as 'a thoroughly impractical theorist'. It seems that only a minor official from the Western Department, Allen Leeper, saw any merit in the ideas and envisaged that at some point in the future Europe would be obliged to organise into a bloc in order to shelter from the global economic pressures, although he foresaw indecision about whether Britain would be involved whilst she retained an empire. Robert Boyce has noted that the separation of economics from foreign policy made it hard for the Foreign Office to observe, and foresee, the potential behind the ideas of the inter-war European movement. This manifested itself with the repeated protests from the Foreign Office that it was being kept ill-informed of the Treasury's reparations policy towards Germany which had consequences for Anglo–French and Anglo–German diplomatic relations.[54]

Aside from economics, the idea of joining Europe was mooted in more physical manners. Given Britain's close geographical proximity to Europe, but divided nonetheless by the English Channel, there was a considerable psychological issue about Britain's separateness. This made the repeated calls for a channel tunnel to be built a particular test case of the extent to which Britain wanted to be close to Europe, and especially France. During the Great War the French had revived the idea of a channel tunnel, in part because new technologies meant that the tunnel extraction might now be possible, but also because estimates suggested that had a tunnel been in place in 1914, then the British Expeditionary Force (BEF) could have been transported to France in three days, rather than three weeks. In March 1919 the French approached Britain to consider the feasibility of joint project review, but the Foreign Office requested that the proposal be left on the table and still had not offered a response six months later. A lobby was growing in Britain via the House of Commons Channel Tunnel Committee. It appeared for a short while as though the Cabinet was favourable too, even if the cabinet secretary Maurice Hankey ensured the drafted minutes avoided registering agreement. Eventually Lloyd George sanctioned the go ahead provided he could be reassured on the strategic implications, the likely impact on Anglo–French relations and the emotional hold of Britain being an island. It ultimately proved to be on this last point that opposition coalesced. The Foreign Office concluded 'our relations with France never have been, are not, and probably never will be, sufficiently stable and friendly to justify the construction of a Channel tunnel'. Arthur Balfour nailed the security problem when he declared 'as long as the ocean remains our friend do not let us deliberately destroy its power to help us'.[55]

Economic crisis

Despite the Dawes Plan the matter of Germany's ability to meet reparations payments continued to be a major issue of concern and, as a consequence, in June 1929 the Allied Reparation Committee appointed the Young Committee to consider whether a fresh solution was possible. At a conference in The Hague the international powers aimed to reschedule Germany's reparations payments. The British government, sensing that the terms were too soft on the French and antagonistic towards Germany, did not welcome the initial report. Snowden, Chancellor of the Exchequer, succeeded in increasing the British share of the reparations receipts, and exacerbating the French as a result. The plan was finalised in January 1930 and offered 'a complete and final settlement' to the problem of reparations.[56] The plan set the final total of German reparations over a 58.5-year period, and divided the payment into two annual tranches of an unconditional sum and a postponable element. It established the Bank for International Settlements and determined the final evacuation of French troops from the Rhineland by 30 June 1930. Britain was reasonably pleased with the outcome of the two Hague conferences. Since coming to power in 1929 MacDonald's Labour government had sought to re-orientate Britain's foreign policy away from the regional focus of Locarno, which it felt undermined the universality of the League of Nations and lacked an emphasis on arms control. According to McKercher, the second Hague conference confirmed that 'Locarno was ceasing to be the focal point of Britain's European policy'.[57] In the autumn of 1929 MacDonald had established a degree of commonality of purpose with the Americans in order to ensure the smooth running of the January conference. During the 1920s American foreign policy might have shied away from political entanglements, but it was willing to pursue economic policies that it thought would enhance its global economic hegemony.[58] The problem was that between the plan being devised, and accepted, a number of significant events occurred that would conspire against its success. On 3 October 1929 Stresemann died whilst at the same time political crisis in France meant that the mantle of political leadership passed to a new generation of politician less accommodating towards Britain and Germany, but the single most devastating event was the Wall Street crash. And it soon became apparent that the Hague deal was causing domestic problems for both the Germans and French which had the potential to spill into the international financial arena.

1929 marks the year that saw the onset of the Great Depression. It was a world-wide economic crisis on a previously unimagined scale which saw the collapse of currencies, of national banking systems, the destruction of international commerce and industrial production, stock market crashes and a rapid increase in unemployment. Originating in the USA, the economic tsunami wave hurtled across the industrial world. The British response was to try and restore confidence in free trade and the abandonment of tariffs, the French in contrast talked of European markets and trading blocs, whilst Briand proposed a form of European federation. Britain herself lurched into political and economic crisis in August 1931, resulting in swingeing public sector cuts and the collapse of the Labour government, to be replaced by a National Coalition government led by Ramsay MacDonald. Amidst all of this the Japanese launched a military annexation of the Chinese province of Manchuria and plunged the League of Nations into crisis. Germany's response was to propose an Austro–German customs union, which would have flouted the Versailles settlements. Memories of the *Zollverein* of 1834, a custom union amongst German states, were brought to mind and inevitably led to concerns that this would result in Austro–German Anschluss. Consequently France blocked the plan, not least because it would have weakened her eastern European alliances, and Austria withdrew from the plan under pressure from its economic sponsors. The British had also opposed the plan, not because they could not see merit in the scheme, but rather because Germany's unilateral action threatened to unravel the degree of European co-operation that had been established with Locarno. Furthermore, with the likely breakdown in Franco–German relations, and possible retaliatory action from France, this was the last thing that Britain wanted in light of the approaching World Disarmament Conference. In this Britain was once again using its role to act as the arbiter of the European balance of power and seeking to prevent Europe becoming two antagonistic blocs.[59] Anglo–French relations were constantly strained during the 1920s and early 1930s. Whether there was a perception of undue harshness in the French attitude at Versailles and subsequent rounds of security negotiations, or whether the French should be blamed for not supporting the pound sterling as the central European banks collapsed after 1931. Yet there was a noticeable softening of British attitudes towards France from 1930. One Foreign Office official observed the growing similarity of objective:

> However irritating and unadaptable she may sometimes appear, the fact remains that of all the Great Powers of Europe France's objectives resemble most closely our own. Both countries have been satiated by the Peace Settlement: neither is striving to obtain anything more. Both only want to keep and develop what they have got. Both, in fact, are seeking peace and security.[60]

As a result of the financial crisis American banks began recalling money they had lent to Europe, fatally undermining the Young Plan. Although President

Hoover managed to garner enough international support for a one-year moratorium, 1 July 1931–30 June 1932, on Germany's payments, the German economy slid rapidly into a deep recession. Because payments were due twice yearly in June and December, the deferral was actually until December 1932. Reports reaching the USA had suggested that the immediacy and acuteness of the European financial crisis required an urgent response. Some have criticised Hoover, suggesting he should have gone further and written off Europe's war debts, but it is evident that the American financial markets would not have tolerated this. Hoover may have secured a pause, but the world powers needed a solution to the problems of debt and reparations. Neville Chamberlain and Herriot convened at Lausanne, along with representatives of Italy, Belgium, Germany and Japan in July 1932 and agreed a replacement plan for the Young Plan. The scale of the economic crisis facing Germany persuaded the allies not to press for immediate repayment, but agreed that Germany could rid her reparations debts by a final payment of 3 billion Reich marks. It was ultimately little more than a gentleman's agreement which was entirely dependent upon securing settlement with the USA (not forthcoming) and Germany making her final repayment (which never happened). In April 1933 the dollar was devalued against gold, and it was evident that the last opportunity for combined international action had passed.[61]

The economic crisis also obliged Britain to abandon its preference for free trade, and instead seek economic strength through imperial unity. The resulting British economic policy was a dual exchange rate and tariff strategy. Britain, having abandoned the gold standard, tried to manage the pound's value on the currency markets at around $3.80 to the pound. From February 1932 tariffs of 10 per cent were levied on all imports, except food and a few specific raw materials. From April all manufactured goods imported were subject to a 20 per cent tariff. Then at Ottawa in the summer of 1932 Britain struck a deal that would give preference to Dominion foodstuffs entering Britain in exchange for British exports being received by the Dominions at preferential rates. Although other world nations retaliated against Britain, the economic revisions appeared to help Britain out of recession more swiftly than her rivals, and by 1934 Britain was the first major country to surpass 1929 figures for industrial production and unemployment began to steadily decline from a peak of 2.8 million in 1932 to 1.5 million in 1937.[62] Still in 1934 Britain owed $4.4 billion (£866 million) to the USA in debt. The 1930s would see a major growth in empire trade. In 1930–38 exports to the empire increased from 43.5 per cent to 49.9 per cent whilst the empire's share of total British imports rose from 29.1 per cent to 40.4 per cent. However, from the Treasury's perspective Britain's recovery was fragile, with concern particularly towards the end of 1937 that Britain's adverse balance of payments suggested a return to recession. Consequently considerable energies were devoted towards policy initiatives that would seek to enhance Britain's export trade.

Disarmament and peace

In the aftermath of Locarno, it appeared that a new spirit of internationalism had emerged with the League of Nations central to this. Reinforcing the League's protocols was a familiar suggestion in the 1920s. Early unsuccessful attempts had come in the form of the Draft Treaty of Mutual Assistance (1923) and the Geneva Protocol (1924). On 24 September 1927 the Poles had proposed banning wars of aggression, although there were those who questioned their sincerity, suspecting this was part of their campaign to get a seat on the League Council. Similar calls were to be made by the Pan-American Conference in 1928. Briand, concerned both for French security and anxious to harness this international enthusiasm for outlawing wars of aggression, made limited proposals which aimed to draw America into the defence of France but which ultimately resulted in the August 1928 Kellogg Pact which condemned wars of aggression. It secured widespread signatory support, even from the Russians who tried to expand it further by the Litvinov Protocol that sought to apply the pact's principals to their eastern borders.

Since Labour had come to power in 1929 one of Britain's objectives had been to use the League of Nations as a vehicle to promote disarmament. Britain had undertaken a series of unilateral steps in this direction during the 1920s, including adopting the ten-year rule that presumed annually that a conflict would not occur within the next decade, and sought to secure arms limitations in specific areas, especially naval, through a series of international agreements. Naval talks in London in 1930 had proved successful and encouraged the British to switch their focus to air and land disarmament. The outcome was the League of Nations World Disarmament Conference of 1932–34 held in Geneva. In advance of the talks Britain began to adopt a dual policy of improving relations with the French whilst encouraging American participation. Importantly too, in light of the Manchurian crisis, the British realised that the utopian concept of disarmament required a dose of pragmatism: armed strength and security were linked and the nation required a minimum strength if it were to cover its responsibilities to the League of Nations.[63] The differing interpretations of 'security' were vitally important here and it was a term frequently uttered by the French. As MacDonald observed, it had 'become the most brazen faced word in the language. She is a French strumpet.'[64] French obstructionism to arms control was a major obstacle and frequently frustrated the British negotiating team, who adopted the usual British position of seeking to mediate between France and Germany. Herein lies the difference between Britain's inter-war and post-1945 position vis-à-vis Europe: after 1945 the Franco–German relationship denied Britain the role of acting as arbiter between the two. The problem for Britain was that if there was no agreement it foresaw a scenario whereby Germany might renounce Versailles and in turn provoke France into re-entering the Ruhr, thus obliging Britain to honour her Locarno obligations.[65] Britain saw the world economic crisis as being linked to the issue of armaments. Not in the sense of rearming to pull out of recession, but rather that reductions in military expenditure would help balance national budgets, and enable the redeployment of national resources towards consumer goods which would stimulate the export market. All of this might suggest that Britain had a formula to follow at Geneva, but according to Kitching the reality was 'an ad hoc policy evolved in response to events'.[66] For Germany the conference offered an opportunity to once more seek to overturn some of the Versailles injustices, especially equality of status in the international arena alongside the right to bear arms. In November 1932 the British proposed that Germany be given the right to have the same military hardware as other nations, but in controlled numbers. In early 1933 Ramsay MacDonald took this further by proposing that Germany could have a partially conscripted army twice the size of that prohibited by Versailles (although Germany was still to be denied an air force). The French reluctantly agreed to the terms, provided there was a trial period before they were obliged to undertake disarmament on their part. But before these agreements could be formalised, Adolf Hitler came to power in Germany and almost immediately began challenging the presumed order. On 14 October 1933 he announced that Germany would be leaving the Disarmament Conference and the League of Nations, but not before Germany had expanded her standing army to 300,000 men and begun preparations to have an air force at a point in the near future. By March 1934 Britain seemed to have accepted that Germany would not only have an army of this scale, but also an air force, and should therefore begin preparations of her own.[67]

Hindsight suggests that Britain should have foreseen the demands, and ultimate consequences, of Hitler's position. However, contemporaries were basing their presumption upon a notion that Hitler would conform to the type of rational and pragmatic leader that they normally negotiated with.[68] Also their sense of recent history encouraged them in the belief that their course of action was correct. A particular explanation for the origins of the First World War had taken strong root amongst the British establishment, one that could be explained by an arms race and alliances. This meant Britain had to prevent Germany from feeling that she was being driven into a diplomatic corner by attempts to form strategic alliances whilst capitalising on any German desire to secure European disarmament by trying to draw her into a series of arms agreements. Combined with the fear of submarines, which had claimed over 3,000 allied ships in 1914–18, these were powerful incentives for the British to seek naval limitations during the inter-war years (Washington, 1922; London, 1930 and 1936). Thus began a period whereby Britain would try to seek a general settlement that would recognise some of Germany's legitimate territorial grievances whilst securing deals to limit the scale and nature of her military revival, on land, sea and in the air. Public opinion in Britain was broadly sympathetic to Germany's revisionist aspirations, although this was framed within a League of Nations rhetoric that was promoted by propaganda groups such as the League of Nations Union.[69]

It was with this rationale that Britain welcomed a German delegation to London in the summer of 1935 to discuss naval strengths. Hitler's offer may have been made in an attempt to secure British sanction for his adventures in central and eastern Europe but the British chose to ignore that and instead maximise the opportunity for pursuing their own strategic ends. The Anglo–German naval treaty of June 1935, and follow-up 1937 agreement damaged Anglo–French relations. Britain had acted unilaterally in including Germany in the European security system.[70] The Anglo–German naval agreements have been portrayed as Britain caving in to German demands, as she accepted the 35:100 ratio offered by Germany, a 'landmark on the road to war'.[71] But recent academic analysis has argued that the British policy was deliberate, structured and envisaged as the first step in a larger scheme for European disarmament and security. The British motivation was to bring Germany back into the security-negotiating fold, and through this ensure that Germany was present at the 1936 London naval talks that could lead to a new global naval limitation treaty. It also committed Germany to developing a continental battleship fleet at a time when British naval strategists feared that the Nazi regime might take a more dangerous route based on submarines and commercial raiders. In doing so Britain was charting a middle way between French encirclement and German unilateral rearmament. It also offered the prospect of further arms control agreements, particularly in the air, because it was not just a naval arms race that the British feared.[72] The rapidly evolving sphere of aircraft manufacture meant that the 'psychological' impact of the aircraft was often greater than the possible reality. Many, in Whitehall, the media and public opinion more generally, were fearful that the technological advances of aircraft, and the scale of the German air rearmament programme, meant that at the outbreak of war (or perhaps even as a wildcat strike) Britain would be subjected to a fearsome aerial bombing assault that would cripple its infrastructure, cause massive civilian causalities and lead to a rapid collapse in morale and oblige surrender: the so-called 'knock-out blow'.[73] The Air Ministry tactic of inflating the fear of a knockout blow from a German aerial assault was not new. The service departments had long been alert to the need to frighten the Treasury into agreeing funds. In 1922 and 1923, the threat was the French air force with projects that so alarmed the Committee of Imperial Defence that they recommended a large expansion in the RAF – that they secured these resources at a time of economic frugality says something about the perceptions of aerial warfare. Yes, the French had the largest air force at this point, but it was in rapid decline, lagging innovatively and production-wise beset by industrial unrest, so the suggestions that it could subject London to sustained and highly destructive bombing were extremely wide of the mark.[74] The German revelation of the Luftwaffe's air parity with the RAF in Hitler's meeting with John Simon and Anthony Eden in 1935 was the greater concern for the British. Overall, Britain was pursuing a general settlement strategy that would create a new treaty system based on Locarno that provided guarantees for both western and eastern Europe, that returned Germany to the League of Nations and which linked into a comprehensive arms limitation agreement. The way to entice Germany to the negotiating table, it was believed, was to offer the carrot of redressing the Versailles grievances. The problem would be that within Europe it was not just Germany who was capable of causing havoc.

Mussolini and Abyssinia

Since October 1922 Italy had been under the dictatorship of fascist leader Benito Mussolini. Italian fascism had long harboured expansionist tendencies and, increasingly anxious not to be outdone by the upstart Hitler, Mussolini was looking for an excuse to develop an Italian empire. Following a border incident at Wal Wal, the Italians launched an invasion of the African nation and fellow League member, Abyssinia, in October 1935. It was a crisis that highlighted the ineffectiveness of the League of Nations and which carried ramifications for the European balance of power. It destroyed the short-lived Stresa front which had only been concluded the previous March between MacDonald, Laval and Mussolini and which had agreed to guarantee the borders of Austria. Although the British cabinet recognised that an Italian annexation of Abyssinia was not a threat to British northeast African interests, they were concerned that public opinion expected them to respond in defence of a League member not least because of Samuel Hoare's 'golden age' speech to Geneva in the early autumn and emphasis given to collective security in the National Government's October 1935 election campaign. Elements within the Cabinet were anxious that if the British acted alone in implementing economic sanctions, without League and French support, Britain could be unilaterally drawn into war with Italy and possibly even Germany. The response was to introduce limited economic sanctions against Italy, but this failed to either halt the Italian campaign or effect their withdrawal, and Abyssinia was eventually conquered in May 1936. The British government reluctantly agreed to the decision to abandon sanctions in June 1936. This was not before the British foreign secretary Samuel Hoare attempted to diplomatically resolve the issue, externally of the League, by agreeing with the French foreign minister Pierre Laval in December 1935 that they should cede a sizeable section of Abyssinia to Italy. When news of this plan leaked in the British press, the public outcry (especially from the Conservative party's backbenchers) was enough to force the Cabinet to withdraw their support for the Hoare–Laval plan and seek Hoare's resignation.[75]

On 6 March 1936, whilst many in London and Paris were continuing to be distracted by events in Geneva and Abyssinia, German troops re-entered the demilitarised Rhineland zone. This was another example of Hitler's knack for timing: seizing a concession the British and French were thinking of offering as a carrot to draw him to the general settlement table. So just as he had frustrated Allied diplomacy over the abandonment of the rearmament clauses of Versailles in March 1935 with the reintroduction of conscription and the announcement of the Luftwaffe, now it was the Rhineland reoccupation. The consequences of this action were potentially enormous. Hitler had not only thwarted one of the central tenets of the Versailles settlement but he had also flouted the Locarno treaty. Hitler's offer of a peace plan added to the conundrum, causing the British and French to pause and consider whether a wider diplomatic solution might be there for the taking. The ramifications for the British were wide-ranging, obliging a fundamental review of both their foreign and defence policies: the government had to decide whether continuing sanctions against Italy were merited, whilst being forced to consider whether the Germans might be prepared to reach a colonial deal in exchange for a general settlement. The realisation also grew that if punitive action were taken against Germany it would in all likelihood push Hitler and Mussolini closer together – the precise thing British policy was trying to avoid. Within the British establishment there was a strong sense that the Rhineland was 'Germany's own backyard', and many were concerned to prevent a French 'overreaction' which might plunge Britain into war defending France and the Locarno commitments.[76] More importantly it became a crisis in Anglo–French relations. Whilst there was a feeling that Britain should not 'fight' for the Rhineland, others, like Austen Chamberlain, were concerned that Britain's failure to react even with sanctions meant the end of collective security.[77] However, there was an overwhelming sense that the French bore at least some responsibility for the crisis, not least because of the provocative signing of the Franco–Soviet pact in 1936, and that Britain should seek to restrain France from any rash action. As one Conservative MP told the House of Commons, 'if we are to be responsible for defending [France's] north-eastern frontier she must undertake not to indulge in political adventures in eastern Europe, which might provoke trouble in which we might be involved'.[78] This certainly echoed a belief that Britain would never have signed the 1925 Locarno treaty had the 1936 Franco–Soviet pact been in existence then. Some believed that this pact hindered the inevitable German expansion eastwards and was consequently obliging Hitler to turn his attentions westward. Throughout the crisis the British government deliberated its response in relation to perceived public opinion, which it sensed as 'strongly opposed to any military action' and that 'many people, perhaps most people, were saying openly that they did not see why the Germans should not reoccupy the Rhineland'.[79] Aside from damaging Anglo–French relations, the crisis refocused discussions on the continuing viability of sanctions against Italy, just at a time when Geneva and elements in the Foreign Office were suggesting that they should be extended to include oil. Critics argued that if sanctions were not to be applied against Germany, then there was little sense in continuing them against Italy. This would enable Britain to recognise the Italian conquest of Abyssinia and allow Italy to return to the negotiating table.

Within the ruling National Government the post-Rhineland crisis situation saw a considerable proportion of its supporters swing in favour of abandoning sanctions. Even Austen Chamberlain, who had been so strongly in support in 1935, reversed his position. The issue went before Cabinet on 27 May and saw Neville Chamberlain, the chancellor, try to persuade the foreign secretary Anthony Eden that sanctions should be abandoned. Eden sought to postpone a decision, arguing that the full bite of the sanctions had yet to be felt by the Italians. Stanley Baldwin decided against an immediate decision in order to allow the Foreign Office to consult with the French whilst giving Eden more time to negotiate with Italy. However, this 'drift' was too much for Neville Chamberlain and he used a speech to the 1900 Club on 10 June to label them as 'the very midsummer of madness'. Chamberlain spoke on the matter without having first consulted Anthony Eden, a serious breach of ministerial etiquette for which he apologised. Privately though, he admitted his intentions had been deliberate 'because I felt the party and the country needed a lead, and an indication that the government was not wavering and drifting without a policy'.[80] Faced with mounting pressure the Cabinet decided on 17 June to propose to the League of Nations the raising of the sanctions, and agreed that this should be announced to the House of Commons first, before any consultation with the French or Italians.

The other consequence of the Rhineland affair was to give renewed prominence to the issue of colonial restitution.[81] Hitler proposed the returning of the British colonial mandates as part of his peace plan. Ideologically this suggestion sent shockwaves through the Conservative party. Baldwin's response was to secretly charge Lord Plymouth, under-secretary at the Colonial Office, with the responsibility of preparing a report on the likely impact of a colonial deal. After several months of consideration Plymouth presented the Cabinet with his findings, concluding that the only benefit of a deal for Germany would be psychological, and ultimately the plans for a colonial deal were shelved.[82] In fact Hitler never had any intention of allowing a colonial deal to obligate him into accepting a European status quo. Rather he was looking towards central and eastern European revisionism and hoping that the offer of colonial talks would lure Britain to the table whereupon they would concede the principal of German eastward expansion in a manner similar to the Hoare–Laval pact.[83]

European flashpoints: Spain to Munich

In July 1936 a new flashpoint occurred in Europe when militarists in Spain, supported by Catholics, monarchists and fascists, began a Nationalist uprising against the left wing Popular Front government. Soon, despite being signatories of the non-intervention pact, Germany and Italy were providing 'volunteer' troops for the Nationalist cause and Russia for the socialists. In Britain the civil war emphasised the divisions between left and right. The Labour party, and public opinion generally, favoured the republican forces, whilst Conservatives tended to side with the insurgent army forces led by Franco.[84] Underpinning these divisions of view were different and sometimes contradictory themes: the influences of war (religion, class sympathy and allegations of atrocities); and the dangers the conflict posed for the stability of Europe with issues about anti-communism, pro- and anti-fascism and perceptions about the threat to British interests.[85] There was a habit for the British right to see only the excesses of the Spanish republican movement just in the way that the British left saw only the excesses of the Spanish right. As the Conservative diarist Chips Channon noted following the fall of San Sebastian in September 1936, the tales of the Reds' 'fiendish cruelties are unbelievable'.[86] British citizens, particularly from the trade unions and political left, also sought to flout the non-intervention arrangements by offering their services to the international brigades. For elements in the British government and Foreign Office there were concerns about the impact the war would have on Anglo–French relations and concerns that should the republican cause survive this might produce a communist Spain, which might present risks for the stability of France and Portugal. The issue of the war occupied a disproportionate amount of parliamentary debating time during 1936 and 1937, as well as being significant matters for the TUC and Labour Party annual conferences, and yet the majority of the political right were indifferent to the war. The involvement of the totalitarian powers in Spain also made the situation precarious – the challenge for diplomacy was to contain this conflict within the Iberian peninsular and prevent it becoming a wider European conflagration. Ultimately, the policy of non-intervention succeeded, only occasionally failing to insulate Europe from the civil war's ramifications.[87] Von Neurath, the German foreign minister, cancelled a visit to Britain in the summer of 1937 after the torpedoing of the battleship *Leipzig* in Spanish waters. The presence of Italian 'volunteers' in the country would continually hamper attempts at Anglo–Italian rapprochement in 1938, whilst the horrors of the bombing of Guernica reminded the world of the dangers of this new aerial warfare.

By early 1937 there was a growing political sense that action was required to separate Germany and Italy. The German grievances over rearmament, the Rhineland and colonies were still viewed as legitimate desires of a nation-state, provided there was no German hint of forcible restitution. The Italians were seen as the more hostile of the two dictatorships, not least because of the potential flashpoint offered by the presence of the British fleet in the Mediterranean. Although the abdication crisis had dominated the political scene at the end of 1936, those with an interest in foreign affairs were increasingly anxious not to be seen as being overly harsh on Italy – a negotiated settlement with one or other of the dictators was required, and the expectation was that Baldwin's successor, Neville Chamberlain, would prove the man to achieve it. In January 1937 the Committee of Imperial Defence was warning that Italy ought no longer to be considered an ally, although she was still not hostile enough to be labelled a belligerent. By December the chiefs of staff were warning the politicians that Britain risked war on three fronts (Germany, Italy and Japan), and that even with the assistance of

France and other allies, she could not realistically expect to fight all three simultaneously and entertain hopes of victory. It was crucial that Britain 'reduce the numbers of our potential enemies and ... gain the support of potential allies'.[88]

Chamberlain's strategy was a dual one: diplomacy supported by rearmament. If one failed the other would be expected to provide Britain with a lifeline. Whilst Britain waited for her rearmament programme to reach maturity it would 'place a heavy burden' on diplomacy.[89] A burden emphasised by the weakness of the League of Nations: 'What country in Europe today if threatened by a large power, can rely on the League of Nations for protection?' questioned Neville Chamberlain in March 1938. 'None' came his reply.[90] During late 1937 Britain was reviewing its rearmament priorities under the Inskip defence review, and it confirmed that a military commitment to the continent remained the least of British priorities, with the army continuing to languish as the 'Cinderella service'. Importantly, though, the decision was taken to switch the emphasis from long-range bomber deterrence to fighter defence, as technological developments in radar as well as a new generation of mono-winged planes, the Hurricane and Spitfire, came into production that made 'aerial defence' a possibility. Paul Kennedy has observed the similarities of the Inskip defence review with the 1891 Stanhope memorandum in order to highlight the long-term trend of appeasement and 'limited liability'.[91] Diplomatically the British appeared uncertain what concessions might bring the Germans to the negotiating table, therefore they needed to establish what it was that Hitler wanted. There was also renewed economic motivation with concern that Britain's fragile recovery from recession was being threatened by a poor balance of trade sheet and overly burdened by the costs of rearmament. An opportunity arose when Halifax, who hated travelling and would assign it to deputies wherever possible,[92] was invited in a private capacity, as Master of the Middleton Hunt, to Germany to attend a hunting exhibition. Although the Foreign Office was suspicious that the prime minister was sidelining it over this event, Halifax nevertheless had a meeting with Hitler. The whole affair could have ended in disaster but for the swift intervention of von Neurath after Halifax mistook Hitler for a footman and went to hand him his hat and coat. The meeting was ambiguous. Halifax's report on his return was as short on specifics as it was fulsome on generalities. Chamberlain appeared to consider otherwise and concluded that perhaps the time had arisen to revisit the issue of a colonial deal, but only as part of a general European settlement. The whole visit had another consequence, for it confirmed to Chamberlain the similarity of view and purpose between himself and Halifax, and some have cited this as the beginning of a rift between Chamberlain and his foreign secretary Anthony Eden.[93]

Anthony Eden directly challenged the Chamberlainite vision for Britain's relationship towards continental Europe in February 1938. It appeared that both men were increasingly at odds about the best manner of approaching a general settlement. Whilst they were in agreement over German policy they found themselves debating Italian strategy. Matters were brought to a climax over President Roosevelt's offer to mediate with the dictators, which Chamberlain rejected without consulting Eden, and then exacerbated by the issue of Anglo–Italian negotiations. Although some in Europe looked towards the USA and USSR to deter the dictators the majority, Chamberlain included, envisaged that the solution of a new security system would always be on the basis of the big European four co-operating.[94] Chamberlain had been seeking to open up alternative channels of communications with the Italians, via his sister-in-law Ivy Chamberlain and Joseph Ball. The Foreign Office, once aware of this, was less than impressed that amateurs were conducting diplomacy upon Britain's behalf. The price for engaging Italy's attentions was that her annexation of Abyssinia should be recognised by the British, essentially re-classifying the invasion as a misdemeanour, and turning a blind eye to the Italian involvement in the Spanish Civil War. Chamberlain considered this a small price to pay for something that was already de facto, and believed that it would remove the stumbling block from negotiating an Anglo–Italian treaty (something that was finally ratified in November). Eden, who had a long and antagonistic relationship with the Italians, and who was being egged on by his closest advisors with assurances that his views carried weight within the Conservative party, determined upon the course of resignation. Ultimately his resignation failed to provoke the expected (and later mythologised) revolt over foreign policy and instead the government succeeded in presenting an image that suggested Eden's resignation was not due to any fundamental dispute over foreign policy but merely the matter of when negotiations with Italy ought to begin.[95]

Meanwhile matters on the continent were taking a turn for the worse. Facing intense pressure from Germany in the opening months of 1938, Austrian chancellor von Schuschnigg sought to trump the Nazis when on 9 March he urged his fellow Austrians to support independence in a referendum. Caught by surprise, Hitler was obliged to improvise an armed intervention and on 11 March German forces entered Vienna. Although the Treaty of St Germain had forbidden the Anschluss, by the late 1930s many in Britain saw it as an unnecessarily harsh clause and were prepared to consider a peaceful Austro–German union in exchange for a European general settlement. The manner of the annexation aroused a range of reactions from outrage to tacit acceptance. Reports of the German methods and the attacks on political opponents and Jews weakened the sense of legitimacy that many felt. Amongst the British ruling classes, there was unease that this should occur so shortly after the resignation of Anthony Eden on 21 February. Did this give credence to the Edenite claims over Britain's foreign policy direction? What it revealed was that Britain's Italian policy had failed to deliver when required. Whilst in 1934 Italian troops had been mobilised on the Brenner Pass to prevent a German putsch in Austria, there was no such replication in 1938. The question arose about whether Britain should intervene. The realists argued that Austrian independence had been lost, that the denial of the

Anschluss had been an inequity of Versailles, and because the Austrians had made no attempt to resist, it was not for Britain to intervene. Others suggested that the folly of Britain's recent relations with Italy, and the implementation of sanctions over Abyssinia, was to blame. Recognising that nothing could be done for Austria, British attention switched to Czechoslovakia.

The Anschluss left Czechoslovakia like a bone in the jaws of a dog, observed the chiefs of staff. Under the Versailles settlement the rights of minority populations had been enshrined in treaties, but by the 1930s these annexes were largely being overlooked. Czechoslovakia had been created in 1919 from the ruins of the Austro-Hungarian empire and comprised a spectrum of different nationalities, including some 3 million German speakers, mainly living along the borders with Germany and Austria, and labelled the Sudentens. The problem for Britain was that if Germany attacked Czechoslovakia, France, under the terms of her alliance with the Czechs, which had been renewed in 1935, would be obliged to support the Czechs. To complicate matters further the Soviet Union had a treaty with the Czechs, so the likelihood of the separatist demands of the Sudetens plunging Europe into general war seemed high. Furthermore, the Poles and Hungarians also had territorial claims on Czechoslovakia. In Czechoslovakia the minority Germany-speaking Sudeten population was being encouraged by Nazi propaganda and a political leadership in cahoots with Berlin. The British response was intended to persuade the Czech government to improve its treatment of its minorities whilst warning Berlin not to undertake anything rash, and also to persuade the French not to think about honouring her commitments to the Franco–Czech mutual assistance treaty. Political debate occurred as to whether Britain ought to offer a guarantee to Czechoslovakia. Chamberlain had resisted the immediate urge after the Anschluss to offer such an arrangement, but was obliged to come before the House of Commons on 24 March to explain the government's position. Informed sources expected it to be concerned with '"realism", which in practice means ... isolation.' Yet on hearing Chamberlain speak they were reassured: 'some of the isolationists feel that we are committed too far, but on the whole it has been a very successful compromise'.[96] In fact, Chamberlain in his speech made it clear that Britain had no treaty obligations to Czechoslovakia and warned the French that they could only expect assistance if directly attacked by Germany; yet he left an air of ambiguity

> Where peace and war are concerned, legal obligations are not alone involved, and if war broke out, it would be unlikely to be confined to those who have assumed such obligations ... it would be quite impossible to say where it might end and what governments might be involved.[97]

Those favourable to a guarantee were in the minority. Most were more fearful of becoming stuck in a European quagmire. Concerns about a German annexation of the Sudetenland grew through the summer, heightened by a diplomatic scare in May that suggested such an operation was imminent. The deepening tension saw Britain move from a position of 'realism' to one of ever deeper commitment; as one Foreign Office official observed after visiting the region in late May, 'we are naturally regarded as having committed ourselves morally at any rate to intervene if there is a European war, and nothing that we are likely to say will remove that impression'.[98] The dispatch of Lord Runciman to the region in August confirmed this impression.

Runciman forlornly attempted to assess the crisis between Prague, the Sudetenland and Berlin, but it was clear that Hitler, in collusion with Henlein, the Sudeten German leader, was pushing the situation to the brink of war. In a bold, and innovative move, Chamberlain and his closest advisors devised a diplomatic coup, Plan Z. This was a personal offer from Chamberlain to fly to meet with Hitler and negotiate a solution to the crisis. In doing so Chamberlain created the modern phenomenon of 'shuttle diplomacy', as he flew to Germany on three occasions to meet with Hitler at Berchtesgaden, Bad Godesberg and finally Munich. After the first two meetings it looked as if the demands being made by Hitler would be impossible to accept, and the British began preparing for war: the navy was mobilised, gas mask distribution begun and barrage balloons set up at key locations around London. On 28 September Chamberlain felt compelled to broadcast to the British nation and explain why Britain was now in such a position. During the course of his talk he referred to the Sudeten crisis as being 'in a faraway country between people of whom we know nothing'. The choice of phrasing has often been held up to demonstrate the isolationist and narrow outlook in Chamberlain's foreign policy vision, but he was merely articulating a view that many contemporaries held. Czechoslovakia was not an traditional British sphere of interest, nor were many enamoured with the idea of fighting for a nation that was the creation of 'woolly headed idealists and extreme nationalists' and for which there appeared to be little militarily that Britain could do.[99] Europe pulled back from the brink when an offer, ostensibly from Mussolini but made at German prompting, called Chamberlain and Daladier, as the French premier, to a four-power conference in Munich to resolve the crisis. Neither the Czechs nor the Soviets were invited to the discussions. In due course, on 1 October, Chamberlain returned to Heston airport proclaiming 'peace in our time' and waving a piece of paper that Hitler and he had both signed on the spur of the moment agreeing friendly relations between Germany and Britain.[100] This was the sugar-coated pill intended to pacify the negativity towards the sacrificing of the Sudetenland (and thereby the Czech's impressive border defence network) to Germany against the wishes of the Czech government (in exchange for France and Britain guaranteeing the new borders), suggesting that this sacrifice had secured a greater goal: the prospect of a general European settlement. Some contemporaries were prepared to defend the agreement on the basis that the Sudetens had been denied self-determination in 1919, and to do so again simply because they were Germans or even because they were supported by the Nazis was not a sufficiently good reason; add to that the lack of Dominion support for war, the British and French unpreparedness for war, and the improbability that the Soviets would intervene on the Czech's behalf, meant a deal had to be reached, no matter how morally repulsive it might be in retrospect.[101] A quip doing the rounds in the House of Commons during the parliamentary debates on Munich likened the crisis to St George, who having failed to rescue the maiden remarked that she would not have been worth it anyway.[102] Since May 1940, Munich has become synonymous with betrayal and humiliation, and following the collapse of communism and Czechoslovakia's return to democracy, Britain has successively sought to atone for the betrayal: both Thatcher and Major would visit Prague offering apologies, and in Major's case symbolically sign a treaty nullifying Munich.[103] Despite many private misgivings, Chamberlain secured substantial parliamentary and public support for his actions.[104] The difficulty facing those who opposed Chamberlain was to what extent could they articulate an alternative vision for foreign policy: the closest to a coherent alternative came in the form of Winston Churchill's idea for a 'grand alliance' in which the western democratic powers would ally with the Soviet Union, and the smaller nations of eastern Europe against Hitler. As the events of 1939 would show, the prospect that this could be achieved were minimal. Nor were contemporaries that convinced it would contain Germany. 'Joining hands', declared Sir John Simon, the chancellor, 'with France and Russia and the rest in a ring round the smoking crater [of Germany] will not necessarily stop the explosion.'[105]

The countdown to war

Expectations that Munich would be the prelude to a wider European settlement were quickly dashed. Although Britain ratified the Anglo–Italian treaty, in November, as a reward to Mussolini for his diplomatic efforts at Munich, Hitler's behaviour only increased the international tension. The Kristallnacht pogrom against German Jews repulsed the world, and raised new questions about the nature of the German dictatorship. If Czechoslovakia had not been considered a natural sphere of British influence then the rumours from early 1939 that Germany was planning a surprise attack on the Low Countries or perhaps Switzerland grabbed the attention. The fear that German bombers would be able to base themselves in Holland and thereby extend their range of attack further over Britain caused considerable anxiety.[106] On 1 February the Cabinet agreed that if either of these countries were attacked Britain would have to go to war. At the same time the British appeared to be edging towards accepting the need for a continental commitment: or at least making verbal and paper pledges. Ministerial statements appeared to make stark declarations of support for France, and Anglo–French staff talks were commenced in March, whilst the Cabinet edged towards accepting the chiefs of staff's arguments for creating a field force at a point in the future.[107] Nevertheless, in early March Chamberlain let it be known that he was hopeful of the possibility of disarmament talks beginning, except Hitler tore up the Munich agreement a few days later and marched his forces into the rump of Czechoslovakia. Britain and France were, although guarantors, powerless to act despite having received intelligence warnings two weeks before.[108] It obliged Chamberlain to announce the end of his appeasement policy in a speech in his home city of Birmingham on 14 March, and on 31 March, under pressure from his foreign secretary Halifax, made an offer to guarantee the territorial integrity of Poland. The Poles responded with a declaration of mutual defence. The British guarantee was then extended on 15 April to Romania, who claimed she was under economic blackmail from Germany, as well as Greece. Then in a Commons statement on 26 April Chamberlain revealed that Britain would not be 'indifferent' to any threats to the Scandinavian nations: Norway, Sweden and Finland.[109] In doing so it appeared that Chamberlain had broken with the traditions of recent foreign policy and obligated Britain to a continental commitment.[110] Some, like Rab Butler, a junior Foreign Office minister, were dubious of the value: 'it gave Russia just the excuse not to defend herself against Germany since we had gratuitously planted ourselves in E[astern] Europe'.[111] This commitment was emphasised by the doubling of the Territorial Army, from 170,000 to 340,000, and the announcement of conscription in April: something the French had been calling for.[112] Yet, this response did not in actuality signal the end of Britain's limited liability position. The first conscripts were not called to the colours until August; the full time service was only for a six-month period and nearly half of the recruits were to be trained in anti-aircraft home defence. The symbolism was in the announcement: reassurance to France, a warning to Germany, and the first conscription in peacetime Britain.[113] Critics of Chamberlain's policies and particularly Munich were arguing by 1939 that if Britain had chosen to stand firm in September 1938 she, alongside France, would have been able to call upon the assistance of Russia, Poland and Czechoslovakia against Germany.[114] Winston Churchill was continuing to promote his idea for a 'grand alliance', which envisaged a network of European mutual assistance pacts based upon the covenant of the League of Nations and 'sustained by a moral sense of the world'.[115] The guarantee to Poland proved more awkward to confirm, and it took protracted Anglo–Polish negotiations throughout the summer of 1939 before formal ratification.[116] Britain's military chiefs lacked confidence in the Poles' abilities to resist a German attack: a verdict confirmed in conjunction with the French during staff talks in April.[117] Jozef Beck, the Polish foreign minister, was only too conscious of the position Poland found herself facing: a resurgent nationalist Germany to the west anxious to secure the Polish corridor, and Soviet Russia to the east still smarting at the loss of territory from the 1919 Polish-Soviet conflict. Matters were complicated by the attempts by the British and French to negotiate an alliance with the Soviets at the same time.[118] The matter of Poland was being used as a stumbling bloc in the Russian negotiations too. Russia argued that she would not agree to any pact unless

Poland agreed too and granted concessions; the Russians were also less than pleased with the Anglo–Polish guarantee, as the wording implied that Britain would support Poland from either a westward or eastern attack, and that it would be for Poland to judge whether its independence was threatened. There was considerable suspicion of the Soviet Union in Britain; many on the political right thought that many of the world's troubles could be attributed to communism, and that Hitler and Mussolini had come to power because of it. This reluctance even reached to the heart of government, with observers sensing that Chamberlain was less than enthused by the prospect.[119] Aside from the ideological distaste for the Russians, Chamberlain was concerned that an alliance risked a repeat of 1914 with opposing blocs being created, and that this would only make the opportunities for diplomacy harder, if not impossible. This undoubtedly contributed to the British failure to establish direct personal contact with Stalin at the opening stages. Furthermore, although the Cabinet agreed on 24 May that it would seek an alliance with the Soviets, Chamberlain inserted a caveat that associated the alliance with the League of Nation's covenant – which would make any military intervention subject to League approval – something not welcomed by Moscow.[120] Ultimately in July William Strang, from the Foreign Office's central desk, was dispatched to Moscow to conduct the negotiations. It was observed that if Chamberlain had been prepared to fly to meet Hitler, then at least he or another senior cabinet minister ought to have tried to negotiate with Stalin – at the very least it would have emphasised the genuineness of the British approach.[121] The talks stalled over the acceptance of 'indirect aggression', which would have given the Soviets the opportunity to interfere in the affairs of the Baltic states. Throughout all of this the Germans sustained their pressure upon Poland, and particularly Danzig, during the summer, making the prospect of war very real. As the pressure mounted upon Poland, British sentiment swung behind the beleaguered nation with grim determination: 'if they really mean business', confessed one diarist, 'we shall really have no alternative but to go in with them.'[122]

Economics and eastern Europe: persistence of appeasement?

Running in parallel with the diplomatic efforts to avert war, the British pursued a series of economic policies that have been categorised as 'economic appeasement', and considered in industrial terms, by some, to have been relatively successful. Economic appeasement offered the possibility of convincing Germany to reject her plans for economic self-sufficiency and increased arms expenditure. It was also thought to increase the influence of the 'moderates' within Germany. Underpinning all of this was an overwhelming concern about the fragility of Britain's economic recovery, and a sense that the economy represented the 'fourth arm of defence'. There had been an Anglo–German Payments Agreement in 1934 that had determined that 55 per cent of the value of German imports to Britain would be used to pay for British exports to Germany with an additional 10 per cent being used to pay off frozen trade debts. In December 1936, recognising that she was experiencing an adverse balance of payments and convinced that rearmament was aggravating this, Britain approached Germany with the offer of a loan in the expectation that they in turn would abandon currency controls and consequently stimulate British exports. However, final agreement floundered because von Neurath cancelled his visit to London after the attacks on German ships in Spanish waters. The 1936 Tripartite Monetary Agreement between USA, Britain and France was a device for managing and co-ordinating exchange rates. In the longer term this marked the beginning of the dollar's post-war role and the beginning of recognition from the USA that it must assume the economic leadership of Europe. Throughout 1938 economic negotiations from the British perspective were driven by a desire to improve Britain's export economy. Staples such as coal and textiles were facing stiff German competition: between 1933 and 1937 Britain's share of the coal export market fell 20 per cent due to German domestic price subsidies. In April 1938 the 1935 payment agreement had to be renegotiated to account for the Anschluss. The Treasury hoped to increase the proportion of German import value to be used for the payment of British imports and for a commitment to honour Austria's debt. Agreement was reached in early July with the promise of further trade talks in September, at which the prospect that they might reached agreement on third country markets, particularly in eastern Europe, as well as the possibility that Germany would join the international coal cartel, was talked about. Robert Hudson, of the Board of Trade, felt that 'if such an agreement emerged it would have great possibilities as a stepping stone to political appeasement'.[123] After Munich British economic attention turned to the Balkans with three aims in mind: to prevent the fusion of the German and Balkan economies; to create a Balkan market for colonial exporters; which in turn would improve the empire's abilities to purchase British exports.[124] The economic appeasement of Germany continued into 1939 with the negotiation of an Anglo–German coal cartel in January. The unilateral activities of Robert Hudson were widely reported in the press in July 1939 over his abortive discussions with Wohlthat, economic commissioner to Goering's Four Year Plan.[125] More discreetly but equally unsuccessfully, Rab Butler, secretary of state at the Foreign Office, was also seeking a 'path of reconciliation' through hoping to encourage renewed Anglo–German negotiations on trade, raw materials, colonies and a naval agreement (as Hitler had renounced the 1935 Anglo–German naval treaty in April).[126]

But these economic arrangements mattered for little when Hitler secured a diplomatic coup 23 August 1939 by reaching rapprochement with the Soviet Union. It was recognised that war was just a matter of days away. As Conservative MP Chips Channon observed, 'Now it looks like war, and the immediate partition of Poland.'[127] The Ribbentrop–Molotov pact, with its secret clauses for the annexation and division of Poland, meant Hitler had secured Germany's eastern front and ensured that any German attack on

Poland did not risk war on two fronts. History suggested that this should not have been a surprise, if one remembered Rapallo, and some accounts also suggest that this was a longer-term Soviet plan.[128] The afternoon that the news emerged, Chamberlain began planning who would serve in a British war cabinet, despite some hoping that a second Munich might be achieved.[129] Within a week Europe was once more plunged into war. On 1 September 1939 at 6 a.m., *Fall Weiss*, the German directive to invade Poland, was enacted and German troops crossed the Polish border. Yet for 48 hours the British and French prevaricated. Some feared that the Allies intended to renege on their guarantee, especially when Mussolini offered proposals for a Munich-style conference. Certainly some in the French political establishment, like Bonnet, were extremely keen to avoid going to war, but more generally the French delayed because they wanted time to commence mobilisation and begin their civilian evacuation plans. The British had no desire to act unilaterally and held back, waiting for the French. A parliamentary and Cabinet revolt eventually forced Chamberlain to issue an ultimatum, and so on 3 September 1939 at 11 a.m. Britain declared war on Germany, followed shortly by the French at 5 p.m.[130] For Neville Chamberlain this was a bitter personal blow and his speech to the House of Commons clearly conveyed his sense of failure: 'Everything that I have worked for, everything that I have hoped for, everything that I have believed in during my public life, has crashed into ruins.'[131] In contrast to 1914, few in Britain wished to fight a war with Germany, but its necessity was grimly accepted. As one MP observed: 'I see heavy hearts, clear minds and grim determination ... No one can foresee the duration of this conflict, the Germans are confident, highly trained, unscrupulous; all the talk of quick decisions is the refuge of unpractical minds.'[132] Italy initially remained 'neutral', although its mere presence tied up considerable Allied forces: As Gamelin, French chief of staff, observed 'If the Italians come in against us, we shall need 5 divisions to defeat them; if they are neutral, we shall need ten divisions to watch 'em; if they come in with us, we shall need 15 divisions to reinforce 'em.'[133] The war quickly took on global dimensions as the Soviet Union, Americans and Japanese were sucked into the conflict. By the time Japan surrendered on 14 August 1945, the military casualties suffered by the British empire were 486,000 wounded and 590,000 killed.

Some concluding thoughts

Opinion divides over whether British foreign policy during the inter-war years, and especially after 1937, was detrimental to maintaining the balance of power in Europe. Critics, like Avi Shlaim, suggest that Britain's continued aloofness and failure to establish a European coalition to resist Hitler meant 'that by 1939 the balance of power in Europe lay in ruins'.[134] Alternatively a view has been offered that suggests British diplomacy to Europe during the inter-war years was based on a premise of limited liability that attempted to take account of the growing constraints of economic interdependence and globalisation.[135] Some suggest that this was ultimately a form of traditional British foreign policy that sought to avoid continental alliances, except with France and the Low Countries. It placed an emphasis on the empire and world trade, whilst believing that defence costs should be capped so as not to be detrimental to the economy. As a consequence defence needs had to be prioritised, with a field force considered the least important aspect. Diplomatically Britain should retain a free hand in order to maintain the balance of power, either by leading or controlling allies, and having the freedom to avoid others' quarrels. Chamberlain's personal diplomacy during 1937–39 was just such a traditional policy and this, according to Paul Kennedy, only ended when Britain guaranteed Poland in March 1939.[136]

However, it is clear that within the political establishment differing interpretations existed over the balance of power. Some, like Austen Chamberlain, subscribed to a continental commitment thesis. They believed that Britain's close proximity to the continent made it impossible for Britain to be aloof. The Rhine River was Britain's frontier, a view that was repeated often during the 1930s. There could be no prospect of peace unless Britain mediated between Germany and France, and economically Britain had to work to constrain Germany's growing economic might. As Nazi Germany became ever a greater threat, then the need to establish the coalition with France became imperative.

In regard to the idea that Britain should have realised the threat posed by the European dictators and stood up to them at an earlier stage: this is unrealistic. Many considered the fascist regimes to be distasteful, but they were regimes adopted by their nations and it was not Britain's role to undermine foreign domestic governments, so one was obliged to find the means of conducting diplomacy with them.[137] It was as Henry Page-Croft, MP for Bournemouth, told the House of Commons during the Munich debates, that if one was to 'run a finger across the map the large majority of the people from Vladivostok to Cape Finisterre are under dictatorships ... if the machinery of civilisation is still to work you have to understand their mentality, you have got to work with them'.[138]

2 The post-war settlement 1940–61

Surveying the international order in the days after the conclusion of hostilities in Europe, Alexander Cadogan, Britain's most senior Foreign Office civil servant, observed that the world was now witness to two and a half super-powers: the United States of America and the Soviet Union, and Britain acting as the half power.[1] For Britain this represented a considerable decline in fortunes. Five years of fighting the totalitarian powers had taken its toll. By agreeing to Lend Lease in 1941 Britain had become economically dependent upon the USA for provisioning the war effort. Whereas in 1938 Britain had been the world's largest creditor, now she was the largest debtor, owing vast sums to the USA, debts that would not be finally paid off until 2006.[2] Britain's gold reserves had been depleted and sterling as a world currency was at the mercy of the strength of the dollar. Based on these economic indices some observers would have suspected that Cadogan was overly optimistic in even ascribing Britain some degree of world power status. Yet by virtue of having been one of victorious powers, and having carried the battle for so long, Britain had secured a position at the negotiating table that established the parameters of the post-war settlement. Added to this was Britain's reassertion of control over much of her empire, giving her a global presence that she hoped could not be just ignored by the Americans and Soviets. It was important, one Foreign Office assessment concluded, that 'Great Britain must be regarded as a world power of the second rank and not merely as a unit in a federated Europe'.[3]

Wartime alliances and redrawing Europe's map

When war had broken out in Europe in September 1939, following the German attack on Poland, Britain had been initially uncertain as to what war aims she was fighting for. Was she fighting to restore the territorial integrity of 1939 Poland, or perhaps even Czechoslovakia? If so, which Czechoslovakia, that of 1918 or September 1938? Would the overthrow of Hitler, or the entire Nazi regime, be a suitable goal or was the total surrender of the German nation the objective? Within the highest echelons of the British government these issues were debated between September 1939 and May 1940, but the political crisis brought about by the fall of the Neville Chamberlain government and advent of Winston Churchill to the premiership, just as German forces unleashed their blitzkrieg on western Europe, removed all debate.[4] The rapid fall of Holland, Belgium and France during ten days in May, obliging the remnants of the British Expeditionary Force to be evacuated from the beaches of Dunkirk, meant that Churchill had only one war aim: the survival of Britain. Yet as the war dragged on and gradually turned in Britain's favour, as the Soviet Union, Japan and the USA became embroiled in the global conflict, so thoughts from 1943 began turning towards how the new international order should be shaped.[5] Given the successful German penetration of the borders of Russia and France, for the second time in a generation, it was recognised that neither of these countries would easily, or quickly, forgive a defeated Germany. Nevertheless, America and Britain hoped that in the post-war era there would be a new form of partnership with the Soviet Union. An expectation existed that if the Soviets were granted a sphere of influence, and a buffer zone in eastern Europe, they in turn would collaborate with western capitalism in the new world order. This would be coordinated through the United Nations, but would be essentially based on a partnership between the "Big Four" – the United States, Soviet Union, China and Britain. This assumption that the wartime alliance could be carried over into peacetime and that the management of Germany would underpin all the Allied agreements up to Potsdam diminished the success of these arrangements. From 1943 at a succession of gatherings the Allied powers began shaping the new political map of Europe.[6] But the alliance of military might did not easily, or harmoniously, translate itself into diplomatic alliances. Strains in the relationships between the Soviets, Americans and British were already apparent. Certainly the British Foreign Office as the war developed was less concerned about the German post-war threat than the Soviet, even if the political leadership of Churchill still hoped for a new working relationship. There was anxiety that Germany might succumb to communism and that this would threaten the European balance of power and necessitate Britain forming a defensive alliance with France and other European nations to form a bloc against Soviet encroachment.[7] The British were already suspicious of American intentions to seek the dismemberment of the British empire. The August 1941 Atlantic Charter which Churchill and Roosevelt had symbolically agreed aboard an American naval vessel USS *Augusta*, off the Newfoundland coast, spoke of the need for 'rights of all peoples to choose the government under which they will live'.[8] America insisted that this applied to colonial peoples, not just those under Nazi tyranny. This provoked Churchill's famous rebuttal: 'I have not become the King's first minister to preside over the liquidation of the British Empire.'[9] Between 1944 and 1945 detailed negotiations were conducted to shape the new political map. The Soviet Union were anxious to carve out a new sphere of influence, which would provide a buffer from Germany and which would give her the diplomatic authority she believed she deserved. Churchill, still conscious of the need to actually win the war, was anxious to keep the Soviets in the war and therefore in Moscow in October 1944 conceded to the percentages deal intended to assign the Balkans to the Russian sphere of influence, whilst Greece would be deemed to be under Britain's interests. With similar intentions at Yalta in February 1945, Churchill conceded the point that the USSR was entitled to a buffer zone in eastern Europe, but believed a guarantee of elections in these liberated states would prevent this buffer zone from becoming a closed Stalinist bloc. Such was Churchill's confidence in his ally's integrity that he rashly declared 'Poor Neville Chamberlain believed he could trust Hitler [over Munich]. He was wrong. But I don't think I'm wrong about Stalin.'[10] Yalta also saw the resolution of what to do with the defeated Germany. It was agreed that Germany would be divided into four zones, controlled respectively by the Soviets, Americans, British and French, that an Allied Control Council would be established to administer Germany, whilst the allies agreed to punish war criminals and oversee the complete demilitarisation of Germany. Although the frontiers of a liberated Poland had been agreed at the Tehran conference in late 1943, Yalta would seal the fate of that country as the Allies granted recognition of the communist led-Lubin provisional government.[11]

The war in Europe reached its finale on 7 May 1945 near Rheims in France, when Admiral Friedeburg and General Jodl accepted the terms of Germany's unconditional surrender. At midnight the next day the war in Europe was over. Victory in Europe (VE) day was greeted with relief by the British people, but the war itself was still not over in the Far East. It would take a further three months and the unleashing of a new terrible weapon, the atomic bomb, on Hiroshima and Nagasaki to bring the surrender of Japan. Yet Europe was also faced with immense problems: the vast numbers of prisoners of war, the swathes of displaced persons, the war disabled, as well as the economic and material retardation brought by five years of conflict. One journalist, whilst relieved to think he would not have to again see London 'ringed by fire', sensed that the population recognised the huge human cost of the war 'for the visible rejoicings have not been anything like as hearty and unrestrained as the Press would have us believe'.[12] The Americans quickly began demobilising their armed forces of 12.5 million men and women and by 1949 had no more than two divisions in the whole of Europe.[13] Nor was it peace: the struggle against Nazism and fascism was to be replaced with the Cold War and East/West ideological battle between communism and capitalism. It also witnessed the physical division of Europe. In part this was due to the actions of the main players on the ground. In the last months of the war, Churchill had argued against allied forces withdrawing from liberated areas that would be allocated to the USSR until a settlement over Poland's borders had been reached, but Eisenhower refused to comply and American forces were pulled back from their bridgeheads over the Elbe. Those countries that saw themselves liberated by Soviet forces found themselves being denied the pledges made at Yalta for free democratic elections and instead passed directly from right-wing authoritarianism to

Stalinist totalitarianism. Only Yugoslavia and Austria managed to sustain a degree of independence.[14]

The defeated Germany was initially divided between the victorious powers. The British zone to the northwest of the country comprised Lower Saxony, Schleswig-Holstein, North Rhine Westphalia and included the cities of Bonn, Hanover and Hamburg. In addition, the German capital, Berlin, which was deep inside the Soviet zone, was divided between the four powers. The cost of maintaining the German British zone was colossal. Seventy per cent of foodstuffs had to be imported. There were 200 million displaced persons in the zone and the cost of administering it was £80 million for the first year.[15] When added to the considerable costs of maintaining Britain's imperial possessions, this was an unwelcome diversion of resources at a time when the fragility of the British domestic economy, and the continued social deprivations being experienced by her population, demanded immediate attention. In Germany the British looked to quickly reintroduce local government, political parties and trade unions to their zone, but matters were complicated by the serious divisions between the allies over reparations. By the end of 1947 the pretence of inter-power unity over Germany had broken down, and the need for a provisional government for the western-controlled sectors become imperative. In order to resist further Soviet encroachment, a democratic westward-looking Germany was required, its borders secured by the western powers with America securing the western powers in return. For some this was little more than a reflection of Britain's long-standing preoccupation with the European balance of power, but this time it required an active continental commitment and the long-term presence of both British and American troops on European soil. The 1948 Berlin Airlift, whereby the western allies airlifted millions of tons of supplies into their Berlin zone over eleven months after the Soviets had blockaded the city in June, only served to emphasise the fragility of the European peace.[16] The outcome was the formal division of east and west Germany with the creation of Federal Republic of (West) Germany on 23 May 1949, and the Soviet-inspired retaliation, the (East) German Democratic Republic in October 1949. It was, as Churchill declared on 6 March 1946, as if 'from Stettin in the Baltic to Trieste in the Adriatic, an iron curtain has descended upon the Continent'.[17] This political and geographical division of Europe was given a military dimension by the creation of the North Atlantic Treaty Organisation (NATO) on 4 April 1949, which saw twelve nations, including Britain and America (signing her first peacetime treaty), pledging to defend one another from attack. The formation of NATO was in the words of General Ismay, the British chief of staff and secretary-general of NATO until 1957, due to the need to keep Germany down, the Soviets out, and the Americans in.[18] The Soviets responded by creating the Warsaw Pact in May 1955. In economic terms, Moscow's satellites were tied to her through the Council for Mutual Economic Aid (Comecon), set up in 1949. The Soviets tried to extend their influence beyond their sphere of control towards the eastern Mediterranean by indirectly supporting the insurgents in the third round of the Greek civil war in 1945,[19] and towards France and Italy via their domestic communist parties, whose leaders obligingly followed Moscow's orders. When the British warned Washington in February 1947 that it would be terminating aid to Greece and Turkey by the end of March, it forced America to act. On 21 March the Truman Doctrine was announced, viewing the world in terms of struggle between democracy and totalitarianism.[20] The USA shortly took over the security of Greece and Turkey. Further deteriorating relations between east and west, following the failure of the Moscow Council of Foreign Ministers in April 1947 to reach agreement on the future of Germany, encouraged the Americans to think about a European bulwark.

American economic aid

The war had wreaked considerable economic dislocation. It was estimated that western Europe's industrial production in 1946 was a third of the 1938 level. The French War Damage Commission estimated that 45 per cent of France's total wealth had been lost. In Italy it was calculated that a third of all assets had been destroyed. The Dutch believed that their total losses were three times greater than their annual income. In Germany there was considerable material and economic damage. Allied bombing proved effective at destroying Germany's domestic infrastructure, for example 90 per cent of Dusseldorf, but surprisingly poor at damaging the industrial fabric: 91 per cent of Volkswagen works machinery had survived the bombing and then post-war looting.[21] Still German industrial output in 1946 was a third of the 1936 figure. As for Britain she had lost a quarter of her merchant shipping fleet and whereas in 1939 she had been the world's largest creditor by 1945 she was the largest debtor, owing £4.7 billion and having liquidated a third of her overseas assets (£1.1 billion). Official estimates suggested Britain had lost a quarter of her pre-war wealth, yet economically Britain was better placed than all of Europe. In 1948, 42 per cent of western European exports were British.

On 5 June 1947 the US foreign secretary George Marshall announced the willingness of the Americans to provide economic aid to European nations.[22] In part a short-term economic solution, it also had longer-term expectations aimed at providing economic and political reconstruction that would create a bulwark against communist encroachment. It is suggested that the Marshall Plan was deliberately engineered to force Europe to move towards political and economic cooperation.[23] Economically the Americans hoped that Europe could be induced to create a customs union that would increase output and productivity, provide a stable platform for economically rehabilitating Germany, and eliminate the problem of dollar deficits. Whilst the American economy could provide Europe with her requirements, the balance of payments was skewed because Europe did not possess the credit to purchase US exports. By 1947 the UK was buying nearly half of its imports from the USA, whilst France, the world's largest importer of coal, was running an annual payment deficit with the USA of $2,049 million. Furthermore many economists were predicting gloomily that it would take Europe twenty-five years to economically recover. The scale of economic and social dislocation certainly seemed worse than 1918 and with the inter-war experiences fresh in the minds of many, observers felt they had good reason to be pessimistic. In May 1947 one US report considered that 'Europe is steadily deteriorating' economically.[24] Even De Gaulle warned the French people in 1945 that it would take twenty-five years of 'furious work' before France would be revived. The aid was also initially available to the Soviets and the eastern European nations under their control, but Stalin rejected the offer and forbade the eastern Europeans from availing themselves of the gesture. This left sixteen western European nations to negotiate with the Americans from July onwards. Problems arose because of disparate aims and expectations of the European countries, and in the end the Truman government decided to limit the aid programme to four years, with annual Congressional approval. The aid was ultimately distributed via the Organisation for European Economic Cooperation (OEEC), replaced in 1961 by the Organisation for Economic Cooperation and Development (OECD).[25] Although OEEC was an American concept it was shaped by the British and French to their own ends, fearful that the American vision offered by Marshall threatened their economic sovereignty. As a result its diplomatic functions were traditional and intergovernmental by design.[26] In turn the OEEC created a series of intergovernmental bodies and committees to oversee specialist aspects of the aid programme. For example, the European Payments Union (EPU) was established in 1950 as a central bank and clearing house for intra-European trade and payments. By end of 1947 the USA had given $15 billion in aid and over the next four years a further $25 billion. Of this Britain secured the largest share, gaining $2.7 billion between 1948 and 1950. Whether the Marshall plan, and its subsequent 'market imperialism', actually achieved its original aims is open to question.[27] American economic assessments of Europe at the time were flawed, and recovery was already well established, and would be enhanced by the stimulus provided by the Korean War. Also the resistance of the governments of Europe, and defence of their own national interests, prevented the Americans from shaping the post-war European economic market to their own vision.[28] As Bevin explained, this was necessary to retain the 'little bit of dignity we had left'.[29]

The Americans had envisaged that Britain could be persuaded to take the lead in moving Europe towards a common customs union, but the British were not keen on sacrificing further economic sovereignty. In Whitehall, the concept of 'western union' quickly evolved from ideas about a customs union to co-operation with the OEEC in order to signal acceptance of Marshall and US assistance.[30] Yet British decision makers were also wary of Marshall's pledges in case President Truman was unable to persuade Congress. As Hugh Dalton, the chancellor, observed, 'Marshall gives the impression of wanting to do something big, but the Congress are completely illiterate in these matters.'[31] Aside from pleading with the Americans to be treated differently from other European nations, the loan that was negotiated with the USA in 1946, of $3.75 billion (or £1.1 billion), was being drained more quickly than anticipated, through military spending and convertibility problems, with the dangers this posed for Britain's dollar requirements. The onerous conditions under which the government had accepted the loan were not without controversy.[32] Many politicians were suspicious of US motives and feared that Britain was now classed as just another European nation, 'another cog' as Bevin characterised it. Parliament only approved the terms, with much soul searching, by 347–100, with many MPs abstaining.[33] The pound was initially forced to a fixed exchange rate of $4.03 to the pound. Then in July 1947, under the terms of the loan, the pound was made freely convertible against the dollar, provoking a disastrous run against it on the currency markets. During the first twenty days of August $650 million was lost. And against this the winter of 1947–48 proved to be one of the coldest and bitterest ever experienced, putting the British economy under further strain. Then in 1949 the Treasury was obliged to devalue the pound by 30 per cent as American pressure, sterling debts and foreign speculation against the pound took their toll.[34] Yet the pound still remained responsible for half of the world's trade, and devaluation enhanced Britain's competitive trading position.

Visions of unity

During the war years, ideas about possible European Union had been floating around the resistance movements and the governments in exile based in London. Visions for a 'new order' were largely confined to the left-wing components of the resistance, but by 1944 elements of the French resistance were advocating a federal supranational structure for post-war Europe to replace the old system of independent nation-states, which held the responsibility for two world wars in living memory. In July 1944 resistance leaders meeting in Geneva signed a declaration calling for a completely new federal and democratic governmental structure to be applied to the whole of Europe.[35] Although this utopianism was to be dashed with the liberation of Europe and the rapid re-establishment of the old nation-states, at the time, if taken at face value, there were some reasons for optimism. 'Official' American opinion did not appear unfavourable to the ideas of European union, after all the USA was anxious that Europe re-establish her democratic and economic credentials as quickly as possible after hostilities finished so that she could play an active role in the containment of communism. Similarly the Soviet Union appeared unconcerned with the concept; communist resistance groups took their lead from the USSR and were participating in such discussions. Britain had proposed in May 1940 the idea of Anglo–French union, in a last-ditch Churchillian attempt to keep France in the war, suggesting that perhaps too some degree of sympathy for the concept existed.[36] At the end of 1940 Eden and the Foreign Office suggested that a war aim might be some form of European federation. This would comprise a European defence scheme, a European customs union and common currency. All these projects may seem wild now [for 1940], but they are in truth little more than the extension of Briand's conception of a European union.[37]

British establishment figures also regularly discussed the matter with the European governments in exile. Individuals like Henri Paul Spaak, the Belgiam foreign minister, and General Sikorski, the Polish head, pushed the cause of European federation whilst Norway's Trygve Lie and Holland's Eelco van Kleffens hoped a European defensive system would prevent a repetition of German aggrandisement, and for some Britons the impact would be long lasting. Douglas Dodds-Parker, who served in the Council of Europe 1965–72, 'became a "convinced "European"' in 1941 after dining with Spaak to celebrate the Special Operations Executive dropping their first saboteur into Belgium, whilst John Maclay, who would help found the Western European Union, credited Jean Monnet, whom he had got to know in Washington in 1944, with getting him 'very interested in the whole European thing'.[38] Within the Labour party, there appeared to be some individual sympathy from the likes of Cripps and Bevin for European unity. Early in 1943 Churchill returned to the issue of European federation and suggested restoring Europe as a factor in the balance of power and remarking, in a direct challenge to the Foreign Office, that the ideas of Coudenhove-Kalergi had merit. He appeared to take this further when he sent a message to the European Congress in March 1943 that a Council of Europe ought to be a post-war objective.[39] Certainly the superpowers were thinking along the lines of some form of post-war European association. At the Moscow conference of October 1944 the decision was taken to establish a European Advisory Committee to see the completion of the war whilst plans for western European regional association, as part of a wider world organisation, were discussed at the Dumbarton Oaks conference in August–September 1944 that saw the creation of the United Nations Organisation.

Third way

In the aftermath of the war, it appeared as though Winston Churchill, now relegated to the role of opposition party leader having lost the 1945 general election to Labour, was to be the champion of this cause. He made a series of speeches, most famously at Zurich University in September 1946, in which he called for a 'United States of Europe'.[40] Whether Churchill was suggesting that Britain should participate in such a process is debatable. In this Churchill was influenced by his sense of 'history'. Much of his inter-war writing had recurrent themes of Britain acting as a facilitator of the European balance of power.[41] His rallying call was certainly well received by European leaders, although less so by members of his own Conservative party,[42] and especially not the Labour party, which hoped a socialist foreign policy could contribute more to the world, which was suspicious of co-operation with political opponents and which failed to accept that European unity was the overriding imperative of the post-war world given its concerns for domestic reform. But it seems more that Churchill was advocating a united Europe in order to provide a resistance to Soviet Russia, with Britain merely seeking to facilitate this unity, whilst retaining independence of action to pursue the Atlantic alliance and reinvigorate the British empire. This tripartite arrangement became known as the 'three circles' doctrine, and whilst advocated by Churchill and many Conservatives, it also informed the foreign policy approach of Labour's foreign secretary Ernest Bevin. The concept was that three circles – the empire/commonwealth, western Europe and America – were overlapping with Britain as the common denominator.[43] This afforded Britain a unique position of influence, enabling her to maintain her leading world role. As would become apparent, the difficulty with this model was the assumption that these three spheres were open to British leadership, and whether indeed they could be sustained and combined. As a future prime minister would concede, little thought was given to how the theory might be practicably applied.[44] Underpinning Bevin's global vision of British foreign policy was a strong streak of anti-communism, something which brought him into conflict with elements of his own party who still saw merit in the Soviet Union.[45] In the opening post-war years he saw that British foreign policy needed to maintain the illusion of great power co-operation whilst actually directing policy towards the creation of a western alliance to constrain Soviet influence in Europe and the wider world. The problem was that in securing this new balance of power, Britain had to accept a role as deputy to the Americans in western Europe. Presenting this as part of a three circles strategy sugared the bitter pill that had to be stomached. Also Bevin hoped if western Europe could be marshalled into a 'Western Union', led by Britain in an intergovernmental format that sought to exploit the strength of the European empires, he could diminish Britain's reliance on the USA.[46] Here Bevin was diverting from Churchill's world view in placing considerably less emphasis on the Anglo–American alliance, and also from many of his colleagues in the Labour party because he was not seeking to establish a 'third way' either ideologically or in terms of a neutral Europe. In September 1946 Bevin had proposed that the government consider the possibility of western European customs union, something which had attracted his attention before the war, and which now carried the expectation of enhancing the west's economic capabilities against the Soviets. Such a proposal brought Bevin into conflict with the Treasury, who wished to preserve Commonwealth trade and for whom greater free world trade was the requirement. The pressing need to defend the convertibility of sterling can largely account for the Treasury's reluctance, whilst the implacable opposition of the Board of Trade arose because it considered that Europe had neither the political stability nor stable exchange rates to make such a proposal viable. Just as had occurred during the inter-war years, Bevin found that between 1948 and 1949 his vision for a third force was continually resisted by the economic ministries of Whitehall. It meant that the difference of emphasis from the key Whitehall departments ensured that 'Europe' became mired in the Whitehall struggle. This was a view concurred with by Britain's Paris ambassador, Duff Cooper, who observed that Bevin could achieve union between Britain and France 'if it were not for other government departments'.[47] It seems too that with the hardening division of Europe, the majority of the left lost interest in the concept of European unity, even as a long-term objective. Yet some in continental Europe hoped that Bevin's apparent support for western union was evidence that Britain was at last enthusiastic about European unity.[48]

It has been debated amongst academics whether British foreign policy under Labour was aimed solely at securing an American military presence in the defence of Europe, or whether there was actually serious support for the concept of a western European 'third force' which would gain Europe a degree of independence from the superpowers. This so-called 'third way' found favour with both left and right in British politics. For Conservatives it was a non-ideological issue, which conceived the matter solely in world power terms, hoping that it offered Britain the opportunity to continue to pursue her role as arbiter of the balance of power, but this time in tandem with Europe in the new east/west division. It was a 'military necessity'.[49] For the left, and individuals likes G.D.H. Cole and Richard Crossman, it was more an ideological idea that would mix a blend of socialist planning, social justice and political freedom.[50] It was felt that Britain and Europe could be strong enough (especially economically) to act independently of both the Americans and Russians, and that in turn the risk of war would be diminished. Central to this debate was the dilemma of whether Europe was a problem for the British and the Americans to solve or whether it was an opportunity for Britain to take. The Czech coup and the Berlin blockade had shown that East–West tensions were escalating and not easily reconcilable. Yet arguments about a European 'third force' were redundant by 1949. On 17 March 1948 Britain, France, the Netherlands, Belgium and Luxembourg signed the Brussels Pact, thereby extending the Dunkirk Treaty of March 1947, which had been a non-binding alliance against German aggression, although not aggression directed towards eastern European countries, and thereby carried echoes of Locarno. Both of these should be categorised as standing 'in a long tradition of British gestures of reassurance to France'.[51] Conceived as a military alliance, looking increasingly towards a Russian threat particularly following the Soviet-inspired coup in Czechoslovakia in February, it also included provisions for greater co-operation in economic and cultural matters. It also established regular ministerial meetings in a consultative council, something that NATO would later copy. The treaty, though, has been characterised as the 'swan song' of Bevin's third force ideas.[52] Some in the Labour party felt that it did not go far enough, observing that a previous defence treaty, Locarno, had failed to keep Britain out of World War II.[53] Historians, like Milward, sense that Brussels was a disappointment to Bevin, who had hoped that the economic protocols of the treaty could have been strengthened so as to provide a platform for a stronger western European union identity.[54] By mid-1948 talks began between the Brussels Pact powers and the Americans about the viability of new defence organisations from which the North Atlantic Treaty Organisation would emerge in 1949, which would, as Michael Foot decided, be a 'pact for peace'. Yet western Europe was no longer to be an independent force but was to hitch its military machine to the American juggernaut. The rapidly hastening Cold War meant that the issue of defence came to the fore as the only short-term solution that could be achieved. NATO gave Britain its military security. Pentagon analysts envisaged the defence of the UK from its US airbases, whilst the plan for the continent was withdrawal and reconquest.[55] For many on the left their growing fear of Russia now began to outweigh their suspicions they held about the Americans, and with this most left-wingers abandoned the objective of European unity. Yet it accentuated the schism between Labour left and right which would plague the Labour party for the next thirty years. Domestically left-wing Labour figures were perhaps unwilling to push too strongly for friendship with Russia, conscious that historic experiences over the Zinoviev letter and the Red scare of the late 1920s, did not play well with the electorate. Third force-ism would momentarily reappear over unilateralism and the Campaign for Nuclear Disarmament in the early 1960s and in the 1980s when Labour proposed a nuclear-free Europe and withdrawal from NATO, but it would never carry the same energy.

Council of Europe

In Britain, May 1947 saw the launch of the United European Movement (UEM), which quickly became a Europe-wide propaganda organisation. Twelve months later it convened the Hague Congress with Churchill as the *president d'honneur*. The British Labour party was so concerned that this was a gathering convened solely for the benefit of the Conservative party and grandstanding Churchill that it refused to sanction its MPs participation (although twenty-seven ignored the edict) and asked other socialist parties of Europe not to send delegates – although in the event only the German and Belgium socialists were not formally represented.[56] From this gathering emerged the expectation that a European parliamentary assembly should be formed. The French government, inspired by Churchill's speech and sensing that the momentum of public goodwill generated ought to be capitalised upon, proposed to the autumn meeting of the Brussels Pact powers that a European Assembly with executive powers ought to be considered. This took concrete form when ten countries agreed to the creation of an intergovernmental organisation, the Council of Europe, a name proposed by Bevin. This body was to comprise of two components: a Committee of Ministers and a Consultative Assembly, taking political delegates from the member nations, and to be symbolically located in Strasbourg at the crossroads between France and Germany. Although the Benelux countries and Italy had hoped for a greater degree of executive power to be granted to the Assembly, inter-governmental characteristics (as favoured by Britain, Ireland and the Scandinavian nations) prevailed, meaning that most power rested with the Committee of Ministers, with the power of veto preserving national sovereignty. This committee also controlled the Council's budget and secretariat and decided the scale and proportions of the signatory nations' delegation and budget contribution. Bevin was broadly supportive about creating the new organisation because it offered a possible future vehicle for organising European economic co-operation once Marshall Aid had ceased, although his insistence on the pre-eminence of the Council of Ministers was interpreted by some as a deliberate wrecking move.[57] The Assembly had only consultative status and was prevented from debating any issues relating to defence, yet a whole generation of British politicians would serve on the Council's Assembly, exposing many, who would subsequently come to champion closer European integration, to the ways of doing European business. As Attlee explained, 'I don't under-stand Europe, but in twenty years' time the party ought to have people who do'.[58] The representatives sent to the Assembly were delegates rather than elected members, the latter concept having been resisted by Ernest Bevin, who feared an elected assembly becoming a 'Pandora's Box' full of 'Trojan Horses'.[59] During the 1961–63 EEC application the majority of former and current Council of Europe delegates favoured entry, and from the back-benches of Westminster provided Prime Minister Harold Macmillan with a reliable source of support.[60] The inaugural session of the Assembly was in 1949 to great fanfare, not least because Churchill attended as head of the Conservative delegation. Yet the experience of the British delegation was mixed; Churchill and his Labour counterpart at one point fell into a very public spat on the Assembly floor over finance issues in a manner reminiscent of the debating chamber of the House of Commons, but this was a style that was both bemusing and alien to the majority of the continental European delegates.[61] Others saw it as a 'jolly', such as Labour delegate Anthony Crosland, who spent his days in bed with alcoholic hangovers.[62] The Assembly did achieve limited success, particularly in the field of human rights, and a sub-committee of the Assembly was responsible for devising a European convention for the 1948 United Nations Universal Declaration of Human Rights. Whitehall was initially very wary of this development, and was con-cerned particularly that it might lead to the overriding of national law as individual citizens sought to appeal directly to an international court of human rights.[63] In October 1950 the government accepted the Convention, but with the proviso that it opted out of Articles 25 and 46, thus beginning a long trend of opting out. Between 1955 and 1980 over 9,000 individual and 10 inter-state applications had been made to the Commission of Human Rights.[64] Despite this positive beginning, to many continental participants, such as Monnet and Spaak, it was evident that first the Labour and then the Churchill Conservative governments were doing their utmost to undermine the Council, as with the refusal to participate in a European army, and by the sending of delegations lacking in seniority and experience.[65] Senior Labour figures were increasingly dismissive, believing that 'the United Kingdom gains little by its membership of the Council of Europe and would be well out of it'.[66] Labour's negativism over the Council of Europe convinced some continental politicians that Britain's interest in intergovernmental institutions was a deliberate delaying tactic that did nothing to benefit Europe. Labour ministers ignored or vetoed the bulk of the Assembly's resolutions.[67] As a consequence Monnet concluded that Britain would not go on a 'mutual journey to an unknown destination' and therefore alternative French-led methods had to be secured.[68] Similarly, Henri Paul Spaak resigned as president of the Council of Europe Assembly in 1952, frustrated that Churchill's government had failed to deliver on its European expectations: having created a vision it was now not delivering the practical leadership.[69] This encouraged them to look for alternative means of securing their economic and political goals. These politicians, sensing the Council to be a lame duck without effective British participation, resolved to find alternative means of securing European unity that could not be scuppered by British intransigence. Contemporary observers could also be forgiven for wondering whether these well meaning, almost utopian, declarations bore too close a resemblance to the failed treaties (such as Kellogg Briand) of the inter-war years and for consequently paying them little attention. There was a sense too that the Council duplicated the functions of NATO, OEEC and the Brussels Treaty and that it was little more than 'a polyglot debating society'.[70] The Council received very little media attention in Britain. Only forty years later with the collapse of communism would the Council of Europe find a new direction for itself as it undertook the task of teaching the ex-communist states democracy and the rule of law.

Schuman Plan

In early May 1950 Robert Schuman, the French foreign minister, invited Attlee's Labour government to participate in discussions to create a European Coal and Steel Community (ECSC).[71] The plan had been conceived in great secrecy by Schuman, Monnet (then head of the French reconstruction committee) and Bernard Clappier. Neither the French coal nor steel industries were consulted, whilst the Quai d'Orsay (the French foreign ministry) was kept out of the loop. The French political establishment was obsessed by the fear of a resurgent Germany. Many, like De Gaulle, had wanted to split Germany up, or at worst hive off her economically important region, the Ruhr. However, the problem for the French was that the German solution was being driven by the Americans, abetted by the British, and took a diametrically opposed approach. The timing of the plan was linked to a forthcoming tripartite conference between Britain, France and America at which the French feared their allies would insist on the lifting of the existing limits on

West German steel production. During the war not all French exiles had been intent on economically and militarily weakening post-war Germany. Some like Monnet and Marjolin developed a view that a democratically prosperous Germany could be economically tied to a unified western Europe. It was hoped that harnessing the economic independence of Germany would in turn lead to a closer bond between France and Germany and thus diminish the risk of war. Certainly some in the American State Department, like George Kennan, were keen on the idea of European economic cooperation. Truman, the American president, called the plan 'an act of constructive statesmanship' and 'a demonstration of French leadership in the solution of the problems of Europe'.[72] Schuman's background may also have some link to the conception of the plan. Although he had been born in Luxembourg, he had become a German citizen and fought for Germany in the First World War, before taking French citizenship in 1919 when Alsace became part of France.[73] On 3 May 1950 the French cabinet had discussed the idea for linking the coal and steel industries of the Lorraine and Ruhr under a supranational High Authority, strictly independent of member nation governments, with sovereign powers. Bidault, the French prime minister, was concerned for the implications for French economic sovereignty, but Schuman's idea secured approval on 9 May. There is some evidence that the Americans were placing pressure on the French to agree to this course of action, and Dean Acheson, the American secretary of state, was in Paris in advance of the announcement en route to London. The German leader, Adenauer, was given a few hours advance notification of the plan, although Schuman was privately already certain of his support. Initially it was only a Franco–German proposal, but other European nations were invited to bring their industries into the organisation, and the French made it clear that only Germany could kill off the idea. The British Labour government was far from enthusiastic and the invitation was declined on 2 June and in doing so, some historians have argued, Britain made itself 'superfluous' to Franco–German rapprochement.[74]

Twelve months later, after an official signing ceremony on 18 April 1951, Belgium, France, West Germany, Italy, Luxembourg and the Netherlands oversaw the creation of the ECSC. The influence of the High Authority was somewhat diluted from its original vision because the ECSC Council of Ministers was given greater powers, and a parliamentary assembly and court were also established. Although from a British perspective it was easy to dismiss this because it did not appear to harm core British economic interests, psychologically it wrested the leadership of Europe away from Britain and began to create the impression of the 'awkward partner'. The decision not to participate demonstrated a mix of British confidence, annoyance and short-termism. There is some evidence that Britain had been lulled into believing that she was the arbiter of European co-operation. In part this arose because of Britain's relations with the USA, but was complacency encouraged by European figures like the Italian foreign minister Sforza, who had told Bevin that Germany could only be contained if Britain, France and Italy cooperated? Some in the Foreign Office objected to the last minute notification of the plan and felt that the French were acting unilaterally over Germany when it was an Allied decision, and featured a region (the Ruhr) that was in the British zone of control. Although it can be debated as to whether in fact various sources had for a while been alerting their political masters in Britain to the types of discussions that were taking place in French economic and political circles, the fact remains that Britain decided not to participate. Economics can largely explain this decision; William Strang, permanent under-secretary, warned 'that we should not be involved in Europe in the economic sphere, beyond the point of no return'. To his mind the surrender of economic sovereignty required would take Britain beyond that point of no return.[75] Britain was not so concerned about the ideas of European federation, federal after all in the 1940s carried connotations of trust, but there was serious concern about the concept of the non-elected High Authority and the idea that signatories were bound to its decisions, thus challenging British economic and political sovereignty. Bevin was scathing, suggesting that the weakness of the French Fourth Republic political system, characterised by fragile coalition governments and challenged on the left by the communists and on the right from the Gaullists, meant it had no sovereignty to sacrifice.[76] The British coal and steel industry was opposed, wishing to concentrate on its global markets rather than Europe, which accounted for only 5 per cent of its exports.[77] It needs to be remembered too that the Labour government had only recently nationalised the coal industry and fought a controversial political battle to do the same to the steel industry. Furthermore she produced half of the coal and one third of the steel of the seven nations likely to participate in the plan. With such production dominance, could Britain really surrender public control over these important staple industries to an un-elected High Authority, especially as the other potential partner states were all dominated politically, not by socialists, but Christian Democrats? The Schuman plan also showed how the matter of 'Europe' translated itself onto the game of British party politics.[78] Nor were matters helped when Parliament met to debate the idea because many were distracted by the outbreak of the Korean War the previous day. It is clear that Schuman only aroused the interest of those at the leadership elite level, or those who had a specialist interest in European affairs, otherwise the majority of parliamentarians were ambivalent, and it is clear that it carried no widespread resonance with the electorate. Yet despite this final observation, the Conservatives, as the opposition party, saw the opportunity to secure political points over the Labour government, and therefore positioned themselves as favouring Britain entering into negotiations. As if to reinforce this, Harold Macmillan and David Eccles put forward alternative plans for a British coal/steel inter-governmental organisation in August 1950 to the Council of Europe Assembly.[79] The domestic argument used, which was to be repeated over coming decades, was that Britain should go into Europe and take the lead; to remain aloof would be fatal; with this opportunity missed, the terms of entry would only become more awkward. And so arose the mythological assertion that somehow Schuman and the ECSC were a 'missed opportunity'. Certainly pro-Europeans like Macmillan may have perceived themselves at this point as being more constructive towards the European project, but this was not how their actions were received from a continental viewpoint. Monnet was highly critical of the Macmillan–Eccles plan, sensing a difference of emphasis from the government, rather than substance.[80] On the other hand, given the Conservatives' support for the Council of Europe and now the Schuman Plan, it had the effect of raising expectations, especially on the continent, about how a future Conservative government might behave on European matters. This was dealt an almost immediate blow when Churchill told his new cabinet in November 1951 'Our attitude is that we help [European Federation], we dedicate, we participate, but we do not merge and we do not forfeit our insular or Commonwealth character.'[81] It is worth observing too that the issue of national sovereignty was clearly debated from this point onwards, something that contradicts current Eurosceptic arguments that it was never fully debated until the 1990s. Linked to this is the consideration of whether Schuman's plans were indeed 'federal'? Such a phrase in the 1940s carried very different meaning to a contemporary audience than it would to a twenty-first century audience. It was less of a political bogey word, and more synonymous with concepts about trust and equality between partners. For some contemporaries these two features just did not exist between Germany and France at this time, and indeed the repudiation of the French Assembly to the Pleven Plan, which would have created a European army and resolved the issue of West German rearmament, showed that federalism was not high on the French agenda.

Defence and Western European Union (WEU)

One of the key problems for the British in the first decades after the end of the war was what to do with Germany. The British had a considerable military presence in West Germany, comprising of four army divisions and the Tactical Air Force. In 1947 Britain had concluded with France the Treaty of Dunkirk offering a guarantee against future German aggression. There was certainly a strand of British thinking that hoped a Franco-British alliance would boost pro-western elements in France and diminish the likelihood of a French betrayal of the capitalist western bloc because of the communist influence in the French government. The physical partition of Germany by the establishments of GDR and FRG made this country one of the flash points of the Cold War, but it ended any immediate prospects for reunification and meant it was all the more imperative that West Germany was rehabilitated to the diplomatic circuit and given the opportunity to remilitarise. The debate about how best to oversee German rearmament brought the British into dispute with the French, who understandably were wary of allowing this to happen so shortly after the end of the war. In Anglo–French relations the importance of history and the appropriating of events and symbols to reinforce and undermine preferences is important. The British had a tendency to frame military relations in terms of the Second World War and the British alliance with the Free French. However, for the French the war was a much more ambivalent experience. De Gaulle harboured dark thoughts about how the Anglo–American alliance sought to exclude French concerns and priorities, whilst many in France, especially in naval circles, had considerable bitterness over the British shelling of French Vichy naval ships at Mers-el-Kébir in 1940.[82]

A commonality of purpose existed between both the foreign ministries of the 1945–51 Labour government and of the successor Conservative administration. Using a premise that western Europe needed to act as a single entity to resist the political advances of communism and the Soviet bloc's military might, meant that Britain displayed a willingness to participate in military alliances such as NATO (1949) and the Western European Union (1952). Part of this was underpinned by a degree of arrogance that suggested that western continental nations were incapable of organising their own military defences against Soviet aggression and British leadership in this arena was required, although Britain was only committed to two British divisions. Not that Britain's European counterparts saw matters in this manner, and the French were keen to extract more precise British troop commitments, no doubt mindful of historic British reluctance to continentally commit. The first signs of this continental disquiet emerged in October 1950 when the French announced the Pleven Plan, an idea to create a European Defence Community (EDC) which would include a European defence minister responsible to a European Assembly, a European Defence Council of Ministers, a single European defence budget and a European joint command. Although some senior British government figures had earlier appeared to propose a similar idea for a European army at the Council of Europe, the Pleven Plan was not well received in Whitehall.[83] Concern was expressed at its federalist intentions, and the absence of a mechanism for withdrawal, whilst scorn was poured on its military competences. The matter dragged on into 1951 and it is evident that the British Cabinet was divided over whether to sanction the proposal. One minister, David Maxwell-Fyfe, promised that the issue was worthy of 'thorough examination', only to be rebuked hours later by Anthony Eden who rejected any concept that Britain could join a European army.[84] Behind this internal debate rested a fundamental dispute about where Britain's loyalties lay: should she look to the continent or was the goodwill of America and the Atlantic alliance of greater importance? There was an anxiety that the EDC proposal was a deliberate French ploy to diminish the primacy of NATO in Europe's defence, and in turn this potentially threatened Britain's unique position of straddling the three spheres of influence: Europe, America and empire. Negotiations continued though 1951 and 1952, when in March Foreign Secretary Eden proposed an alternative plan. It was suggested that the various western European communities should come together under the auspices of the Council of Europe. The ECSC and the European Defence Community should use the secretariat and assembly of the Council of Europe. This complemented a British desire to strengthen the intergovernmental nature of the Council of Europe, and also offered a chance to assuage French fears about a resurgent Germany by hitching the German rearmament programme to the western European defence system. However, there were also hopes within the Foreign Office that reforming (or 'killing ... in its present form') the Council of Europe would provide the opportunity 'of beating a decent retreat from Strasbourg'. The Eden Plan was not well received in Europe, with many suspecting that this was a deliberate attempt to sabotage attempts at closer European cooperation, and in order to smooth over counter-proposals from Schuman, by July 1952 Eden was insisting that the changes should occur 'within the framework of an organisation in which we play a full and active part'.[85] Yet if it was to be the British who derided the Pleven Plan, it ultimately received its coup de grace from the French when her parliamentarians rejected it in August 1954. David Bruce, the US ambassador in London, concluded it was 'the greatest missed opportunity in modern European history'.[86]

In contrast, sensing an opportunity to safeguard NATO's primacy, Eden then suggested that German rearmament should be made an issue for NATO. He proposed an extension to the 1948 Brussels treaty to allow the membership of West Germany and Italy, thereby recognising West Germany as a sovereign nation and permitting limited and controlled rearmament and membership of NATO. In exchange, Britain agreed to maintain its military presence in Germany. Thus the Western European Union (WEU) came into being in October 1954. The WEU's council and secretariat were based in London, whilst the parliamentary assembly was in Paris. Membership of the assembly was drawn from the Council of Europe delegations, and the activities of both organisations' assemblies overlapped. Ultimately, WEU was little more than a paper tiger; most of its functions were merely duplications of either the activities of the Council of Europe or NATO, but importantly it enabled Germany to re-enter the international order in a manner that both reassured the French and assisted NATO in maintaining the military balance of power in Europe. It improved relations between member states, as shown with its role in the negotiations over the transfer of the Saar region from French to West German control in 1955. British ministers were smugly satisfied that the whole experience had re-established British leadership in Europe, ensured the primacy of Atlanticism, and demonstrated the primacy of inter-governmentalism over federalism.[87]

Messina and the Treaties of Rome

The British government might have felt that WEU had dealt a long-term blow to the integrationist agenda, but many continental politicians were anxious to find alternative forums. A multinational meeting of the six ECSC members was convened at Messina, Sicily in 1955 to begin just such discussions about the possibility of a customs union. Britain was then invited to participate in the detailed discussions to be held in Brussels and chaired by Spaak, but determined the meeting worthy only of the presence of a civil servant from the Board of Trade, Russell Bretherton.[88] It was hoped amongst the Six that by not making the acceptance of supranationalism a precondition of joining the discussions then the British and the Dutch would feel able to participate. It was certainly an issue that vexed the Foreign Office and it remained 'haunted' by a fear that Britain would lose its sovereignty if it participated in plans for federation. Pro-Europeanists like Harold Macmillan, the foreign secretary, hoped that Britain could exert influence through participation, but still only referred to the Messina process once in his diary.[89] The Treasury supported by the Bank of England and the Commonwealth Relations Office were unsympathetic to the concept. All of this meant resisting American pressure, with the Foreign Office having it clearly stated by the American embassy in London that Eisenhower supported the discussions whilst the State Department let it be known, when the British suggested it should be discussed within the framework of OEEC, that they saw no conflict or overlap. The British Whitehall discussions about the viability of the proposals were considered by the Mutual Aid Committee (MAC) working group, chaired by Burke Trend, under-secretary at the Treasury. That this was a working party and not a sub-committee should be taken as indicative of its lowliness of priority. Britain's trading patterns certainly suggested that membership of a customs union would be detrimental. Only 14 per cent of British exports went to the Six and only 25 per cent to the whole of Europe, whilst 50 per cent went to Commonwealth countries. Officials were concerned that membership of a customs union would result in discrimination against Commonwealth trade, particularly agricultural products, which constituted 50 per cent of their exports to Britain. British growth rates did perhaps indicate problems: British growth rates 1950–55 were 2.9 per cent, compared to 4.4 per cent for France, 6.3 per cent for Italy, 9.1 per cent for Germany and an average of 6.2 per cent for the Six.[90]

Some in the Board of Trade wondered whether Britain could negotiate a preferential arrangement on this aspect and also observed that raw material exports from the Commonwealth were mostly tariff-free in the Six. Britain's share of exports from Commonwealth countries was also in decline, from 39 per cent in 1938 to 27 per cent in 1956 with 64 per cent of that coming from New Zealand, 31 per cent from Australia and 17 per cent from Canada. Despite this ministers felt unable politically to surrender on preference. At the end of October the conclusions of the MAC review determined that the establishment of a common market would be prejudicial to Britain if she joined and 'if possible, should be frustrated ... We cannot count on the project collapsing of its own accord.' On 11 November 1955 the decision to withdraw Bretherton from the Spaak committee was taken. There appeared to be little appetite for the matter either in Cabinet or Parliament (indeed Cabinet never once discussed the Messina initiative and Parliament did not discuss the issue until Robert Boothby tabled a parliamentary written question in June 1956),[91] and many were sceptical about the French commitment to the proposals, particularly given their recent actions over EDC.[92] There is certainly some evidence to support this assessment, for even Spaak was concerned as late as February 1956 that Paris would scupper his plans; however, the British had not foreseen the fallout from the Suez crisis.[93] Britain's unilateral decision to halt and withdraw her forces from the joint Anglo–French military operation against Nasser's Egypt upset Paris, damaging Anglo–French relations at a point when the French government was having reservations about the customs union plan not involving the British, and consequently determined them to seek closer co-operation with the Federal Republic of Germany. Also there was little appetite more widely in economic circles in Britain. The main British economic interest groups, such as the Federation of British Industries, National Farmers Union, National Union of Manufacturers and Association of British Chambers of Commerce, were unprepared in 1955 for the concept of a customs union, and their interest, and eventual support for the concept, only grew after 1957.

When Bretherton was withdrawn there was confidence that the proposed trade alliance had little to offer Britain. The manner of the British withdrawal did cause offence, especially when it became apparent that they were seeking to sabotage the discussions by encouraging the Germans to withdraw too and encouraging American hostility by suggesting that a customs union was incompatible with global trade liberalisation.[94] The Foreign Office, basing its assessment on repeated comments by German economics minister Erhard, presumed that Germany was lukewarm to the idea of a customs union. However, they placed undue emphasis on the influence of Erhard's economic arguments in the German government and inflated his influence over European policy. In fact, Adenauer took the view that economics were not applicable and that German membership would be for the greater good of Europe.[95] The Six ensured that Macmillan was well aware of their anger when he attended the WEU Ministerial Council meeting in December 1955 and then the NATO Council meeting in Paris.[96] Some have interpreted the attempts at sabotage as recognition that the Six were going to succeed and that this customs union would damage Britain if she were excluded.[97] In May 1956 the Six agreed that their Brussels talks should provide the platform for negotiating a common market. The French government, acutely aware that its Assembly could repeat its EDC actions, sought to ensure that French concerns about colonial trade and transitional periods were assuaged. The British then decided to abandon their covert opposition and moved to counter-balance the emerging EEC. Consequently the Six reached agreement on 25 March 1957 and signed the Treaties of Rome, which created the European Economic Community and Euratom; these came into being on 1 January 1958.

In October 1956 the Conservative government had proposed Plan G, a form of European free trade area in industrial goods (an emphasis intended to placate the party's farming lobby). It was hoped this would include the Six, Britain and any other members of the OEEC who wished to join. Therefore Britain was proposing association rather than membership and seeking to safeguard her relationship with America and the Commonwealth. A Free Trade Association had first been raised in the autumn of 1955 as part of ideas about how to counter the Messina process and lure the Six into the OEEC. When it was clear that this would not happen, FTA was mooted as a possible alternative to the Messina process. Only in the autumn of 1956 did FTA become a policy aimed at complementing the Common Market plans.[98]

Whilst it is generally accepted that Suez drove London to seek to restore the Anglo–American alliance in preference to seeking a European solution, Macmillan's government did appear to be giving fresh impetus to European policy, by seeking to supplement its free trade area plans with proposals for political and defence co-operation. Selwyn Lloyd's 'grand design' was a Foreign Office plan to regroup the various European parliamentary assemblies (Council of Europe, Western European Union, NATO, Common Assembly of Coal and Steel Community) under one single parliamentary assembly to cover all aspect of 'western cooperation'. However, the proposal found little favour with anyone. This 'grand design' included 'radical' proposals for realigning Britain with the Six in the field of developing thermo-nuclear weapons under the aegis of the Western European Union.[99] That this was proposed four days before Eden resigned as prime minister over Suez, makes it all the more significant. It suggests too that the Foreign Office was trying to wrest European initiatives away from the economic departments of Whitehall. However, the Cabinet rejected the nuclear plans in January 1957, not least because they were felt to run in conflict with a post-Suez strategy of giving primacy to Anglo–American relations. Thus only the proposals for institutional assembly reform went before the governments of Europe. Some, particularly the Germans, suspected these were part of British plans to delay the final stages of the Treaties of Rome. Austria, Sweden and Switzerland, as members of the OEEC, rejected the assembly plans simply because they involved defence, whilst the Eisenhower administration made its hostility very clear to the British. Matters were not helped by the British seeking to gain WEU approval to withdraw conventional British forces from Germany so that the British Army on the Rhine would only total 50,000 (a 30 per cent reduction), as required by Duncan Sandys' defence review, which was seeking to recast Britain's strategy away from conventional forces towards a nuclear deterrent. As Macmillan admitted to his diary, 'the reception of our plan for cutting our forces was pretty chilly'.[100] For many it questioned the extent of Britain's 'Europeanism' and disturbed the French who sensed it was an attempt by Britain to reduce its continental commitment. It suggested too that between the failure of the Eden plan in 1952 and the next five years the British were continuing to demonstrate their insensitivities to the concerns of the Six, and their failure to learn from past mistakes.

Free trade area

In August 1957 Reginald Maudling was given responsibilities for conducting further free trade area negotiations with the seventeen member nations of the OEEC.[101] The Six, recognising that there were considerable differences of opinion amongst themselves over free trade, feared that Maudling's bilateral negotiations during this period were part of a British attempt to scupper the newly agreed Treaty of Rome. It is evident too that the Interim Committee, established by the Six to cover the period between signature and formal creation of the EEC, resented the distraction of trying to negotiate a free trade area when their priorities lay in establishing the institutions of their new community and formulating policies. The French were also anxious that a common market could not be grafted onto a free trade area, and feared that the French economy was not sufficiently insulated to cope with the competition of free trade. Also, fears were expressed that if other members of the Six, especially the Germans and Dutch, accepted free trade it might diminish their adherence to the Common Market goal. Furthermore there were concerns about British Commonwealth trade and agriculture. The Six were not swayed, and the British miscalculated the influence Germany held over France. During the summer and autumn of 1957 it became clear that the Six were not going to be moved towards the British proposals, and despite various attempts to water down the British concept to make it acceptable, including bringing agriculture into the equation, ultimately nothing could reconcile the French to the British position. In April 1958 the French government fell. For the next six weeks the prospect of civil war loomed over France, until General De Gaulle returned from political exile, assumed power on 1 June and founded the 5th Republic. De Gaulle had been an outspoken opponent of EDC and had been highly critical of the Treaties of Rome, which led some to hope that he might look more favourably on the free trade concept. However, in De Gaulle's eyes Britain had blotted its copybook by appearing indifferent to his proposals for a three-power directorate of NATO, and recognising that French public opinion was strongly opposed to free trade, he vetoed participation. The plans to exclude foodstuffs and for Commonwealth preference had to be diluted, and faced with effective French intransigence the British were forced to admit that it was a failure. It was a failure in no large part due to poorly conceived British negotiating plans.[102] Its failure suggested the inconsistency of Britain seeking to align with Europe whilst still harbouring ambitions of maintaining a relationship with the Commonwealth and America. FTA also showed that Britain had miscalculated the extent to which the Six wanted Britain to participate in European affairs.[103] What is noticeable is that the Five supported France, putting aside their own differences on free trade because of 'loyalty to the Treaty of Rome'.[104] It was the first crucial test for the fledgling EEC and it passed. The British press was under no illusion as to whom to blame. On 18 November *The Times*' leader was headed 'France the wrecker' and there was widespread speculation that a trade war might erupt in western Europe.

Some historians have characterised Britain's unwillingness to participate in Messina as a missed opportunity.[105] Others have portrayed it as less a rejection of the EEC as a conscious strategic decision by Britain to pursue an alternative strategy that at the time was perceived as being in Britain's better interests.[106] An even more damning interpretation is the suggestion that Britain just failed to analyse the situation correctly and take account of the recent changes in the international context.[107] Some contemporaries retrospectively concur with this last assessment. 'We stood aside', opined Peter Thorneycroft in the 1980s, 'because there was no strategic decision in the British Cabinet to play a part in Europe'.[108] On the one hand the British government could excuse itself from not signing up to the Treaties of Rome. The 1956 Suez crisis, arising from the Anglo–French invasion of the Egyptian canal zone and the subsequent humiliating withdrawal in the face of international, and especially American, condemnation had cost the career of prime minister Anthony Eden and demonstrated the nadir to which British world power had sunk. Harold Macmillan, Eden's successor at Number Ten, had the distraction of rebuilding Anglo–American relations as well as establishing his own position whilst the treaty negotiations were reaching their climax. Many had doubted that the Six would ever be able to set aside their differences and reach agreement; others inclined to the view that it mattered not, as the proposed EEC could do no economic harm to Britain, and were thankful that Britain's Commonwealth trade and agricultural products were subject to the Six's decision to include their overseas territories within the EEC tariff boundaries.[109]

The spring of 1959 saw testing times for the European project. Germany and France rebuffed the High Authority of the Coal and Steel Community's plans for dealing with the rapidly mounting coal stocks. Concerns abounded about the French's commitment to supranationalism, further there were concerns that De Gaulle's growing hostility to NATO might force the Germans to choose between this military alliance and the new French relationship. The likelihood that Adenauer could step down as German chancellor, with the prospect that Erhard, an advocate of free trade, might succeed him, caused anxiety for many 'Europeanists'. Consequently any suggestions that the EEC might return to the issue of its trading relationship with the wider Europe was met with hostility, and encouraged the argument that the Community should seek to hasten the Treaty of Rome timetable and consider measures for deepening the ties between the Six.

EFTA alternative

Having excluded itself from the Treaties of Rome and having failed to secure a Free Trade Area instead, Britain, at the instigation of the Swiss, had to settle for a much smaller industrial European Free Trade Association (EFTA) comprising seven member nations (Denmark, Norway, Sweden, Austria, Portugal and Switzerland) which was signed into being on 21 November 1959.[110] This commitment to EFTA would make it even harder for Britain to reach rapprochement with the EEC; it suggested too that Britain had not yet reached a point of seriously considering joining the Common Market. When Parliament had debated the prospect in February 1959 there appeared to be a degree of consensus between the rival front benches that Britain should seek association with the Common Market, but the means by which this could be achieved were unclear; only the Liberals deviated, advocating that Britain seek EEC membership.[111] When the House returned to the matter in December to approve the government's actions in establishing EFTA the debate was poorly attended, with most speakers wishing to concentrate on the prospects for reaching agreement with the Six rather than in discussion of EFTA. When the Liberals divided the House, believing the government should have gone further in trying to associate with the Common Market, the government's majority was a comfortable 185–3.[112] One wit, playing with the number of members each organisation had, suggested Europe was now at 'Sixes and Sevens'. Critics believed that EFTA was far too small to compete with the EEC or America. Supporters countered with the argument that such a trading bloc, because it was British-led, would liberalise trade. It was even optimistically suggested that its creation would oblige the Six to abandon the EEC and join with EFTA to create one large free trade area. Certainly some of the Benelux countries were anxious to secure arrangements that covered the entire OEEC sphere. The EEC Commission's response was to refuse to sanction any further discussions with the Seven: free trade only made economic sense in a growing global market if it was embedded in a structure of economic union, or if it was part of a world wide free trade agreement. Others members of the Six were relieved and hoped that the discussions amongst the Seven would distract them from the calls for a wider arrangement. Furthermore, many 'Europeanists' looked at the EFTA agreement as a retrograde step, it being little more than a commercial agreement.[113] Matters were made more complicated by De Gaulle's vision for Europe, which began emerging from May 1960, and the reaction of the Six. De Gaulle's placing greater emphasis on the nation-state strained relations with Adenauer, who believed in supranationalism. De Gaulle was also making proposals about monetary and cultural union, something some in the Six suspected was a French tactic to create an alternative authority to diminish the responsibilities of the European Commission. De Gaulle appeared to be more favourable to confederation. In their discussions the Six tried to be guided by three negotiating positions: a wish to ensure that the Six developed within the framework of NATO; to ensure the independence of the established Communities and to provide them with a framework for future growth; and to provide the possibility for future federal objectives to govern their procedures.

Some concluding thoughts

It became quickly apparent that EFTA was not the economic solution that Britain was seeking; indeed there is considerable evidence that they had only reluctantly signed up in 1959. But politically, the prime minister during 1959 was distracted by the problems of East–West relations and détente and the likelihood of fighting a general election. However, behind closed doors in the confines of Whitehall planners began considering the possibilities of whether Britain ought to join the EEC. This conversion began strongly taking hold from the spring of 1960, which challenged the prospect that a Europe-wide free trade area could ever be negotiated and which then questioned whether some form of associated status with the EEC was actually in Britain's best interests. Civil servants Frank Lee and Herbert Andrew, alongside Chancellor of the Exchequer Peter Thorneycroft, have been credited as key figures in the Whitehall conversion. Lee chaired the Economic Steering Committee in 1960 which was concerned with examining the possibilities of finding accommodation with the Six and which concluded that politically it was in Britain's interests to join the Common Market. Senior figures began making positive statements about Europe. Selwyn Lloyd told the Assembly of the Council of Europe that 'we regard ourselves as part of Europe, for reasons of sentiment, of history and geography'; furthermore he regarded it as 'a mistake' for Britain to have not joined the discussions to form the Coal and Steel Community, and that despite having associate status since 1956 this was not the same as being a member.[114] In the spring of 1960 government departments were instructed to examine the articles of the Treaty of Rome and report in detail on the likely implications membership would entail, both in policy and financial terms. In a House of Lords debate, Lord Boothby, long an advocate of European co-operation, warned Macmillan that Britain would have to work hard to remove the Six's suspicions of Britain's motives, but that 'the time has come to jump' and join the Common Market.[115]

3 The application phase 1961–75

Over the decade of the 1960s Britain was to make two bids (1961 and 1967) to become a member of the European Economic Community (EEC), before finally achieving success at the third attempt in 1970. In that time Britain had to overcome the hostility of France, and seek to resolve problems concerning the position of British agriculture and her trading relationship with the Commonwealth. Throughout, the applications were presented as free trade exercises that were economic necessities if Britain was to survive economically on the world stage. For critics this was a radically dangerous departure, which threatened to irreparably destroy Britain's imperial links, and yet others viewed it as little more than an attempt to reinterpret the three circles – Europe, America and the Commonwealth – with Britain at the intersection.[1]

To apply or not?

The decision to seek EEC membership was not a snap decision, but rather an evolutionary change of position that had occurred over a period of years. A multiplicity of factors, both domestic and external, can explain Harold Macmillan's decision to apply for membership in 1961. There existed a strong elite European lobby, in the forms of ministers like Sandys, Kilmuir, Soames and Thorneycroft and from backbenchers like Geoffrey Rippon, Peter Kirk and Maurice Macmillan. Given Macmillan's sympathy for European co-operation it's perhaps unsurprising that he surrounded himself with likeminded individuals. At the same time there was evidence of changing attitudes amongst the business community, for example Lord Chandos and the Institute of Directors as well as the Federation of British Industries.[2] The press was also changing its position. The *Observer, Economist* and *Financial Times* all supported an application from 1960, and were followed in 1961 by the *Sunday Times, Daily Telegraph, Daily Mail,* and *The Times.* Only Beaverbrook's *Daily Express* was opposed. There can also be a danger of exaggerating the negative influence of the farming lobby, although at the time Conservative analysts estimated that between 70 and 80 Conservative seats were at threat from the farming vote. Many large farmers were favourable to entry; one regional survey of farmers in the east Midlands found 42 per cent favourable.

Lord Netherthorpe (National Farmers' Union president 1946–60) was inclined to support entry, although his successor Harold Wooley was opposed.[3] This was akin to the experience of cabinet minister Rab Butler, whom many saw as the agricultural conscience in the government. He agreed to support entry after a tour of farming constituencies convinced him that the community was largely favourable to entry.[4] Nor can outside circumstances be overlooked.

The growing Soviet threat from 1961 with the technological resurgence of the USSR following their successful Sputnik space programme, the building of the Berlin Wall and Macmillan's failure at détente with Khrushchev once more gave emphasis to the need for European co-operation against the communist threat. At the same time Britain's relationship with America meant that London had to heed the views of Washington. The failure of the British nuclear Blue Streak missile programme in April 1960 emphasised Britain's defensive vulnerability, and placed a reliance on the US Skybolt system for a nuclear capability, making the Anglo–American alliance all the more significant to Britain. Yet some observers also interpreted it as a turning point that made an application to join the EEC inevitable.[5] After the difficulties over American disapproval about Suez, the relationship was tense. The Eisenhower administration saw EFTA as an unnecessary complication. Their support for European unity can be seen through the significant, but covert funding, that the USA was injecting into the European federal movement.[6] There was concern in London post-Suez that if Britain did not begin to see Europe in the same light as the USA, the latter might well begin to look to other Europeans, notably West Germany, for the special relationship. Kennedy told Macmillan in April 1961 that should Britain join the EEC it could only enhance the Anglo–American relationship. Furthermore, there were economic concerns that American inward investment was flowing towards the EEC rather than Britain. In 1960 for the first time half of American direct western European investment was directed towards the EEC and only 40 per cent to Britain. It was hoped that Britain's EEC membership would reverse this trend. It is clear that the British discussions were taking place against a backdrop in which the four strategic components underpinning Britain's world status were in varying degrees of crisis: the nuclear option, the Commonwealth relationship, the Anglo–American alliance and Britain's mediatory role between the two superpowers. The economics may have been deemed 'secondary' at this point but they were still concerning. Over the 1950s Britain's international trading competitiveness had declined sharply from 25.5 per cent to 16.5 per cent whilst West Germany's share had risen from 7.3 per cent to 19.3 per cent. Commonwealth trade had also declined significantly and by 1962 Britain's exports to western Europe were higher than its exports to Commonwealth countries.[7] A noticeable trend in Britain's trading patterns developed during this period, no doubt in part due to the expectation that Britain would join the EEC. Between 1960 and 1962 in the three years that Britain was being penalised by tariffs from the Six and exploiting market advantages by tariff cuts of 20 per cent on trade with the Seven, exports to the EEC rose by 55 per cent whilst exports to EFTA went up only by 33 per cent.[8] The potential fragility of the British economy also weighed on the minds of decision makers. Whilst the UK economy was growing solidly this did not compare as well against EEC members' economies. Problems with the balance of payments had produced a cycle of stimulating demand only then for the necessity of restrictive measures to damp down the flood of imports. It was suggested that EEC membership would offer the British economy a greater platform for stability. The retreat from empire, especially in Africa, also suggested to Britain the need to consider alternatives. Attempts at bolstering the colonial 'circle' were not proving successful via the Commonwealth, not least because of the desire of former colonies not to appear subservient to previous masters.[9] Suez had illustrated only limited Commonwealth support, and then the decision to expel South Africa in 1961 against British advice illustrated that this 'circle' was haphazard. What the above all served to do was reinforce the narrative of 'decline' that was playing on the minds of many politicians. This can be seen by surveys of elite British opinion. Of those questioned in 1959, 72 per cent saw Britain as the third superpower. By 1965 this had declined to just 39 per cent with only 8 per cent expecting Britain to sustain that position to the end of the century.[10] For Philip de Zulueta, one of Macmillan's advisors, Britain had 'to join the European game in order to stay in the world power game'.[11] Labour's leading Europeanist, Roy Jenkins, was just as sanguine about necessity: 'we would do better to live gracefully with them than to waste our substance by trying to unsuccessfully to keep up with the power giants of the modern world'.[12]

Macmillan's success in the October 1959 general election, returning with an increased majority, meant that fresh thought could be given to Britain's relationship with Europe. The collapse of the free trade area talks in 1958 and a growing sense that EFTA was of peripheral relevance re-focussed the attentions of the British government. Attempts were made during 1959 to repair the damage in Anglo–German and Anglo–French relations by ministerial visits to Paris, and a visit to London by Adenauer, the German chancellor. The British may have adopted a strategy that was designed to demonstrate to the Six that Britain was sympathetic to their objectives and was undertaking her own Europeanisation; however, as with Selwyn Lloyd's January 1960 proposals for reform of Western European Union (WEU), the British were also seeking to warn the Six not to develop too independently of NATO and WEU on political and defence matters. On 13 July 1960 the British cabinet took the decision to 'draw closer' to Europe. The reshuffling of the cabinet and the promotion of key Europeanists to relevant posts consolidated this decision. Duncan Sandys, an early advocate of European unity, was moved to the Commonwealth Relations Office; Soames, also seen as another enthusiast for Europe, was sent to Agriculture, and Edward Heath, who had made his maiden speech supporting the Schuman Plan, was made Lord Privy Seal with special responsibility for European affairs, with the added responsibility of being a member of the Foreign Office and its spokesman in the House of Commons. Thereafter hints were being made that Britain might wish to join the ECSC and Euratom, and linked to these was the suggestion that this was part of a process favoured by Macmillan whereby Britain would secure 'associate' EEC status.[13] However, the European leadership was not enthusiastic about this concept, even if some were anxious to secure British membership in order to dilute the influence of French president, De Gaulle. Monnet, in a television interview, thought that Britain had to accept the whole European process or not at all. The Six were wary of these British overtures in part because of differences amongst themselves on how the Common Market should develop, and particularly the Common Agricultural Policy, and a fear that the British would use these uncertainties to undermine the customs union and develop a free trade area. Britain continued to drop hints that it was interested in membership by making statements to the Council of Europe and the Western European Union.[14] Miriam Camps' analysis of the British decision to seek membership portrays it as being motivated by a strategic concern, rather than an economic one. There was an anxiety over whether the EEC could survive after De Gaulle and Adenauer left office, and a growing sense that a stable EEC with Britain participating was perhaps the easiest way of bolstering the Atlantic alliance, both politically and economically.[15]

The Cabinet agreed to back an application on 21 July 1961. During the Cabinet discussions no reference to sovereignty can by found in the minutes until the meeting of the 24 July when it was observed that the opposition of the anti-marketeers (those Conservative and Labour MPs opposed to entry) in Parliament appeared more concerned with presentational tactics.[16] It seems that officials at the Foreign Office were more relaxed in their approach to the potential loss of sovereignty, certainly in comparison to before the Suez crisis. This suggested a changing understanding of the idea, moving away from one defined as a concept of independence from external forces (something so brutally exposed as untrue by the Suez crisis) towards a more relative concept of seeking the greatest possible international influence. Political sovereignty was another matter, but one which the Foreign Office thought hardly mattered that much as it was a domestic political issue that could be controlled by party and political management.[17] Sovereignty was also specifically considered by the Lee Committee, which concluded that whilst there would be instances whereby Britain had to accept majority decisions that were at variance with her interests, because at least two other nations were likely to be joining with Britain it was unlikely that Britain would be isolated on too many occasions, thereby minimising the dangers of qualified majority voting.

The first application

When Prime Minister Harold Macmillan announced his intention to bid for membership he emphasised that Britain would have to resolve three issues during negotiations with the EEC: the relationship of other EFTA nations with the EEC, the agricultural exports of the Commonwealth to Britain and the position of domestic British agriculture. He also stressed that it would strengthen the unity of the western free world. When questioned as to why he was choosing to apply under Article 237 (membership) rather than Article 238 (association), Macmillan responded that the economic difficulties remained for the Commonwealth whichever route was taken, but that association would mean Britain 'would have no influence in Europe'.[18] Given the twelve months of speculation about an application being launched, observers were surprised at the relative low-key manner in which Macmillan made his speech to the House of Commons.[19] The Irish and Danish quickly followed the British lead and requested membership in July 1961, followed in May 1962 by Norway. In March 1962 Britain finally applied for membership of ECSC and Euratom.

The saliency of Europe was certainly increasing in parliamentary terms. In the thirteen months between the first major parliamentary debate on EEC membership in July 1960 and the announcement of an application, European policy took up 1.5 per cent of debating time. This was twice as much as occurred during the Schuman Plan and twenty times as much as during the first few years of the European Coal and Steel Community. In the period of the actual application the figure would creep slightly higher to 1.7 per cent, which amounted to 854 columns of the official parliamentary report *Hansard*. Of this just under 18 per cent of the statements were made by government frontbenchers, meaning that backbenchers were given nearly four fifths of the debating time.[20]

In these debates parliamentary opponents, both Conservative and Labour, were fearful about the potential loss of sovereignty, both parliamentary and economic. They began rehearsing the arguments that would sustain their campaign for the remainder of the century during the full-dress debate on 2–3 August, which lasted thirteen hours.[21] The sovereignty argument would remain a feature of the domestic discussions about Europe, but never became a direct agenda item during the Brussels talks. The debate produced relatively few strong 'pro-European' speeches, with those of Roy Jenkins (Labour), Peter Smithers (Conservative) and Charles Pannell (Labour) being most notable; however, in general, the sentiment underpinning most speeches was a grudging sense that in view of the lack of other alternatives the government must seek membership. The government won substantial parliamentary approval for beginning the negotiations, although Macmillan had felt it necessary to play the 'loyalty card' by threatening resignation if he was defeated.[22] In the event only one Conservative voted against the Government although the level of voting abstention amongst Conservative backbenchers forewarned Macmillan of the need to negotiate satisfactory entry arrangements. Edward Heath, Lord Privy Seal, was now charged with leading the negotiations in Brussels.

Whilst the majority of the Conservative parliamentary party had agreed to support Macmillan, despite many having private misgivings, the Labour party was much more divided over the matter. Indeed for this party 'Europe' would be another of those ideological skirmishing grounds that marked out Labour's battle between left and right. Most of the Gaitskellites, veterans of the unilateralism and clause IV battles, were in the pro-entry camp, alongside some of the left. In the anti-entry camp were the majority of the left, some centrists and right-wingers, although there was some blurring of the boundaries. Likewise the distinctions within the Conservative party over Europe were less clear-cut than first perceptions suggest. Conservative anti-marketeering was largely perceived as a right-wing phenomenon that was populist, chauvinistic and reactionary. The association of right-wingers like Anthony Fell, Ronald Bell and Lord Hinchingbrooke appeared to confirm this assessment, and yet it was much more amorphous and there were no neat ideological left/right divisions.[23]

Pro-entry campaigners saw value in seeking to portray the issue as being above party politics, hence a preference for multi-party campaigning groups. The Common Market Campaign was launched in May 1961, under the chairmanship of former diplomat Lord Gladwyn, now a Liberal peer. Roy Jenkins the Labour MP was a vice-chairman. Inside the Labour party the pro-entry camp formed themselves into the Labour Common Market Committee and claimed to have the support of 80 MPs: a mixture of federalists, socialists who saw a united Europe as the first stage towards world government, and social democrats who believed that Britain joining a large market would enhance the mixed economy. Alongside these there were many differing individual motivations for supporting the case for Europe.[24] Conservative Europeanists involved themselves in the all-party European movement, but avoided establishing an explicit Conservative European campaigning group, at least initially. Instead they chose to operate through support for the cause at internal party committees, such as the Foreign Affairs Committee, and the various policy groups that were established within their party structure to help formulate European policy.[25]

The antis within Labour were motivated by a diverse range of factors: those from the left who saw the EEC as a hindrance to socialism and feared it would restrict the freedom of a Labour government; others, such as Michael Foot and Peter Shore, who feared for British sovereignty and the British constitution. And as with the Conservative anti-marketeers, anti-German, anti-French and anti-Catholic sentiments also had their roles to play. The Conservative parliamentary opponents to entry were quick to form themselves into the Conservative Common Market Group. Although only numbering a maximum of forty backbench MPs, these were the individuals who abstained in August.[26] The antis' leadership centred around Derek Walker-Smith, Robin Turton, Peter Walker and Lord Hinchingbrooke. But these were all backbenchers and the reality was that the anti-marketeers of 1961–62 lacked a leader with the sort of public standing capable of converting the parliamentary irritation into a major embarrassment. As Macmillan observed disparagingly, 'I see no Disraeli among them; not even a Lord George Bentwick.'[27]

Anthony Eden, now ennobled as Lord Avon, was the national figure the anti-marketeers had hoped would assume the leadership. As a former party leader, prime minister and foreign secretary his views would have carried considerable weight, but despite his many misgivings about Europe, Eden was unwilling to cut the ties of loyalty and commit open rebellion.[28]

With formal parliamentary approval the way was clear for the Macmillan government to begin discussions with the EEC. These talks began with the Six on 26 September, although the first ministerial meeting only occurred on 10 October. At this point Heath made it clear that Britain accepted the basic features of the Treaty of Rome – a common external tariff, a common commercial policy and a common agricultural position, but they were seeking special provisions and a transitional period before full membership. Further meetings in November agreed to establish specialist working parties to seek to hammer out the finer detail, before finally in May 1962 detailed negotiations began. The complexities of the challenge facing the British were enormous and often conflicting. Not only was Britain negotiating with the Six, but simultaneously the Commonwealth, the EFTA nations, and the United States. It had to convince the Six that Britain was ready to become a full member of the Community and not plead a special position or seek to undermine from within. It had to show the Commonwealth that it was not being sacrificed, and the EFTA countries required convincing that it was still committed to free trade. Additionally, the uncertainty of domestic opinion meant that the government had to ensure that it was alert to the concerns of its electorate; as Miriam Camps suggested, the government 'took an enormous, but necessary, gamble on the development of public opinion'.[29] Macmillan had also couched Britain's application in a manner in which the decision to apply would only be taken once the terms of entry had been negotiated. The TUC took the view that 'laying down definite and inflexible conditions of entry ... could adversely affect the UK's negotiating position which was already weak'.[30] Some historians would concur and have been critical of this approach and the decision to make entry pre-conditional.[31] It is felt that had Britain made an open unconditional approach then the outcome might have been very different. The attitude of the French was anticipated as the largest stumbling block to entry. The French had successfully tailored the Treaty of Rome to their own advantage and had a coherent sense of the new structure of the Community. British membership was likely to skew the new balance of power, and given De Gaulle's express desires to return France to a position of pre-eminence on the continent this was likely to prove problematic. What the British negotiators hoped was that De Gaulle would recognise that Britain offered a useful foil in his battle against the concept of supranationalism and that British accession might usefully diminish the moves towards deepening integration. The biggest surprise for the British was that rather than entering negotiations around seven governments, she instead found herself negotiating as one government versus the Six.

The slow pace of the negotiations did little to reassure many in Britain, in particular the Beaverbrook press that was seeking to arouse popular opposition to entry especially over sovereignty, and the agricultural community (especially the horticultural sector) who feared entry would damage their livelihoods. Populist opposition was also being aroused by the Anti-Common Market League (ACML), which launched a propaganda campaign and held a series of mass meetings across the country designed to highlight to the government the extent of popular opposition. Reports that meetings of the ACML were attracting large rural audiences and being addressed by dis-affected Conservative MPs caused a certain degree of alarm about the potential threat to safe Conservative seats. The whole issue of Europe deeply divided the Labour party, but leader Hugh Gaitskell ensured official policy was one of declared opposition to the EEC and which attached five 'essential conditions' that would need to be fulfilled before a Labour government would consider an application. Was this a historical precedent that Gordon Brown in 1997 would look to when ruling out membership of the euro unless five conditions were met? The party's internal divisions were given very public display at its 1962 party conference, an event likened by one historian to 'a monument to disunity'.[32] It was a position that the Conservatives sought to exploit for party political gain, since it enabled them to present themselves as relatively unified on the matter in both policy and personality terms at the expense of their opponents. It also allowed them to position themselves as the forward-looking party, with Rab Butler famously telling the 1962 Llandudno Conservative conference: 'For the Labour party 1,000 years of history books. For us the future.'[33]

That said opinion polls conducted during 1962 appeared to suggest that the anti-marketeers were garnering support. Support for entry had peaked in December 1961 at 53 per cent before falling back to 36 per cent in June 1962.[34] There was a rally in the numbers supporting entry during the summer of 1962, only for that to steeply decline during the autumn as the government faced a number of by-elections with anti-common market candi-dates standing, most notably in South Dorset where the scale of the anti-marketeer vote was enough to deprive the Conservatives of the seat to Labour's advantage.[35] There were two features of the opinion polls that indi-cated potential problems for the government. There always was a significant proportion of those polled who offered no opinion, suggesting that these voters required significant reassurances. Also, the level of confusion about matters European suggested the government needed to go to greater lengths to educate opinion about Europe. Polls showed that two-thirds did not know whether Britain was a member of the EEC or EFTA, or else gave an incorrect answer.[36] Macmillan's government was in a difficult position. It wanted to continue to be positive about the pace of negotiations and was banking on a successful application to re-launch itself and reverse its slide in the opinion polls, an anxiety reinforced by heavy by-election losses during 1962, such as in Orpington. However, because it was in the midst of negotiations it felt restricted from saying too much publicly for fear that this would hamper Heath. Macmillan even went as far as forbidding his ministers from making any specific statements on Europe lest they could be used against the government either by its critics or the Six.[37] The negotiating pace was not helped either because the Six were still trying to reach agreement amongst themselves on the precise nature of the Common Agricultural Policy (CAP), and until this was resolved they could not resolve the matter of British agriculture. Some historians, like Camps, believe that generally the British had entered the negotiations having learnt from their mistakes made during the free trade negotiations. The British appeared much more sensitive to the European perspective, were more alert to the weaknesses of their own position, and avoided getting hung up over procedural arrangements. They did misjudge the Six's attitude to a transitional period, in which they presumed they would be granted a degree of latitude to apply the necessary adjustments to policy and structural procedures, whilst the Six saw it precisely as a period of transition in which all aspects of the eventual system would be reformed to meet the new criteria.[38] Britain had hoped to be faced with a single figure conducting the negotiations, in the manner that Spaak had done during the Rome drafting process, but the French vetoed this idea, possibly because they were concerned that this individual might be too willing to make concessions in order to achieve a successful outcome. Equally the matter of foodstuffs and the Commonwealth were issues peculiarly British, problems stemming from historical experience that were not always understood by their European counterparts and which did not necessarily offer simple solutions. Historically Britain had become used to cheap food prices due to a mix of preferential Commonwealth trading arrangements and a productive domestic agricultural sector. Although the British were already thinking about reforming their system of agricultural subsidies, it was evident that membership of CAP would end subsidies and increase competition. It would also end the policy of imperial preference, which had underpinned British/Commonwealth trading arrangements since the 1932 Ottawa Agreements. Because some Commonwealth nations depended almost entirely on the UK as a market for their exports there were real concerns that EEC membership would be the death knell of the Commonwealth, and this prospect did tug at the emotional heartstrings of some within the political establishment. These Commonwealth ties were not easily understood on the continent, despite the French and Belgians being imperial powers themselves. In personal discussions with General De Gaulle at the Chateau de Champs, 1–2 June 1962, it appears that Macmillan thought he had persuaded the French president of Britain's sincerity. Certainly the joint press release indicated that the two leaders had agreed there was a 'community of interests' between Britain and France. Yet there was no softening of the French position at the Brussels talks and the British negotiators were frustrated to find the French still insisting on full acceptance of the Treaty. When the negotiations adjourned in August for the holiday season Britain and the Six had still failed to achieve an 'outline' agreement. This may have gone some way towards reassuring the anti-marketeers that the British government was not rushing into agreement, and indeed signalled the potential failure of talks, but for the government it was considerably frustrating.

Just as the French government used the negotiations as a tool in the battle for domestic political supremacy, so too in Britain the Conservative government saw a successfully concluded negotiation as a vital element of their domestic electoral tactics. In 1962 Macmillan's domestic position was under threat. The huge defeat inflicted at the Orpington by-election in March 1962, suggesting a resurgence of the Liberals, when added to rising unemployment, concerns over Commonwealth immigration, and scandals over the George Black spy ring and the Vassall and Galbraith affairs, were all denting Macmillan's 'Supermac' reputation. Some hoped for an idealistic focus on European policy: 'Young people', declared one young Conservative student, 'want to take part in something that is above the level of ordinary politics. The ideal of the Common Market could fill this need.' Iain Macleod, the party chairman, shared similar frustrations: 'the natural destiny of this country lies in Europe. Very difficult to get this over to the public, as we cannot embarrass Mr Heath by pronouncing that we shall become the leader of Europe.'[39] Macleod was hoping to re-launch the Conservatives as the 'party of Europe', but the longer the negotiations dragged on the more painful it became: without any 'hard news' of success in the negotiations 'we are going to go on suffering', he reported to the prime minister. Macmillan's response was that it was best to leave organisations like the Federation of British Industry and Britain in Europe to continue to promote the European message, as 'their statements do not commit us'.[40] In the autumn of 1962 the government faced a series of by-elections, which included the interventions of a number of anti-Common Market candidates, appearing to confirm the volatility of the issue. Certainly the pace of negotiations was frustrating many in Britain and increased the calls from those who wished to see Britain seek an alternative to EEC membership. Public opinion's support for entry appeared also to be in steep decline from October 1962. The reality was that once in the negotiations, the government had little choice but to remain at the table.

The veto

As it was, De Gaulle dealt the application a fatal blow on 14 January 1963 when he infamously declared 'non' to British membership during a press conference. Although the British made a last ditch attempt to save the negotiations, a meeting on 28–29 January 1963 confirmed the failure of Britain's application. De Gaulle's decision had been motivated by a multitude of factors, largely underpinned by French nationalism. The Cuban Missile Crisis and the Nassau agreement between Macmillan and Kennedy on the nuclear Polaris missile had reminded him of the reliance of the British on America.[41]

And he increasingly viewed Britain as an American 'Trojan horse', fearing 'in the end there would appear a colossal Atlantic Community under American dependence and leadership which would soon completely swallow up the European Community'. Britain's background was 'insular' and 'maritime' and her links with her Commonwealth emphasised her differences from the continent. Thus his conclusion was that Britain had an economic and political perspective that was out of sync with the Six and therefore she was not ready for accession to the EEC.[42]

For Macmillan the veto demonstrated his inability to secure interdependence: to both strengthen Britain's relationship with America whilst making his country 'European'. Furthermore, the squabbles over the Commonwealth's position that the EEC negotiations had highlighted, also suggested that this bond was rapidly weakening. The veto seriously damaged the credibility of the Macmillan government. The *Daily Mirror* might proclaim 'Halleluiah', but Macmillan's critics were quick to apportion blame, suggesting that the government had failed because it was not sufficiently European in outlook and was still seeking to maintain the Atlantic alliance. For the government it was clear that De Gaulle and the French were to blame, and it did little to dampen that claim, recognising that this at least deflected the worst of domestic criticism from itself.[43] Retaliation came in the form of cancelling the planned visit by Princess Margaret to France in March.[44] The Europeanists within the government were concerned too that such a stratagem just played into the jingoistic hands of the anti-marketeers, and risked leaving the Liberals as the sole 'European' party in Britain, possibly a dangerous tactic given their recent revival at by-elections. Yet despite this, Anglo–French relations were not irreparably damaged, collaboration still continued on the Channel Tunnel and the supersonic Concorde Anglo–French aircraft project. Collaboration, and rivalry, also continued in the realm of military procurement, until France's 1966 withdrawal from NATO. For example in 1964 there was agreement on collaboration over the Martel air-to-air missile project, as well as a series of helicopter development projects (Lynx, Puma and Gazelle) and the production of the Jaguar strike aircraft. For the British, though, these collaborations were not based upon a desire to promote Britain's Europeanness but rather were a series of pragmatic responses to immediate circumstances and often without the assent of the industrial partners involved. In contrast the French saw these as part of a system that was bolstering Europe's military independence. What ultimately emerged was a legacy of bitterness and rivalry between the two nations' aircraft industries and those involved in procurement, which mirrored the diplomatic impasse.[45]

De Gaulle's actions in unilaterally vetoing the British application were not universally welcomed by all the members of the EEC, but it is evident that whatever misgivings they may have had over France's behaviour, this could not be allowed to interfere with the wider challenge of making the Community work. However, De Gaulle was to test the resolve of these member nations in the first full-blown crisis that the Community faced in 1965. The crisis arose because of the move towards giving the European Parliament budgetary control and stripping national government of this power. This was a move towards supranationalism that was unacceptable to De Gaulle. His vision of the Community was of economically co-operating nation-states, and so any move towards political unity threatened French sovereignty. De Gaulle's actions were dramatic. He withdrew the French representative and from 6 July 1965 boycotted all meetings of the Council of Ministers. It transpired that the matter of the budgetary powers had been an excuse to provoke a crisis so that De Gaulle could block the transition towards majority voting in the Council of Ministers. For the French the abolition of the national veto was a far greater challenge to national sovereignty and would remove the ability of a nation-state to block any changes it disagreed with. After some torturous negotiations, the 'Luxembourg compromise' was agreed whereby if any state considered a proposal to be a threat to its national interests, it could exercise a veto, even after majority voting had become standard practice. De Gaulle also insisted on symbolic changes to the role of the European Commission in order to clip its wings and remind it that it was a representative of the member nations rather than the supreme authority.[46] In a significant institutional amendment the Six agreed in April 1965 to merge the three councils of the three European Communities into a single Council, and to the merger of the ECSC High Authority with the commissions of Euratom and the EEC into a single European Commission, reforms that would come into effect in July 1967.

The argument that British entry was necessary because of increasing economic competition carried considerable favour with British business leaders. The Federation for British Industry (FBI) had initially urged Britain to participate in the Messina talks, and then in the EFTA negotiations. On each of the three occasions Britain made an EEC bid: 1961, 1967, and then in 1970 (but now as the Confederation for British Industry, CBI) it was favourable to entry. In 1961 there were conditions attached and references to necessary safeguards, but by 1967 such assurances were no longer required. Smaller businesses (with less than 200 employees) were marginally less enthusiastic than larger ones about entry, but it still figured at 80 per cent in 1968. Nevertheless the FBI/CBI leadership was more favourable to entry than its wider membership, but it saw educating its membership as one of its key leadership roles, even liaising with the government over publicity campaigns.[47] In contrast the National Farmers Union, which represented about 80 per cent of farmers and was led by Harold Wooley (1960–66), was strongly opposed. At least one motivation for the NFU's national leadership was a concern that EEC membership would diminish the privileged negotiating position on prices and subsidies that the NFU had previously enjoyed with the Ministry of Agriculture. Considerable efforts were made throughout the 1960s to try and convince the NFU of the necessity of joining the EEC, even though less than 5 per cent of the British workforce were employed in agriculture. The government was aware that the earlier FTA talks had endured significant delays because of the success of NFU lobbying. This was particularly important because the NFU adopted a promotional approach to the matter, ensuring a constant stream of press releases and information on the subject, much of which was being reported in the press and therefore was influencing public opinion. The results of the government's efforts were mixed. Hostility appeared to be increasingly confined to smaller farmers, hill farmers and horticulturalists, but there was a sense that the community more widely was open to persuasion.[48] The Macmillan government largely sought to ignore the attitude of the trades unions to EEC entry, even though this sector was pragmatic on the matter. The Trades Union Congress (TUC) with the free trade proposals had made considerable emphasis upon the safeguards required for full employment rather than the opportunities for economic growth offered by the trading arrangements. By the 1960s it was advocating entry, and more individual unions were reaching the same conclusion. The September 1961 TUC annual conference voted in favour of conditional entry, but with conditions that were more akin to the government's position than Labour's. Aside from economic considerations, the union movement hoped that entry would harmonize living standards in Britain with those on the continent, and furthermore they were aware that their sister organisations in Europe had much greater access to policy makers of the EEC than they enjoyed in Whitehall. The participation of these interest groups in the Europe debate played a significant role in depoliticising the issue in advance of the 1961 application. This would change from August 1961 in part because the economic ministries were no longer primarily responsible for the negotiations, because the mass media became embroiled in the issue and also because the issue became a matter of partisan contention for the political parties. EEC membership was increasingly packaged as an economic measure, and done so in order to weaken the political saliency of the issue.[49] In advocating safeguards the Macmillan government in 1961 was seeking to mollify the specific economic concerns of the major economic interest groups.

With the failure of the 1961 application 'Europe' played unsurprisingly little role in the 1964 general election, which saw Harold Wilson's Labour party victorious, although with only a narrow majority. The Conservatives had downplayed Europe during the contest, not wishing to draw attention to the failure of their 1961–63 negotiations. In contrast Wilson had tried to look futuristic, talking about the 'white heat of the technological revolution'. Wilson's 1964–66 administration also made one significant European concession, the implications of which went largely unnoticed at the time, but which in retrospect were to prove highly significant for national sovereignty. On 7 December 1965, without any discussion in Cabinet or Parliament, using a Royal Prerogative, and implementing it through the Council of Europe, Wilson announced that Britain would accept Articles 25 and 46 of the European Convention on Human Rights. This meant that Britain conceded that the European Court of Human Rights at the Hague had the right to overturn the sovereign decisions of Parliament and British judiciary should a British citizen seek to appeal to their judgement. By 1999, the Court had partly or wholly found against the British government on 50 occasions, on issues such as the use of corporal punishment in Isle of Man, the equality of adult homosexuals in Northern Ireland, the rights of Irish republican terrorist prisoners held in the Maze prison, and the rights of the press to publish articles considered to be in the public interest, often causing considerable political irritation in Westminster.[50] During the Maastricht negotiations it is unclear whether British officials realised the implications of allowing human rights, as protected by the European Human Rights convention, to be enshrined in the EU's constitutional law.[51]

The 1967 application

A further election in 1966 saw Wilson's majority enhanced to 96 and with it came thoughts about the possibility of a fresh application for EEC membership. During the campaign Wilson had spoken of securing entry 'given a fair wind', conditional on Britain retaining the freedom to buy food and raw materials from the cheapest markets. The Conservatives had committed themselves to seizing 'the first favourable opportunity', but only 50 per cent of their candidates had thought Europe important enough to mention in their election addresses.[52] The matter of a British application had been discussed at a number of meetings of the WEU in 1966, with government ministers trying to make it evident that Britain was prepared to discuss entry terms, whilst French representatives made it clear that France was in a position of 'benevolent waiting'. The 1966 Queen's Speech indicated Britain's willingness to seek entry so long as 'essential' British and Commonwealth interests were 'safeguarded'. Matters were not helped by the controversy over the value of sterling and the balance of payments. In July 1966, George Brown, chancellor of the exchequer, had failed to persuade Cabinet of the necessity of devaluation and again during the autumn of that year vigorous cabinet discussions ruled out devaluation as a prerequisite to making an EEC bid. In November the government decided on a 'new high-level approach'.[53] In the new year of 1967 Wilson and Brown visited the main capitals of the Six to establish the parameters of an application. The visits revealed that, from the British perspective, the sticking points would be the operation of the Common Agricultural Policy, with its structural impact on British agriculture as well as concerns about rising food costs, the risks for the UK budget and balance of payments. From the EEC's perspective financial regulations, regional policies and the need to negotiate special terms for New Zealand trade and the Commonwealth Sugar Agreement were to be the issues. Parliament had debated a possible application in November 1966. The Labour party itself remained deeply divided on the matter of Europe. In February 1967, 107 Labour MPs, objecting to Wilson's exploratory talks, signed an early day motion recalling Gaitskell's five conditions and demanding the protection of essential British and Commonwealth interests. Reports suggested that the party's divisions extended to the Cabinet, with some ministers such as Douglas Jay, president of the Board of Trade, privately fearing the economic consequences of membership. For these reasons of intra-party disunity Wilson was anxious that government and Whitehall 'should to the utmost of our power' seek to confine debate 'between Governments and not on the floor of the House of Commons or in the columns of the press'.[54] Consequently contemporary critics complained that the application was being imposed upon an unsuspecting public and parliament.[55] Furthermore Wilson concentrated European policy making amongst a small elite within the formal and informal power structures of Whitehall.[56]

The application was formally announced on 2 May 1967, not only for EEC membership but also of ECSC and Euratom, and received the tacit approval of the Conservative opposition now led by Edward Heath.[57] Likewise bids were made by Denmark and Ireland. Parliament approved the application on 10 May by 488 votes to 62 (34 Labour and 26 Conservative voting against and another 51 Labour abstaining). Internally within the Labour government there appears to have been little expectation of success. Richard Crossman, a cabinet minister with keen Eurosceptic beliefs, voted for the application, confident that De Gaulle would again use his veto.[58] But as he confessed to his diary, the internal party divisions and the likelihood of failure meant he 'felt gloom and depression and knew that we had trouble ahead'.[59]

With De Gaulle still president of France expectations of success were muted, and his 16 May press conference on the problems of the British application appeared to confirm the predictions. Consequently British consideration was being given to possible alternatives. The 'alternatives' debate involved both pro-Europeanists, who wished to bolster a future British application if this one was vetoed, and the anti-marketeers, who were seeking to prevent Britain aligning itself with the EEC, and revolved around three visions: Commonwealth preference, EFTA (European Free Trade Association) or North Atlantic Free Trade Area (NAFTA). The reality was that in the context of the late 1960s none of these were realistic options, and the inability of the anti-marketeers to successfully articulate a viable alternative to EEC membership proved, and continues to prove, their Achilles heel. NAFTA was rejected in the belief that the USA would use it to send exports to Britain whilst giving the EEC capital and technology. Wilson had already told the German chancellor, Kurt Kiesenger, that although 'other solutions ... existed' the government 'believed they all represented a second best'. However, some observers were concerned that Wilson appeared less than enthusiastic about entry, but again it seems that this was a deliberate strategy to seek to pacify ministers hostile to entry.[60]

The terms of the debate changed with this application. Labour had ditched Gaitskell's five conditions, and with the significance of the Commonwealth having dramatically declined, they were looking to the modernisation of British industry and associated research and development. The wider Labour party was still deeply divided over the matter. On the extreme of the debate some pro-Labour marketeers wished to see a federal Europe, but the majority of pro-Europeans took a more pragmatic approach that favoured signing the Treaty of Rome and then seeing how the EEC evolved. The Labour antis, driven by pragmatic concerns for gaining power, had deliberately pushed 'Europe' back as an issue. This did not mean that the private debate was over, and it revolved around the extent to which the EEC was devoted to free competition. Nor at this stage was it a debate characterised by a clear left–right division.[61]

There has been considerable historical debate about why Wilson launched the second application. In large part it can be seen as part of a re-evaluation of Britain's position in the world. The fallout from the Suez crisis, the rapid move from empire to Commonwealth, an organisation about which Wilson was largely disillusioned,[62] and Britain's emerging economic shortcomings, made membership an attractive option. Whilst there is little unanimity as to when Wilson decided on the need to make an application,[63] the key point is he did, largely motivated by the changing realities of global power, but also because of a sense that there was a party political gain to be had over the Conservatives, now being led by the Europhile Ted Heath. When Heath welcomed rumours that France would accept British entry, Wilson scored political points by accusing him of 'rolling on his back like a spaniel'.[64] So despite Wilson's association in the 1950s with a left-wing perspective on foreign policy (he resigned in 1951 over the rearmament budget and had demanded an end to Britain's nuclear deterrent), by the time he was prime minister, he was very much moulded in the Bevinite world role tradition.

Wilson visited Paris in June and held talks with De Gaulle, telling the French president that he did not see the problems associated with the British application as 'insoluble'.[65] The Six had meet in Rome in May and recognised the British application, but when the EEC Council of Ministers met in early June the meeting broke up before discussing the application because of the Middle East crisis arising from the Arab–Israeli Six Day War, which had prevented the attendance of the French, West German and Italian foreign ministers. When the Council of Ministers was finally able to discuss the issue in July, despite the ministers of Belgium, West Germany, Italy, Luxembourg and the Netherlands being prepared to hear the British application, Couve de Murville, the French minister, insisted that the Six needed to agree amongst themselves on the merits of enlargement first before inviting the British to make their case for membership. In October the European Commission published its preliminary conclusions on enlargement, indicating that the accession of the four applicants would strength the Community without diluting its fundamental objectives, provided the individual applicants accepted particular arrangements, especially on GATT, the Community's associational agreements and in Britain's particular case over the economy, the role of sterling and the Community's monetary system.

This mattered not. De Gaulle did indeed veto the second application on 27 November 1967, citing Britain's economic position, especially monetary matters, believing that sterling following its devaluation was 'incompatible' with the common market and that Britain's poor balance of payments record would have threatened the Community's foundations.[66] That same month Wilson had been forced finally to accept the 'unmentionable' – devaluation – and the pound's value to the dollar was cut from \$2.80 to \$2.40, a cut of 14 per cent. Robert Armstrong, the Cabinet secretary, also believes it was De Gaulle wanting to have the last word on the matter. Whilst Lord Con O'Neill, in his official history of the 1970 application, would suggest that the French were concerned that English would become the primary language of the Community's institutions and that this in part explains the motivation behind their hostility.[67] In private De Gaulle was still harking back to themes persistent in 1963, his fear of the 'mortal sin of Atlanticism' and fears of the negative impact Britain would have on the ethos of the Community.[68] Yet this assessment was unduly harsh on Britain. It was clear between 1967 and 1968 that Labour was repositioning Britain, financially, imperially and militarily, in a manner that represented a fundamental change. Britain's imperial commitments were slashed, with troops stationed in Singapore and Malaysia being halved. In January 1968 the Cabinet agreed to retreat from its east of Suez commitments (except Hong Kong); whilst relations with Rhodesia were highly strained over that country's universal declaration of independence (UDI) and ties with South Africa and Australia weakening, with the former because of apartheid and with the latter's shifting into the American sphere of influence. Relations with the Americans were strained too; Wilson's decision not to help in the Vietnam War angered Washington, as did the scrapping of the contract for American F-111 aircraft. Furthermore, in February 1968 Wilson had rejected an American offer for a joint sterling–dollar area and a twenty-five-year loan to aid sterling. To accept would have made a British entry into the EEC an impossibility. Given the Labour party's recent difficulties over unilateral nuclear disarmament, there were some within the party who were wary of the concept of a 'nuclear' military Europe, as Heath and the Conservatives appeared to be advocating. To some observers Britain was finishing the decade in a worse position that it had begun, without an empire, a near fatally weakened special relationship and a new European role blocked by De Gaulle. The EEC negotiations were finally killed off in the Council of Ministers in December with the French insisting that any resumption must be conditional on an improvement in the UK economy.

The second EEC veto did not prevent Britain from continuing its European co-operation in other arenas, but wherever Britain encountered France relations were strained. In February 1969, Britain extended its co-operation arrangement on atomic energy, originally agreed in 1958, with Euratom for a further two years. The continuing poor relations between Britain and France were played out at the WEU during early 1969, which ultimately led to a French boycott at the Council and a souring of relations over the 'Soames Affair'. In 1968 after De Gaulle's second veto the Belgians sought to use the Council of the WEU to discuss measures of security that fell outside the remit of the Treaty of Rome. This was seen as a deliberate snub towards the French and a clear attempt to keep Britain involved in European activities. Then in 1969 the deteriorating Middle East situation was placed on the WEU's agenda. France boycotted the meeting, and subsequent ones for more than a year. Compromise was finally reached when Britain's third attempt at gaining EEC entry was begun and the WEU agreed it should not stray into matters of the Community's remit. The French objections arose because of British-inspired plans for reform of the WEU that would have created a seven-member European 'foreign policy community'. France felt that the WEU in trying to push this arrangement through was ignoring the principle of unanimity. Matters then worsened as France protested to Britain when it appeared that Christopher Soames, the British ambassador in Paris, had leaked details to WEU partners and the press of plans by De Gaulle to revise NATO and enter negotiations with Britain about a free trade area in Europe. This was symptomatic of the decline in Anglo–French military relations during the 1960s. The French, who had been militarily independent of NATO since 1966, were insistent on maintaining independence in defence matters and were wary of Britain's continued commitment to NATO and the Americans, yet the potential for collaboration existed, particularly in the missile sphere. The British had expertise in warhead design whilst the French were technologically advanced in missile propulsion and development. But 'national' interests sometimes overrode the desire for collaboration. The French and British were both in competition trying to sell their Mirage and Jaguar strike aircraft in the same markets. In contrast, military links between the British and Germans were quite extensive during the 1960s. In part this was due to the close relationship between the two defence ministers Denis Healey and Helmut Schmidt, in part to collaboration in military procurement, and because of co-operation between officials and military staff in NATO and training, particularly tank training, in both north Germany and Britain. In 1968 Britain agreed with Germany (with Italy as a third partner) the Multi-Role Combat Aircraft project (which became known as the Tornado) and which would become the fighting aircraft for these nations in the 1980s. The irony was that the continued Anglo–French rivalry prevented any trilateral collaboration between the three countries.[69]

The 1970 application

Despite the 1967 veto it is clear that Wilson anticipated making a fairly swift repeat application probably once he had won a third general election and expected De Gaulle would soon be obliged to leave office. His decision to go to the polls in June 1970 was motivated by improved economic results and signs in the opinion polls that suggested Labour was opening up a lead over Edward Heath's Conservatives. It also represented a tactical call based upon concerns that public support for Labour was volatile, and would abandon Labour if economic and industrial problems arose over the summer, so the decision was taken to plump for June rather than hold out until October. On the day, exit polls suggested that Wilson's gamble had paid off; however, as soon as the declarations started, opening with Guildford, it became clear that the Conservatives were going to pull off a surprise victory.[70] Given Heath's European credentials, it was widely expected that he too would seek membership of the EEC. Yet the Conservative election manifesto had avoided any overt commitment to making a third British application and merely acknowledged a wish to open negotiations. This was in direct contrast to its 1966 manifesto, which had pledged to 'seize the first favourable opportunity'. Similarly, the party's candidates had downplayed the matter with nearly two-thirds failing to even mention Europe in their election addresses, and only 3 per cent of public addresses during the campaign had made the case for membership.[71] Nevertheless, Heath had come to the view that by having not been there at the beginning of the Community's creation, with each passing year the terms and conditions of entry became more unpalatable, or at least less favourable to Britain. The predecessor Labour government had already published a white paper in February 1970 on the economic effects of membership suggesting that the impact of entry would be less than 1 per cent of gross national product. This was why in May 1970 Heath had urged the Six to allow British entry 'on terms which are tolerable in the short term and clearly and visibly beneficial in the long term'.[72] By 1970 conditions seemed more favourable to Britain than on the two previous occasions. A new French president was at the Elysée Palace after Georges Pompidou had won the June 1969 presidential election. Positive soundings had been received from various European officials, including the signal from a summit of EEC leaders at the Hague convened to discuss the re-launching of the European project, and it was believed that a number of the obstacles to entry had been resolved. The 1968 Basle agreement had diminished the problems of sterling whilst many Conservative policy commitments, especially the pledge to introduce value added tax (VAT), pointed to a willingness for harmonisation between British and EEC policies. Consequently Heath launched Britain's third application twelve days after the election victory, with the hope that their entry would see greater competition and choice and an improved standard of living across the Community. The negotiation team was led initially by Anthony Barber, and then by Geoffrey Rippon after a Cabinet reshuffle caused by the sudden death of chancellor Iain Macleod. As with previous applications, the negotiation process was drawn out, but the tone was more optimistic than previously. That said the negotiators were under no illusions. Rippon admitted that the Treaty of Rome was 'four pages of principles and four hundred pages of exceptions'.[73] The issue of the CAP rules, agreed in July 1966, would have to be resolved not least because of British fears that it could increase food prices by as much as 20 per cent. Commonwealth trade was a problem, particularly in those areas where the EEC already produced surpluses such as butter. There were still concerns about the position of Britain's balance of payments as well as what impact monetary union would have on sterling as an international currency. The issue of how long a period of transition would be required prior to full membership would have to be settled. It was accepted that a British application would run in tandem with ones from Ireland, Norway and Denmark.

Prior to the negotiations opening the Six had managed to resolve the budgetary dispute that had rumbled on since 1965 at the Hague summit. France finally agreed to accept it, realising that she was likely to be the net beneficiary of the system and fearing also that if the matter were not resolved before British entry then the whole system might have to be renegotiated with the risk that it would not be so favourable to them. In addition they agreed to the objective of achieving economic and monetary union by 1980, through a common system of economic management and the adoption of an exchange rate system to link together the national currencies. Importantly, unlike previous applications Heath was not seeking to challenge and amend EEC policies; rather he was willing to accept the EEC position as it was.

The negotiating positions of each side were put forward to a special meeting in Luxembourg on 30 June 1970. Then from September a series of ministerial and delegation meetings was conducted before a series of Council of Ministers meetings between May and June 1971 concluded the main phase of the negotiations. It was not all plain sailing; contention arose over Britain's financial contribution to the EEC and her ability to pay, Commonwealth sugar and dairy products, and the key issue of sterling. In December 1970 Britain had proposed that its budgetary contribution should rise over a five-year period to a maximum of 15 per cent of total contributions to the EEC. The French wanted payment immediately, and the talks stalled for a three-month period. Anxious that this might be a prelude to a French veto, Heath determined upon a personal visit to Pompidou.[74] Here Heath successfully allayed the French president's concerns about wishing to play a European role, and he secured an important monetary concession from Heath to reduce her sterling balances. Of course, Pompidou also saw in British accession the possibility to counter-balance the growing economic might of Germany and the suggestions of possible German reunification that were concerning many in Paris. Further, by agreeing to enlargement of the Community the EEC was embarking upon a commitment to both widening and deepening its role, matters that were to provide Britain with fundamental and recurring problems in the future. This time there was no French obstructionism, despite concern from some like Chaban-Delmas, the French prime minister, that enlargement might challenge the Community's 'fundamental principles', and a French referendum approved enlargement in April 1972.[75]

Britain's relationship with the Americans could no longer be held against entry. In many respects the Federal Republic of Germany had become America's most important European ally, even if the Vietnam War did place the relationship under stress. Economically the German miracle demanded American attention. She produced one-fifth of the world's exports of manufactured goods, easily outstripping the Americans and roughly doubling those of Britain. The increased strength of the Deutchsmark was challenging the dollar, forcing it off gold. Militarily, the German contribution of 274,000 troops to the defence of Europe was larger than American contribution and dwarfed Britain's. Furthermore the growing diplomatic confidence of West Germany, especially Brandt's policy of détente with East Germany, was once more raising the possibility of German reunification. At the same time under Heath, Britain was distinctly cool about the special relationship. He thought it odd, given British trade with the USA only amounted to 8 per cent, that it was necessary to maintain a Washington embassy with 750 staff whilst the proportion of trade with the EEC was 20 per cent and rising and yet in Brussels there were only four staff officers and clerical support.[76] Nixon's decision in August 1971 to suspend dollar convertibility and terminate the Bretton Woods system antagonised Britain and America's other trading partners. There was also concern in Whitehall that discussions on anti-ballistic missiles at the 1972 strategic arms limitation talks (SALT), between the USSR and the USA would safeguard their own positions whilst leaving the Europeans exposed. The relationship was brought under further strain by the Indo–Pakistan war, which erupted in December 1971. Britain refused to intervene, and, anxious that the USA's siding with Pakistan would only drive India further into the Soviet sphere of influence, refused to support an American UN resolution demanding a ceasefire. Heath assumed that with British EEC entry, the French, German and British squabbles would be terminated, providing the conditions for greater foreign policy co-ordination, giving western Europe a greater cohesion and consequently enhancing the European nature of NATO. Heath articulated a view that 'an eventual European defence system … might also include a nuclear force based on the existing British and French forces which could be held in trusteeship for Europe as a whole'.[77] It would secure Britain and France greater international status due to their global commitments, nuclear capabilities and membership of the United Nations Security Council. There was certainly concern in European capitals that in the event of a nuclear war, the Soviets and Americans would refrain from using their strategic nuclear arsenals in order to preserve their homelands and instead obliterate Europe with tactical nuclear weapons. Furthermore in terms of relative weighting in the NATO alliance, the USA might appear to spend a greater proportion of its GDP on defence-related matters but the Western allies provided between 80 and 90 per cent of the land forces in Europe. And to prove this, with entry Heath made it clear to the Americans that he would not act unilaterally with them, but only in consultation and co-ordination with his new European allies.[78]

Entry and renegotiation

The conclusion of the negotiations in June 1971 led to the publication of a white paper outlining the necessary legislation and began a lengthy parliamentary battle as Heath steered the European Economic Communities bill through 300 hours of debate, and 104 voting divisions. Calls for a referendum were brushed aside by Heath, who argued that MPs were representatives of the people and in a representative democracy the will of the House of Commons was sovereign. The 1971 Conservative conference overwhelmingly endorsed the entry terms by 2,474 to 324. Yet this did not prevent the Conservative anti-marketeers in Parliament from repeatedly seeking to defeat the government. The Commons witnessed the largest rebellion since the Norway debate of May 1940, on 28 October 1971 when one-fifth of back-benchers rebelled. Still Heath won the vote 356 to 244. Over the coming months variously thirty-nine Conservatives rebelled, but the connivance of Labour pro-Europeanists with the Conservative whips ensured that the government never lost a vote, even though many were victories by the narrowest of margins. In July 1972 the bill was given its third and final reading.[79] In the interim the negotiations had continued to seek to resolve a number of outstanding issues, not least on the common fisheries policy, which had come into force in February 1971, and particularly irked the Norwegians, but which also raised problems for the British. Eventually a deal was reached in December agreeing that national governments could apply six-mile limits around parts of their coastline but with a clause that intended to review this arrangement within ten years. At the official signing ceremony on 22 January 1972 Heath had a bottle of ink thrown over him by a protestor, but such an action was not going to stop Britain formally joining the EEC on 1 January 1973 (and simultaneously leaving EFTA), alongside Ireland and Denmark. The Norwegians, after a referendum, rejected their government's successfully negotiated entry terms.

As to the cost of entry, this was less than clear. In December 1969 the UK's Institute of Directors published a report indicating that greater economic growth from entry would be offset by higher labour costs and that those industries dependent on either raw materials or benefiting from tariff protection from Community producers would suffer. That same month the Confederation of British Industry had also concluded that entry would be advantageous to British and EEC industries, but only if the entry terms did not provoke deflation in Britain. The government had sought to downplay the likely rises in food prices and the scale of contribution to the EEC budget. 'Disingenuousness' is how one historian has categorised it.[80] When the European Commission officially revealed figures in 1980, Britain's net contribution had been closer to £1 billion, when at the time pro-market campaigners had offered claims of £200 million. One reason that the government was keen to downplay the costs of entry was due to the internal Conservative party polling which showed that rising food prices, followed by concerns about the loss of sovereignty, were the most significant issues troubling the electorate.[81] There was certainly awareness that the EEC was a 'dynamic' structure, which often took decisions, which extended the authority of the Community's institutions to new areas, but the government was not overly keen to publicise this. There were moments of frankness from Heath's ministers during the accession debates. Geoffrey Howe admitted that the EEC 'would evolve and continue to evolve', and in the same debate Heath admitted it was likely that additional treaties would occur and majority voting would be introduced. Entry was presented as a trade-off between the loss of virtual autonomy against the influence gained. Furthermore it was expected that future integration would be policy orientated rather than institutional and this would not threaten Parliamentary sovereignty.[82] For Heath sovereignty meant autonomy, and autonomy was best gained through influence. A 'myth' has gained currency that somehow in 1971–73 there was no discussion of the developing nature of the EEC and the ramifications this may have for British sovereignty. This is evidently not that case, and as Teddy Taylor (a Eurosceptic who resigned as a junior minister in 1971 in opposition to entry) admitted Heath 'didn't hide the consequences. The tragedy is that few listened.'[83]

Despite the 'educational' efforts of the Heath administration, via the European Movement, many voters were still largely ignorant of what the EEC presented the British people with. In signing up to the Treaty of Rome, Britain was now obliged to work within a new organisational structure. There was the European Commission, which was the executive arm of the Community and which had three functions: the right to initiate legislation; to act as guardian of the treaties; and oversee the day-to-day management of the Community. It was both a full-time civil service and 'government' of the EEC, with a President of the Commission assisted by a number of commissioners, nationally appointed but expected to act as the conscience of the Community. Initially there were nine commissioners, a figure that expanded to thirteen with enlargement in 1973. Christopher Soames, the former British ambassador to Paris, and George Thompson, the former Labour cabinet minister, were appointed by Heath as Britain's first commissioners in October 1972. Throughout the 1970s complaints persisted that the behaviour of commissioners was too partial to their national government's interests. If the European Commission had the role of initiator, then the Council of Ministers was the forum that could aid or reject its plans. It was made up of national government ministers, one from each state appropriate to the subject under discussion. The chairmanship rotated between member nations, in line with a six-month rotation of the presidency of the European Council. Enlargement increased the size of the Council from six to nine in 1973. Each member's votes were weighted according to a formula, which rewarded the larger member nations. Before the 1973 enlargement there were 17 votes, with 12 required for qualified majority decisions, and thereafter this increased to 58 votes with 41 required for majority decisions. The legal apparatus of the EEC was the European Court of Justice, with a permanent member from each member state, and which was common to the EEC, ECSC and Euratom and based in Luxembourg. Under section 2 of the 1972 Treaty of Accession, European law secured primacy over British law. Its responsibilities included the legal interpretation of the treaties, adjudicating in disputes over

Community law and in making binding judgements. Before the first enlargement there were seven judges and two advocates-general. The number increased to nine and four respectively in 1973. During the late 1960s and 1970s the continued operation of the ECJ 'kept alive the vision of the Community as something more than a trade alliance'.[84] Its treatment of the Treaty of Rome as not just a treaty but as a constitutional instrument with provisions enforceable by law gave the EEC an ever wider remit. The European Assembly (Parliament from 1979) was formed from Article 108.3 of the Treaty of Rome and divided between Luxembourg (where the secretariat is based), Brussels (where the committee meetings are held) and Strasbourg (where the plenary sessions are conducted). With each phase of enlargement the membership has expanded from 142 at conception to 198 in 1973 to 410 in 1979 when the first direct elections were held. Britain's initial delegation size was 36 although it was actually smaller because the Labour party did not at first take up the seats allocated to them until after the 1975 referendum.

Did the average British citizen notice any immediate differences over becoming an EEC member? It seems that public opinion in the majority now viewed entry as a positive thing, although from 1976 this would slide very rapidly into reverse.[85] There was, however, a high level of ignorance about the nature of the EEC.[86] In public opinion there was certainly a change in how the public compared Britain with the EEC. Fewer people now believed that Britain had a higher standard of living than the EEC, more thought that the EEC had greater holiday entitlements, higher wages and a more significant world role than Britain.[87] Government departments were instructed to consider the harmonisation of their methods with those of Europe in their sphere.[88] In a sense this had already begun as far back as 1961 when the Halsbury Committee of Inquiry was established to consider the question of decimalisation. This decision was taken in March 1966, with the first new coins entering circulation in April 1968 before D-Day on 15 February 1971. Furthermore, the Conservatives had decided in opposition to introduce a value-added tax (VAT), believing it 'would be powerful evidence of "meaning business" as far as the Community was concerned'. The huge volume of work done in opposition for the adoption of VAT is difficult to comprehend without realising its European context, and became party policy on the understanding that the European Commission was prepared to accept different rates between countries.[89]

However, Heath was unable to reap the political benefits from his success. Persistent inflation, strike action and low growth rates seriously hampered his government's tenure in office and in February 1974 Heath was ousted from office. The EEC played its part in his demise. Former Conservative cabinet minister Enoch Powell had urged Conservative anti-marketeers to vote Labour, whilst the Labour opposition had pledged them to renegotiate the terms of Britain's entry whilst promising a popular vote on membership. These pledges were a reflection of Labour's own internal splits on Europe and were a compromise offered by Wilson to try and hold his party together.

Wilson formed a minority government on 4 March, and shortly, through James Callaghan, delivered the renegotiation request to the Council of Ministers in Luxembourg in April 1974. Top of the renegotiation agenda were the issues of CAP and Britain's budgetary contribution to the EEC. In June, in recognition of the potential impact of European affairs, measures were announced to give Parliament greater scrutiny of developments. More frequent debates were promised on matters European, as well as the allocation of part of question time to Community affairs, whilst monthly announcements would be given to Parliament outlining forthcoming Community business as well as promising six-monthly reports on the government's attitude to Community developments. In addition select committees on the European Community were established in both Houses of Westminster. When a second general election in October 1974 gave Labour a narrow majority of four seats, the need to keep his party unified on Europe obliged Wilson to press ahead with plans for renegotiation and a referendum. The promise of a referendum not later than June was made on 23 January 1975 to the House of Commons, a move that has been likened to an 'opportunistic u-turn'.[90] The Dublin European Council meeting in March 1975 saw the conclusion of the renegotiation at which a compensatory refund mechanism was agreed, as well as a statement of intent to reach agreement on continued access to New Zealand dairy produce after 1977. Ultimately the renegotiated terms were merely tweakings, but Parliament overwhelmingly endorsed them by 396 to 170 in April 1975. The referendum pledged in January was now timetabled for June. Within the Cabinet, though, there were very real divisions over the merits of recommending the renegotiated terms. Seven ministers, Michael Foot, Eric Varley, Barbara Castle, Tony Benn, Peter Shore, William Ross and John Silkin, took a dissenting line. There was concern that the EEC's supranational ambitions restricted a Labour government's room for manoeuvre and further that the EEC was a tool of capitalism whose market-led policies discriminated against the workers. When a special Labour conference debated the terms on 26 April 1975 it voted 3.7 million to 1.9 million to leave the Community. Labour's split over Europe was symptomatic of a growing schism in the party that over the next six years would see the grassroots move leftwards, and elements of the party's right split off to form the Social Democratic Party (SDP) in 1981.

Organisations immediately sprang up to promote the referendum. The 'Yes' campaign was directed under the umbrella of the Britain in Europe (BIE) group led by Con O'Neill, the former Foreign Office diplomat. The rival camp was the National Referendum Campaign (NRC) led by Neil Marten, Conservative MP for Banbury.[91] Both groups were multi-party coalitions, but each experienced problems arising from traditional party political antagonism. Both Wilson and Thatcher (now Conservative leader) restricted themselves to only addressing 'Yes' rallies comprising of their own supporters. Whilst the NRC 'No' group witnessed divisions between left-wingers like Tony Benn and Barbara Castle and right-wingers like Enoch Powell. The outcome of the 5 June referendum was a two-to-one majority accepting the renegotiated terms and Britain remaining a member of the EEC. Only in the Western Isles of Scotland was there a majority for the No campaign. Financially, the No campaign operated on a shoestring. Whereas the Yes campaign had raised nearly £1.5 million to fund their campaign, the No campaign in contrast only secured £8,000 with a further subsidy of £125,000 being given by the government to each side. Also the No campaign lacked the support of the press, with only the *Morning Star* offering assistance. The No campaign divided between those who spoke about high food prices and those who spoke about the loss of sovereignty. In addition they argued that there was a risk of unemployment, especially in those regions furthest from the continent. The rebuttal from the Yes campaign was that new jobs would be created because of membership, and that Britain had to realise that it had no alternative to membership, whilst reassuring voters that membership did not risk British traditions. The scale of the electorate's rejection of the No campaign's arguments appeared to suggest the irrelevancy of anti-marketeerism. The rapid closure of the NRC's twelve regional offices and 250 local branches appeared as confirmation.[92]

Some concluding thoughts

During the application phase the concept of Europe evolved, at least presentationally. Membership of the EEC was presented as an economic necessity that would provide Britain with renewed strategic significance. Entry would enable Britain to resume her role as the arbiter of the balance of power. Were there alternatives that Britain could have chosen? She could have remained with EFTA, although the scale of this trading bloc and the changes being experienced by Britain's trading patterns suggested future difficulties if they did. The same applied to the Commonwealth preference option. The most commonly 'new' alternative mooted was the idea of a North Atlantic Free Trade Area (NAFTA) – this enjoyed two periods of active promotion, 1967–69 and 1995–2000 – but whilst the language, customs and laws may share a closeness with the USA, this concept always carried little weight with Washington. The negotiation process had been treacherous and the domestic ratification equally torturous, but the referendum result was closure. The challenge it now presented the political establishment with was for it to make membership work and to find Britain's place in Europe.

4 Britain in Europe
From EEC to EU, 1975–97

The 1975 referendum outcome meant that Britain was confirmed as a member of the EEC. Following this the question to be answered was to what extent this membership would actually impact upon Britain's political, economic and social culture and lead to 'Europeanisation'. Initially British opinion towards the EEC was largely positive. This was short-lived. From 1976 onwards opinion became increasingly hostile, in part encouraged by negative press coverage critical of the Common Agricultural Policy and issues relating to fishing quotas. It became a matter of 'them' and 'us', none more so than in the portrayal of the British and French as 'opponents'.[1] Following the hijacking of British lamb lorries in January 1984 the *Sun* invited its readers to submit anti-French jokes. There was a growing sense that the EEC was unable to respond to the global economic uncertainties of the late 1970s and early 1980s. Consequently the early years of British membership have been seen as a 'barren decade'[2] in which 'nothing was achieved'.[3] The *Economist* in March 1982 carried a pictorial front cover of the EEC's gravestone, inscribed:

> Born March 25, 1957
> Moribund March 25, 1982
> Capax imperii nisi imperasset[4]

Yet this proved, and has continued to prove, to be one of many premature obituaries for the EEC.

European Parliament

One of the most immediate areas in which the EEC impacted was in representation to the European Parliament, resulting in European elections in 1979. When Britain joined the EEC in 1973 a delegation of non-elected British representatives began attending the European Parliament. Initially, only the Conservatives and Liberals sent delegates as the Labour party boycotted the concept until 1975. At the Paris summit in 1974 it was agreed that direct elections to the European Parliament should be introduced, and it was the responsibility of each member nation to secure the necessary domestic legislation to ensure that elections could take place in 1978. In Britain the debate involved two issues: should Britain participate in elections to an assembly that might usurp the legitimacy of Westminster? And if elections were adopted what electoral system should be used? Could they be conducted under a proportional representation (PR) system, and might that prove a precedent that ensured its implementation for Westminster elections? In the event, Britain caused the Europe-wide delay of the elections after Labour's direct elections bill had its proportional representation element rejected by 319 votes to 222 in December 1977. This resulted in the bill having to be reintroduced and the elections delayed until 1979. The PR element clause had been a trade off for Callaghan securing Liberal support to maintain his administration's majority. When the first direct elections under first-past-the-post were held on 7 June 1979 the Conservatives won sixty out of the seventy-eight seats on offer and gained 51 per cent of the vote. However turnout was low at only 48 per cent. This suggested voter apathy towards Europe, but also may have been due to voter fatigue, the electorate having been asked to turn out the previous month to vote in a general election, one which saw the Conservatives returned to power and the premiership of Margaret Thatcher. Observers were reassured, though, because the European election result mirrored the national outcome of the previous month.

Regional funds and European political co-operation

The October 1972 Paris summit agreed to establish in 1975 a Regional Development Fund (ERDF) to give assistance to the EEC's own 'backward' areas, something which had been a long-standing call from the Italians. The British and Irish, who both had endemic regional problems, were concerned that by both being late entrants to the EEC and by being on the periphery of the EEC that they would be excluded from enjoying the benefits of the Bonn-Paris axis, so they supported the Italian proposals. This was something that Britain could expect to benefit from, except that Heath refused to allow revenue from Britain's North Sea oil discoveries to be ploughed into Europe and thus the Germans refused to make any significant contributions to the Fund. Its intention was to stimulate economic development in the least prosperous regions of the EEC. Cynics suggested its motivation was bribery by the wealthier members to the poorer peripheral members to buy their support for closer economic co-operation. Protagonists suggested that it would enable the various member states to reach more or less equivalent stages of development. ERDF required local government to submit schemes for support, which countered agricultural poverty, brought about industrial change or provided infrastructure, to their national governments. These would be forwarded to the EEC, with the expectation that the national government would match any funding offered by the EEC. The awards would be decided by a quota system.

Over time they have evolved to become a major element of regional development for regions in all the member nations and have become the second largest budgetary expenditure following CAP. In 1975 ERDF was allocated 4.8 per cent of total EEC spending. By 1987 its allocation was 9.1 per cent of total EEC spending.[5] The expectation was that this scheme would make a fairer European-wide regional policy so as to ensure that areas that might be poor in a national context were not singled out for preference by a national government when a objectively more deprived region in another member state was not receiving any state support. Furthermore these funds have been used by the Commission to encourage the Europeanisation of regional development projects, such as the Welsh Development Authority established in 1976, as opposed to simply ones of national self-interest. The ERDF rules were revised in January 1985. From the outset Britain became one of the main beneficiaries of the system with 28 per cent of the pool, after Italy with 40 per cent. Once Spain joined she moved into the slot as the second largest recipient.[6] The problem proved that with enlargement the new accessionees were eligible for increasingly large proportions of the funding pool, which meant that the largest contributors, Britain and Germany were expected to increase their funding.

Monetary instability, the USA's break with dollar convertibility and the rise in oil prices marked the end of Europe's economic golden age and impacted upon the EEC's plans to move to the next phase of integration during the 1970s. The steep rise in oil prices, with Europe acquiring 80 per cent of its oil from the Middle East and North Africa, caused a European-wide recession, but with increasingly divergent experiences. West Germany's inflation for the period 1973–80 ran at 5 per cent compared to Britain's 15 per cent. The number of unemployed in the EEC rose from 5.9 million in 1973 to 10.6 million by 1982. The ambitious plans agreed at Paris in 1972 were no longer viable and with a rapidly diminishing political commitment it seemed that the plans for further integration were receding. Some academics were arguing by the early 1980s that the EEC had reached a state of equilibrium. Whilst it had managed to absorb the worst of internal and external crises of the 1970s it appeared to be ill equipped for future challenges. A similar view was reached by a Chatham House analysis.[7] For Britain, the shocks of EEC membership were profoundly felt, both financially and psychologically. July 1977 saw the end of the transitional period for Britain, requiring full abolition of intra-community tariffs. When Britain secured the presidency of the EEC in the first six months of 1977, Callaghan made it clear that Labour and Britain opposed any challenge to the sovereignty of national governments. He emphasised the need for national control over economic and regional policies and insisted that the Community needed to reform its budget procedures: refrains that would sound increasingly familiar under the Thatcher government from 1979. The 1970s may have been one of stagnation for the EEC, but the experience was profoundly important in shaping the attitudes of the member states. It moved the obsession with full employment to one of concern for inflation. It also led to a questioning of the welfare social services model and the state's role. Reform was on the EEC's agenda but not necessarily in the manner Britain hoped. Prior to the accession of Portugal and Spain, in 1986, many in the EEC had sought to extend the use of majority voting and reduce the opportunities for member nations to invoke the 1966 Luxembourg compromise veto. Reforms had been proposed numerous times and floundered with the ghosts of the 1969 Barre Plan, the 1970 Davignon report on political unification, the 1972 Vedel report on the European parliament to the 1976 Tindemans report and the 1979 'Three Wise Men's Report' on the EEC's institutional structure stalking the corridors and committee rooms of Brussels and Strasbourg.

European Political Co-operation (EPC) and European Monetary System (EMS) were 'the two exceptions to the general record of stagnation'.[8] EPC was agreed by the Six in 1970 and aimed to give the Community a foreign policy profile that matched its growing economic might. EPC put into practice a long-held French view that foreign policy co-operation could be conducted in parallel with economic policy, and outside the formal procedural protocols of the Community treaties. Yet it was quickly apparent that economic policy could not be separated from foreign policy and that the organs of the Community needed at least a consultancy role in any EPC discussions. The adoption of EPC saw the EEC beginning to establish a single European voice on the diplomatic circuit. Dialogue was begun with the Arab states from 1974 as OPEC began rapidly raising the price of oil. One of its first successes was the achievement of presenting an EEC verdict to the Conference on Security and Cooperation in Europe that resulted in the 1975 Helsinki Accord. This began a thaw in East–West relations as America and the European countries recognised the Soviet Union's eastern borders. An independent EEC voice began to be heard in the problems of Latin America whilst in the United Nations members of the EEC began adjusting their voting behaviour and acting with a degree of European unity; however, as successive foreign policy crises through the 1980s and 1990s would show, national interest still persisted, suggesting that to label it a success was premature. Still EPC persisted. The 1981 London Report concluded that where issues of security had a political bearing then these could be discussed under EPC arrangements. Ultimately Title 111 of the 1986 Single European Act formalised and institutionalised the practices, and created a small EPC secretariat in Brussels that would codify EPC into treaty.

Towards monetary union

The EEC had been working towards monetary union (EMU) since agreeing to it at the Hague summit in 1969. Luxembourg's prime minister Pierre Werner was charged with developing the plan. The Werner report published in October 1970 aimed to establish a system of Community central banks and central authority for economic decision making. The concept was an ambitious one and was welcomed by Germany, yet initially it looked prone to failure, not least because France objected to its supranational nature. The initial mechanism for achieving EMU was a system nicknamed the 'Snake', which tried to hold exchange rates between currencies in narrow fluctuation bands, which varied against the value of the dollar. However, uncertainty on the world economic markets between 1972 and 1974, as the Bretton Woods system collapsed in March 1973 and then global oil prices soared following the outbreak of the Yom Kippur War, irreparably damaged the credibility of the system and one by one member currencies, including the pound in 1972, the franc and lira in 1973, were forced out of the system. Although the Tindemans report proposed continuing with the Snake by 1977 it had in effect become a Deutschmark zone.

The European Monetary System (EMS) was a Franco–German proposal offered by Helmut Schmidt and Valery Giscard d'Estaing in 1978 to tie together the exchange rates of the EEC member states in an Exchange Rate Mechanism (ERM), thereby formalising economic co-operation with the long-term objective of achieving economic convergence. It also included plans for a European Currency Unit (ECU), a weighted average of all EMS currencies, which was suggested could ultimately become the single currency of the EEC. The Callaghan Labour government ruled Britain out of participating, suspecting that its motives were primarily political and aimed to enhance the momentum for political union, and that the whole proposal would only serve German interests.[9] Certainly the Germans, as the main protagonists, were seeking to provide a European solution to dampen inflationary pressures on their economy and minimise the impact of the world recession. In rejecting British participation, Callaghan was looking to the Americans and a global solution, believing that through stimulating growth recession could be climbed out of whilst believing existing international structures, like the International Monetary Fund, offered the means for currency stabilisation.[10] The Conservatives, after lengthy consideration of EMS, decided to play party politics and pledged in their European manifesto of 1979 that 'we shall look for ways in which Britain can take her rightful place within it'.[11] Once more, the Conservatives were using Europe as a tool of political opportunism, in a manner similar to the Churchill opposition in the years before 1951. On assuming power in 1979 the Conservative cabinet's enthusiasm immediately waned as Treasury advice argued that the conditions were not yet suited to British entry into the EMS. As Nigel Lawson confessed it was 'a hideously complex and awkward issue, both economically and (more importantly) politically'.[12] Yet despite the lack of British participation the EMS could be judged a success, and in part this owed much to the weakness of the German economy in the early years of the scheme, making it easier for other members to maintain their parity with the Deutschmark, whilst working to drive down their own inflation levels. Once the German economy recovered by the 1990s the growing strength of the Deutschmark would challenge the viability of the system.

Budget

How the EEC was funded was one of the most significant and controversial issues to face the member nations in the late 1970s and early 1980s. The EEC was not a subscription club, but rather a form of means-tested contributory group. A complex system of financing the EEC was agreed in 1970 before Britain joined. The model derived income from three streams: customs duty levied on imports to member states; levies on agricultural trade with non-member countries; plus a proportion of member states' sales tax (VAT in Britain). In 1973 Britain contributed 8.64 per cent of the EEC's budget, a figure that climbed significantly thereafter. The 1971 white paper had warned that British contributions would be high, not least because the EEC's preference for 'own resources' penalised Britain with its extensive external trading links. From the 1975 renegotiation onwards the British net contribution to the EEC rose rapidly from £168 million in 1976 to £948 million in 1979. Although the contribution Britain received from the CAP budget fluctuated in between £181 million in 1977 to £371 million in 1979, this was a relative fraction of the benefits Britain's counterparts were receiving.[13] This made Britain the second largest donor to the Community after Germany, despite being the third most impoverished member of the Community.[14] Treasury officials were calculating in 1979 that membership was costing Britain £1 billion a year.[15] It was observed that British tourism benefited from 7 million EEC visitors, that 42 per cent of Britain's exports went to the EEC, and 44 per cent of the EEC's exports came to Britain. Furthermore it was suggested that 2.5 million jobs were reliant upon EEC business.[16] When these figures were considered alongside Britain's relatively poor import/export balance of payments it was evident that the cost of EEC membership was politically significant. In the view of the Treasury, 'abolition [of the Common Agricultural Policy] is the long-term goal and every little war is a step towards or away from that goal'.[17] CAP was established in 1962, and arose from Article 39 of the Treaty of Rome. It accounted for over 50 per cent of the Community's budget and aimed at a unified market for agricultural products within the Community. From the point of British entry it made agriculture one of the most Europeanised aspects within the British government. Prices were fixed annually by the Council of Ministers, which because of national self-interest and the nature of inter-governmental bargaining has tended to over-inflate these prices, resulting in over-production and agricultural surpluses. During the 1980s Britain, along with the Dutch and Danish governments, pushed for reform of CAP, but with little success, except in managing to restrict agricultural expenditure. Opposition from those member states with relatively large agricultural sectors, as well as the agricultural lobby itself, made it difficult to secure wholesale changes. At the beginning of 1983 the Commission reached the conclusion that the over-supply of milk in the Community required one of two solutions: either lower prices on milk or the imposition of quotas. Ultimately they favoured the latter, but the problem proved to be securing member state agreement. Britain favoured a lower total milk quota. Because of the failure to secure agreement in the autumn the Commission then sought to exert pressure on national governments by proposing the alternative policy of 12 per cent price cuts, a threat which forced the agriculture ministers to agree to a quota arrangement in March 1984. In an increasingly global market, many perceive CAP as European protectionism, and suggest that it has been globally damaging for emerging Third World economies.

On assuming office, Thatcher was swift to warn the EEC that she was not prepared to sacrifice domestic social and economic improvements for the bankrolling of the Community. Arguing that for every £2 contribution Britain received back just £1, Thatcher began promoting the cause of a British budgetary rebate. Until 1984 the budget rebate issue threatened to disrupt all EEC matters. The hostility displayed by fellow EEC leaders towards Thatcher's position was apparent even to her critics, some of whom felt she was poorly treated at the 1979 Dublin summit.[18] After this diplomatic cold shoulder Thatcher retaliated by threatening, in March 1980, to withhold Britain's VAT contribution. This adversarial approach was certainly controversial, even amongst her own advisors and some Cabinet members. Francis Pym, the defence secretary, was concerned that Thatcher was whipping up anti-European sentiment amongst the British electorate and simply alienating Britain's European partners.[19] The tone of Thatcher's attacks was not solely geared to the EEC leadership, but was also directed towards the British electorate. In adopting her nationalistic approach, Thatcher's European rhetoric was intended to shift the blame for some of Britain's domestic woes and mitigate the deep unpopularity with which her premiership was then viewed. As another Cabinet critic observed, 'a running row with our European partners was the next best thing to a war; it would divert public attention from the disasters at home'.[20] In May 1980, Peter Carrington and Ian Gilmour successfully negotiated a temporary twelve-month solution whereby Britain would be given two-thirds of the rebate that was being demanded. Further compromise was required in June 1982, after Britain vetoed agreement on agricultural prices, threatening the functioning of the CAP, before the matter was finally resolved at the Fontainebleau summit in 1984 when the two-thirds rebate was confirmed. In retrospect Thatcher had come to view the Fontainebleau deal as a compromise too far, and suggested that foreign secretary Geoffrey Howe had been too quick to concede owing to his excessively romantic visions of European consensus.[21] The reality was more that throughout her dealings with Europe until 1988, Thatcher always started from a position of intentional resistance before moving to a compromise position.[22] Indeed, one highly ranked Council of Ministers official observed that no-one paid any attention to British objections, for they realised that on the important questions Thatcher would eventually either concede or let the other Council members decide, while vainly proclaiming her opposition in principle.[23] As one journalist observed, Thatcher's European views were like a religious faith, where the individual thinks they ought to be atheist but cannot take themselves beyond fluctuating between attending church and then observing atheism.[24]

External affairs and domestic politics

Contextually Europe was not the central feature of the early years of the Thatcher premiership. Domestic economic policy, rising unemployment, which was pushing nearly 3 million, and the power of trade unions, especially with the miners' strike of 1983–84, and the privatisation of the 'family silver' all had great prominence.[25] British inflation peaked at 26 per cent in 1976, and despite recovering in 1978–79, rose again thereafter, pushing 20 per cent in the opening years of Thatcher government. The second oil crisis of 1979 was largely to blame and then compounded by the 1980 decision of the American Federal Reserve to restrict the growth of the US money supply, which pushed up American interest rates and the value of the dollar. Although the price of oil was doubled, this did not directly affect Britain because she exported as much oil (thanks to the North Sea) as was imported. The global market was restricted and demand for British exports was weakened, something then aggravated by the continued strength of the pound on the currency markets, when the EMS countries' currencies were falling against the dollar.

External events were highly significant too. Events in Iran with the Islamic Revolution overthrowing the Shah and then seizing American hostages brought an end to the Carter presidency in America. The Soviet Union's invasion of Afghanistan, roundly condemned by the EEC in January 1980, suggested a resurgence of the Cold War, something the presidency of Ronald Reagan aggravated through resorting to an arms race. In Poland the rise of Solidarity briefly threatened the Soviet-sponsored dictatorship of General Jaruzelski. More directly, events involving Britain, such as the Falklands War (1982–83), and the American bombing of Libya (1986) launched from bases in Britain, focussed much more attention on the Anglo–American relationship than the Anglo–European, whilst the public protests against the installation of cruise missiles and the American arms build-up brought Anglo–American relations directly to mainland Britain.

The Falklands crisis, prompted by the Argentinian military's seizure of South Georgia and the Falkland Islands in the southern Atlantic, presented a significant challenge for the EEC. Britain, and Thatcher personally, lobbied fellow EEC member nations extremely hard to ensure that the EEC sided with Britain. On 10 April 1982 the EEC declared short-term sanctions against Argentina, including a ban on imports and on the sale of military arms. The speed with which the Community acted on sanctions was impressive, as it was unusual. The Commission hailed the sanctions as the toughest yet imposed by the Community, especially when compared to those imposed upon Poland and the Soviet Union in 1981 following the declaration of martial law.

Thatcher in the House of Commons acknowledged the sacrifices being made: 'The decision cannot have been easy for our partners given the commercial interests at stake.'[26] The EEC took 20 per cent of Argentina's exports, and West Germany had particularly close trading links. The EEC viewed sanctions, which were effected on 17 April, as an alternative to military conflict and it is evident that some member states had sacrificed national interest for the greater good of the EEC. However, behind the scenes there was considerable disquiet and it was by no means a foregone conclusion when EEC foreign ministers met on 19 April that the united front would be maintained. The Irish were particularly aghast at the continued use of sanctions after the sinking of the *Belgrano*, an Argentinian light cruiser, and their government was under intense domestic pressure to lift restrictions. But concerns about EEC punishment, especially in the area of farm subsidies, persuaded Dublin to avoid unilateral action. Behind the scenes, some saw an opportunity to trade support for Britain's Falklands strategy with squeezing concessions from Britain on the EEC budget and CAP. On 8–9 May there was a particularly acrimonious meeting of EEC foreign ministers in Belgium. Britain apparently threatened to leave the EEC if sanctions were not renewed. The Irish and Belgian governments proposed that concessions from Britain over the budget dispute, and its current action of stalling the increase in food price support under CAP, could be matched by EEC solidarity over the Falklands. On 18 May the Council of Agricultural Ministers took the highly significant step of disregarding British opposition to farm price increases and took a majority decision to implement the changes. This was highly controversial given in theory that Britain had the power of veto in this area under the Luxembourg compromise, and the Council was in effect introducing majority voting in this area. Yet, Britain chose to let the issue ride because of its continuing search for EEC support. Britain then took a reduced budget rebate of $875 million on 25 May in exchange for the EEC agreeing to the indefinite renewal of sanctions.[27] When diplomacy failed, the British task force, which had sailed from Britain on 5 April, began the liberation of the islands on 21 May, finally securing the Argentinian surrender on 14 June. For Thatcher the 'mixed' response of the EEC suggested the need to enhance the organisation to ensure future support for a 'troubled' member nation.[28] The EEC's public support for Britain did have unintended domestic consequences, namely that it convinced some of last remaining Conservative anti-marketeers that they could no longer continue their hostility to the Community.[29]

This was less the case for the Labour party, with Europe still remaining a significant ideological divider. The October 1980 party conference had voted in favour of withdrawal from the EEC. Shortly afterward Callaghan resigned as party leader and was replaced by Michael Foot. The party reinforced this EEC hostility by enshrining the withdrawal pledge in their 1983 general election manifesto, or 'longest suicide note in history' as Gerald Kaufman characterised it. This would ultimately remain a manifesto commitment until 1988. Opposition to Europe came from two distinct perspectives in the party.

There were those Labour figures who opposed the EEC because they feared that it was a capitalist club that would frustrate a Labour government's policies, then there were those more fundamentally opposed to the concept of the EEC because of concerns about the potential loss of sovereignty it threatened. The 1983 manifesto argued for an Alternative Economic Strategy involving large-scale state intervention and economic controls. But not all Labour MPs were so accepting of the party's Euroscepticism. Historically the party's divisions over Europe were very evident and it was clear that the pro-Europeans in Labour would be willing on occasion to put country before party, as did the seventy Labour MPs who co-operated with Heath's Conservative whips over the 1972 EEC bill. However, the divisions became even more significant, resulting in the defection of the Gang of Four (David Owen, Shirley Williams, Roy Jenkins and Bill Rodgers) to form the Social Democratic Party in March 1981 following the Limehouse declaration of January, which attacked the 'isolationist, xenophobic and neutralist' trends in the Labour party.[30] It would be overstating the point to suggest that Europe was the cause of Labour's split, but it was an important element of a cluster of issues that prompted the party's schism. The near electoral annihilation that the party experienced in 1983, with Thatcher in part benefiting from a 'Falklands bounce', were to oblige Labour to undergo a significant ideological evolution such that by the beginning of the 1990s they had become the pro-European party.

Organisational rivals

After the period of stagnation that the EEC appeared to have experienced during the 1970s, the European Commission hoped to revive the European project by recruiting additional members. The expansion of the EEC, with Greece (1981 – who had associate membership from November 1962), Spain (1986) and Portugal (1986) joining did raise questions about the best means of operation for the EEC, and given the agrarian predominance of these nations, suggested that the timing of Britain's concerns about the EEC's budgetary and agricultural policies was apposite. Enlargement also meant that it was no longer solely Britain who was the nation expressing disquiet. All three of the new accessionees had recently had democracy restored after lengthy periods of dictatorship, and by being brought into the EEC were ensuring that their loyalties remained with the west, and particularly in the case of Greece, that they remained within the sphere of NATO.[31] Not everyone was anxious to be an EEC member. Greenland held a referendum in February 1982, which saw 52 per cent in favour of withdrawal, and this was formalised on 1 February 1985.

There is a danger of characterising and evaluating Britain's relationship as if the EEC were the sole avenue of European co-operation. It could occur in areas of technological business development, such as with Concorde, or with membership of alternative inter-governmental organisations. Despite enlargement the EEC still remained one of several different European organisations. The EEC's rival European organisation was the European Free Trade Association (EFTA), which comprised Switzerland, Sweden, Norway, Finland, Austria and Iceland. Britain had been a member until she chose EEC membership. In 1985 EFTA had a higher gross domestic product per head of population than EEC: $11,750 compared to $7,575. However, the EEC's bureaucracy dwarfed it. Whilst the EEC employed 17,000 civil servants, EFTA had only seventy-one employees, nine of whom were part time. English was EFTA's working language, so had no need for the 5,000 linguists and translators that the EEC employed. But EFTA was heavily dependent on the EEC for trade, having become the EEC's largest trading partner.[32] An EEC-EFTA free trade area was established in January 1984. Another comparator is that by 1990 NATO employed 2,300 officials at its Brussels HQ whilst the EU had 14,000 located in the city.

Although the 1981 London Report on EPC had offered the potential for a political security dimension to be added to the EEC's remit, the issue of European defence was a complicated one due to 'variable geometry' – the fact that defence is considered by a vast array of committees and different organisations, some within the EU, some external and some part-EEC. That NATO had assumed overall responsibility for the defence of western Europe added additional complexity to the matter, especially since France had withdrawn in 1966. Italo–German plans for a Defence Council under EPC were poorly received, not least by the British who had consistently fought to ensure that the primacy of NATO was not challenged. In the arena of defence WEU, after a period of hiatus, was reactivated and there had been moves towards greater bilateral co-operation on defence procurement and military training. Evidence of Mitterand's concept of a two-speed Europe was apparent in French plans to revitalise WEU in late 1984 as a forum for European defence co-operation. This represented a shift in French military policy, as France had not contributed to discussions on European security issues since De Gaulle had withdrawn the country from NATO in 1966. Also despite EEC enlargement, WEU remained a membership of seven. It was proposed that WEU should consider enhancing the European pillar of NATO. Germany and France sought to co-operate militarily, establishing a 4,000 strong Franco–German brigade. The Agency for the Control of Armaments, initially created to oversee German rearmament in the 1950s, was given a fresh remit to oversee arms control and wider security issues. The British initial reaction was one of scepticism, but ultimately acceptance of the proposals in October 1984. Furthermore European co-operation on the Eurofighter was initialised. West Germany, Italy and Britain had co-operated in the mid-1970s on the development and production of the Tornado aircraft, plus plans for the Ariane space research programme and the Airbus airliner project. The reforms were taken further in 1987 with the adoption of the 'Platform on European Security Interests', which sought to confirm WEU's position within a broader framework of western European defence and as a mutual European support pillar within NATO and as a forum for arms control and disarmament. The intention behind reforming WEU was not solely one of ensuring a European identity within NATO; it was also down to European distrust of American strategic policies. The 1986 Reykjavik summit between Reagan and Gorbachev appeared to confirm suspicions that America would be perfectly willing to act unilaterally, independently of NATO if it served her interests. WEU continued to expand. In 1988 Spain and Portugal joined. As Spain remains outside NATO, as with France, WEU membership was an opportunity for co-operation with their neighbours. WEU also succeeded in co-ordinating military operations, ensuring a naval presence in the Gulf region during the latter stages of the Iran–Iraq War, and then in 1990–1 with the First Gulf War to liberate Kuwait, ensuring co-ordination between their forces. The limitations of WEU though were clearly apparent and evidenced with their unwillingness to commit grounds troops to the Yugoslavian civil war until the conclusion of a lasting truce.

Towards a European economic and foreign policy?

Despite the early successes of the EMS, it was evident by the early 1980s that it had failed to revive Europe from its economic doldrums. The Germans and Italians began speculating about whether a form of collective economic planning implemented through the institutions of the EEC, rather than by national governments, would better insulate Europe from the fluctuations of the world economy, and the strengths of the Japanese and American economies. This disillusionment with the poor economic performance was particularly keen in West Germany. In 1981 German foreign minister Hans Dietrich Genscher proposed strengthening the powers of the Community's institutions. Italy saw potential in these plans and Italian foreign minister Emilio Colombo gave the plans further backing at the European Council meeting in London in November 1981. This process gained impetus with the June 1983 Solemn Declaration on European Union, which timetabled a plan of action to revive the process of closer integration, and the European Parliament's adoption of the Draft Treaty on European Union proposed by the Italian MEP, Altiero Spinelli, in February 1984.[33] Differences within the Community began to emerge during 1984 about how reform should develop. In May 1984 Mitterrand, in his capacity as President of the European Council, had made a speech calling for the re-launch of Europe through a process of renegotiating the 1957 Treaty of Rome and moving towards areas of common policy in the realms of transport, communications and defence. If necessary, Europe would have to achieve these as a 'two-speed Europe'. In contrast Britain was making calls for 'practical' measures to reform the EEC's modes of operation including reducing the size of the Commission and streamlining various Community procedures.[34] Within the Thatcher leadership elements were beginning to believe that moves towards a European single market would help secure free market ideas, whilst curbing inflationary pressures was an opportunity to develop 'Thatcherism on a European scale'.[35] *Europe: The Future* (1984) was a deliberate attempt to ensure that the driving force for these changes came in the British mould. The proposed introduction of majority voting in the Council of Ministers and plans to increase the scrutiny remit of the European Parliament, alongside plans to establish an internal European market, appealed to the Thatcher government.

The Fontainebleau summit agreed that a committee, chaired by Irish senator Jim Dooge, should investigate institutional reform. The Dooge committee produced its final report in March 1985, recommending that an intergovernmental conference be held to consider the wider use of qualified majority voting, reducing the size of the Commission and increasing the powers of the European Parliament and establishing a permanent secretariat to co-ordinate future co-operation. However, the British, Danish and Greek members of the committee opposed the idea of an intergovernmental conference and secured support for their view at the March 1985 Brussels European Council meetings. Yet a few months later in June at the instigation of Italian prime minister Bettino Craxi, the Milan European Council voted in favour of an intergovernmental conference to consider the institutional reform question. Although the British, Danish and Greeks continued their opposition, they agreed to attend the conference. Prior to, and following, the Milan meeting various member nations put forward reform plans aimed at either closer European union and/ or institutional reform. The British, through foreign secretary Geoffrey Howe, suggested the establishment of a small foreign policy secretariat, for greater co-operation on security issues and foreign policy, the extension of qualified majority voting and the acceleration of moves towards a common internal market. A Franco–German counter-proposal called for a 'treaty on European union', and likewise looked to greater foreign and security co-operation. These two documents were to form the basis for the inter-governmental discussions during the autumn of 1985. Creating a single internal market would require revisions to the Community's founding treaty, but there was momentum for change. For Jacques Delors, the new Commission president, the creation of a single currency would eliminate the exchange rate risks and high transaction costs, thereby creating a true single market. The problem for Britain was the federalist tone of much of the proposed changes. Thatcher lost the battle to prevent an inter-governmental conference to consider alterations to the Treaty of Rome at Milan in June 1985, but she determined upon a strategy of negotiating within the system in order to dilute the worst demands of the federalists. The successful outcome of this was seen at the Luxembourg European Council in December, which agreed the creation of the single market by December 1992 for people, goods, services and capital. The plans for institutional reform were restricted to the extension of majority voting and increasing the numbers of commissions and MEPs, and minor reforms to the powers of the European Parliament giving it a veto over any single-market legislation.[36] A new chapter of the Treaty was added covering 'Social and Economic Cohesion'. Plus the development of a secretariat to support European Political Cooperation (EPC), the foreign policy dimension of the EEC, was included. The responses to this agreement were mixed. In Britain Thatcher reported to the House of Commons her view that these reforms could be achieved without Treaty revisions,[37] whilst the Italians expressed disappointment that the reforms had not been radical enough. Delors admitted that the reforms were not as extensive as some had hoped but they were inevitably a compromise. Nevertheless he felt that national economic interests needed to be overridden if the Community was to shake off 'Euro sclerosis'. The response of the European Parliament was to initially vote against them 243–47 on 11 December, a decision reversed in the new year. Thatcher gave her full authority to the Single European Act (SEA) not least because Lord Cockfield (her former Cabinet minister and now EEC commissioner) was the architect and she signed the agreement in February 1986. Yet only nine of the twelve Community members signed. Italy, Greece and Denmark all initially delayed their signatures, until domestic reservations could be overcome.

During the 1980s, and especially the latter half, the EPC became increasingly active. Sanctions were variously imposed upon Iran, Poland, the Soviet Union, Argentina and South Africa. The number of statements being issued by the EPC rose from 25 in 1983 to 81 in 1988 to 99 in 1989 as the Iron Curtain collapsed across eastern Europe.[38] The weakness of EPC rested in the non-binding nature of its statutes even when formalised under the Single European Act. As a consequence 'national' interests have often overridden 'European' interests. This can be clearly illustrated in the example of southern Africa, an area of former colonial interest to many of the EEC members and consequently full of historical 'baggage'. The independence of Mozambique and Angola in 1976, and events in Namibia and Rhodesia, led the EEC to issue a business code of conduct for European firms operating in the region. As the South African apartheid regime began to descend into political violence in the 1980s, pressure grew for the implementation of sanctions. An initial package was agreed in 1985, but was rejected by Britain, Germany and Portugal (the former colonial powers in the region). During 1986 after considerable political wrangling a minimum package of sanctions was agreed banning new investments and the importation of iron, steel and gold. The opposition of Britain and Germany ensured that stiffer sanctions were not implemented and that coal, which represented 15 per cent of South Africa's exports to the EU, was excluded. With the release of Nelson Mandela in 1990 signalling the final phase in the ending of apartheid, 'national' interests can again be seen to be at work. Britain unilaterally announced the ending of sanctions and her preparedness to authorize new investment, even before the EPC had discussed the issue.[39]

Single European Act

Europe's decision to create an internal single market by 1992 required national governments to ensure this was enshrined in domestic legislation.

The ratification process in Britain was relatively straightforward. With Thatcher's political authority and a large majority it was seen as a foregone conclusion, and for the Conservatives was relatively uncontenious because it was being portrayed as an example of British leadership and as something that business and the City of London wanted. The parliamentary debates witnessed widespread absenteeism, and opposition at the third reading was restricted to forty-three MPs. One backbencher exasperatedly observed that the turnout was 'a measure of the way in which European debates have almost become a part of our domestic scene ... they rate slightly below Scottish housing debates'.[40] The SEA would only achieve its position of significance retrospectively. Indeed, one Treasury insider observed that their response was that it 'was a one-week wonder', a view 'hardly credible in the light of what happened later'.[41] Other European-related events were also distracting the political establishment and media. One was the Westland affair, resulting in the resignations of Michael Heseltine and Leon Brittan after a split over whether to support a European helicopter consortium with a purchasing order for Westland helicopters in preference to the American firm Sikorski. However, with the SEA, not for the first time, the British had mistaken European statements of position as being of little relevance, and held the expectation that the SEA would herald a long period of calm. This was misplaced. Consequently whilst Thatcher was presuming that the creation of the single market marked the topping out ceremony of the Community building project, 1992 was ultimately viewed, not least by the European Commission, as the opportunity for building an extension. This interpretive ambiguity arose because of the vagueness of the language used in the preamble of the SEA and the title of Article 20, which enabled the EC to force the pace towards a single currency. Even amongst those favourably disposed to the European project there was frustration. Geoffrey Howe observed that

> in domestic politics one had at least the feeling of being able to control the speed and manner in which policies developed. But in the Community we often seemed to be on a remorselessly moving carpet.[42]

It reflected the contrasting perspectives on how Europe should develop. For Jacques Delors Europe was a bike: you kept pedalling or else you fell off. He certainly belonged in the camp which was disappointed that the Single European Act did not go as far as the European Parliament's draft treaty and that the reform accepted had only been what was deemed absolutely necessary to allow the freeing of the market. A further dimension was added by the emergence of Mikhail Gorbachev in Soviet Russia from 1985. His *Perestroika* market reforms in Russia and eastern Europe, and his *Glasnost* desire for better relations with the West, opened up the prospect of new trading relationships with eastern Europe, but also raised the possibility of German reunification. For Mitterrand and Delors these developments were evidence of the need to accelerate the pace of integration.

The economic and political turmoil unleashed by Gorbachev's reforms saw nationalist movements re-emerge in many of the Soviet republics and a gradual weakening of Moscow's political control. In August 1991 the process of disintegration was hastened after a failed coup by hardline communists. Reassured that Gorbachev had ruled out military action against separatists, many Soviet republics asserted their independence and the Baltic states sought international recognition for their newly acquired freedom. At the same time Gorbachev's foreign policy was heralding the rapid end of the Cold War and the nuclear arms race, formally announced at the Malta summit in December 1989, and heralded with the 1987 Intermediate Nuclear Forces (INF) treaty. Those eastern European countries tied to the Soviet Union by the Warsaw Pact had since the 1980s been suffering with poor economic performance, food shortages in even the basic foodstuffs and experiencing environmental degradation, all of which was undermining the authority of the communist regimes. The speed of the collapse of the eastern bloc system was swift as it was historic. The first signs of change emerged in Poland in the summer of 1989 when Lec Walencza, leader of the Solidarity movement, which had emerged from the shipyards of Gdansk, took power. Changes soon occurred in Hungary, and suddenly whole regimes were being swept aside, and in the case of Romania resulting in the summary execution of Nicolae Ceausescu and his wife on Christmas day. The newly liberated eastern European countries now sought to implement democracy and market-led economies. This was to prove extremely painful economically and socially, and it was at the time by no means apparent that the fragile democratic system could survive. East and West Germany were quick to reunify, adopting a common currency in July 1990 followed by full political union in October and nationwide elections in December. The collapse of communism also brought an end to the Warsaw Pact, which was dissolved in 1991, and the new democratic nations began negotiating the phased withdrawal of the Soviets' Red Army.

Single currency

By 1988 proposals were put forward for the creation of a European Central Bank and the conversion of the ECU into a single European currency. For Britain this was a direct challenge to national economic sovereignty, consequently provoking Thatcher to reject British participation in the European exchange rate mechanism. This set Thatcher on a collision course with European Commission president Delors. The prospect of an erosion of sovereignty and her belief that in time the extension of the EC's powers, from 1992, would mean that the vast majority of economic, financial and social legislation would originate from Brussels, alarmed her unduly. This provoked Thatcher, in a speech in Bruges in September 1988, to declare that 'We have not successfully rolled back the frontiers of the state in Britain, only to see them re-imposed at a European level, with a European super-state exercising a new dominance from Brussels.'[43] The outspokenness of Thatcher's speech was profound, both domestically and within Europe. Domestically, it suggested that Thatcher was abandoning her centrist position within the Conservative party and moving it further rightward, which ran the risk of undermining her leadership and creating schism. It suggested too that Euroscepticism was moving into the mainstream, legitimising views that previously had been dismissed as those of cranks and extremists. It could also be interpreted as an admission of failure: a recognition that Britain had failed to use negotiation to secure her national self-interest in Europe and that still fifteen years after entry Britain had yet to find a satisfactory position in Europe. In articulating what could be interpreted as a vision of Europe as a Europe of independent states which co-operated closely, but which drew back from economic and political union, Thatcher provoked a counter-reaction from her European counterparts who determined that even more far-reaching reforms to the EC were required, with or without Britain.[44]

Once more Germany and France had become the driving forces behind European reforms. Historically, although both these countries had pushed forward closer integration, their national perspectives on it had not run in tandem. Germany had long seen political union as a complement to monetary union. France in contrast wished to extend its own influence in Europe and saw this as best achieved through an inter-governmental Europe. The fall of the Berlin Wall in 1989 refocused views. Germany wanted to accelerate unity in order to reassure those fearful of a new German supremacy. The French too hoped a common currency would curtail the economic might of Germany. They decided that exchange rate controls were not enough, and that monetary union was the answer if they were to isolate their own economic strategies from global pressure. This view was particularly strong after she was forced to devalue the franc in January 1987. Germany took the view too that by demonstrating her willingness to sacrifice her own currency on the condition of currency stability, what better way to show her European credentials. In June 1989 at the Madrid European Council, Thatcher reluctantly agreed that sterling could join the ERM provided it was within a broad band of 6 per cent. In return she believed she had secured agreement to postpone the next stage of implementing the common currency until after further discussion. Behind the scenes in the British cabinet the whole matter of the ERM was threatening a split. An axis had formed between Geoffrey Howe, the foreign secretary, and Nigel Lawson, the chancellor, both of whom threatened resignation unless Thatcher conceded to joining the ERM. That two of the most senior Thatcherites were at odds with their prime minister suggested that Thatcher was finding herself increasingly isolated. Thatcher's response was to reshuffle her cabinet and move Howe from the foreign office, a humiliation he did not quickly forget. And in October 1989 Lawson resigned citing the persistent intervention of Thatcher's economic advisor Alan Walters, a trenchant critic of ERM, in Treasury affairs. It seemed that European affairs were spilling into almost every dimension of government.

Thatcher's demise and the rise of Major

The events of 1989 in eastern Europe and the Soviet Union which heralded the collapse of the communist regimes was the most significant re-ordering of the world's political, military and economic geopolitics since the end of the Second World War. It required the complete overhaul of all the assumptions upon which western European leaders had based their policies for the past forty years. At the same time it opened up a whole prospective range of opportunities, not least for West and East Germany, for whom now the prospect of German reunification was very real. Despite Chancellor Kohl promoting reunification, and even Mikhail Gorbachev appearing in early 1990 to accept the principle of reunification, Margaret Thatcher persisted in her opposition, fearful of the emergence of a fourth German Reich. In this view Thatcher was out of step with much of British public opinion, of which the majority favoured reunification, although with some apprehensions about the economic implications of a united Germany. Thatcher found it very difficult to set aside her own ideological suspicions of Germany, and her vision was dictated by a particular Cold War mindset. Her views were echoed by political ally Nicholas Ridley, who in an interview with the *Spectator* outspokenly accused the Germans of seeking the hegemony of Europe through the economic policies of the Bundesbank, an interview that ultimately cost him his Cabinet position.[45] In mid-July 1990 a memorandum of a meeting at Chequers was leaked detailing a meeting at which a select group of historians had been asked to analyse the German national character and the transformations in German politics, and which did little to hide the anti-German sentiments within the prime minister's entourage.[46] In September 1990 in talks in Moscow the four Allied Powers finally agreed to relinquish all their rights and duties towards Germany and Berlin. A major British anxiety was whether Germany would remain a member of NATO; some were concerned about the emergence of a neutral Germany; whilst others speculated whether bilateral German-Soviet relations might improve along the lines of the 1922 Rapallo Treaty.

When European leaders convened in Rome in October 1990 the summit called for an intergovernmental conference on monetary and political union, a process that would eventually become the Maastricht Treaty. Thatcher was deeply troubled by this decision. For her the Madrid agreement had ruled out the need for an intergovernmental conference, and so this decision to continue to move forward the plans for monetary union raised issues about the balance of decision-making power in Europe and begged the question as to whether Britain actually had any political leverage. The Rome summit also brought Thatcher's leadership to crisis point. She had managed to further anger Geoffrey Howe by making a briefing to journalists which contradicted the official Foreign Office negotiating position, and which made an attack on the role of Jacques Delors. Then Thatcher compounded the crisis by making a robust statement in the House of Commons in which she once more attacked

Delors and his plans to make the European Parliament the legislature for the Community and the Commission the executive: 'No, No, No' was her cry.[47] Convinced that there was now a fundamental division between himself and the prime minister, Howe resigned. At his resignation speech to the House of Commons he placed the disagreement over the substance of European policy at the root of his departure, likening the experience to being akin to a cricketer being sent to the crease only to find that his bat had been broken by his own captain. Within days Thatcher was subjected to a leadership challenge for the Conservative party from Michael Heseltine, and although not actually defeated her majority was insufficient to suggest she carried the support of her party, so she resigned. John Major emerged the ultimate victor from the subsequent contest and, as both prime minister and leader of the Conservative party, was presented with the challenge of leading the British negotiating team to Maastricht and of overseeing Britain's participation in the First Gulf War, as a US-led coalition sought to dislodge Saddam Hussein's Iraqi forces from Kuwait.

It appeared from the outset as though Major would offer a less abrasive manner of dealing with Europe. In March 1991 he spoke of the need for Britain to be at 'the heart of Europe'.[48] Such statements were not well received by the increasingly vocal Conservative Eurosceptics, but Major sought to pacify these critics by reassuring them that he would not 'accept a treaty which describes the Community as having a federal vocation'.[49] This meant Britain would not join the EMU, nor would it accept Community interference in the spheres of foreign, defence or domestic policy, and the plans for a Social Chapter could not be accepted if it meant threatening economic competitiveness. He favoured the enlargement of Europe and subsidiarity, an idea which meant more decision making should occur at the national, rather than regional or European levels. The difficulty was that the Dutch, who had the presidency of the Community, were looking to ensure that federalism was part of the draft Maastricht Treaty. Major also had to contend with increasingly awkward relations with a Germany still miffed at the perceived Germanophobia of his predecessor.

Maastricht's ratification

Major returned from the negotiations in December 1991 claiming success: Britain had secured opt-outs from the single currency and the Social Chapter and succeeded in removing references to federalism from the treaty's text. On closer inspection it was evident that Major had actually compromised. Whilst he had preserved the intergovernmental nature of the Community's institutions and retained parliamentary sovereignty over matters relating to currency and taxation, the treaty had agreed to establish a 'pillared' structure whereby the role of the Community expanded into areas relating to foreign and security policy and matters relating to justice and home affairs. Yet when Parliament met to debate the treaty on 18–19 December MPs appeared broadly satisfied, with only seven Conservatives voting against and a further three abstaining. Major's attentions were now diverted to the need to fight a general election and respond to the prospect of electoral defeat, as the opinion polls suggested would be the case. Yet against the expectations, Major won a majority and now had to oversee the ratification process of the Maastricht Treaty. This appeared to proceed quite smoothly: the bill received its second reading on 21 May, with only the opposition of twenty-two Conservative MPs. As the bill moved to the parliamentary committee stage it appeared as though the ratification would be 'tedious but sure'.[50] Furthermore, it appeared as though the momentum towards integration was being checked by a less than enthusiastic reception from the peoples of Europe.

The smooth ratification process changed with the Danish nation's 'No' vote on 2 June. It re-energised the Eurosceptics in Britain and threw the whole British legislative process into disarray. The decision was taken to abandon the bill and reintroduce it in the autumn after the Irish and French referendums. During this time Britain would be taking its six-month turn as president of the Community. During this period of delay, the Eurosceptics appeared to gain support and credibility. Eighty-two Conservative MPs signed a 'fresh start' early day motion in June advocating a renewed look at Europe's development. The argument was being made that Maastricht was a step too far, challenging the sovereignty of the nation-state and moving Europe in a fundamentally new direction. Europe was no longer a common economic market, which the British people had accepted by referendum in 1975, but a radically different entity, a European Union seeking economic, monetary and political unity.

Europe's tests: Yugoslavia and exchange rates

Maastricht had made 'defence' a provision of the EU and took the first steps towards formalising the relationship between the EU and WEU. At the same time the WEU confirmed that its mission was dual: strengthening the defence component of the EU and enhancing the European dimension of the Atlantic alliance. Practical problems arose. In 1991 three EU signatories (Denmark, Greece and Ireland) were not members of WEU. And, given the WEU's role of maintaining the Atlantic alliance there were three members of NATO who were neither members of WEU or the EU (Iceland, Norway and Turkey). The solution was to offer full membership of the WEU to all EU members, to grant associate membership to the other non-EU but European NATO members. This left the small matter of turning treaty pledges into practical actions. This was to be achieved by organisational changes such as relocating the WEU secretariat from London to Brussels with a view to eventually synchronising meetings between the WEU and the EU. It would also ease liaisons with NATO. Plans were also advanced for a Franco–German military brigade which some perceived as the first step towards a European army.[51]

The war in the former Yugoslavia was the first test of the new foreign and security policy pillar of Maastricht, but it is recognised that it failed. Successive EU special envoys were despatched to the region including Lord Carrington, David Owen and Cyrus Vance, but the EU quickly realised that it could do little more than offer a diplomatic solution. EU military estimates suggested that a force of 100,000 troops would be required if the EU was to militarily intervene and it was accepted that this scale of military, combat ready, forces could not be achieved. WEU naval and air forces did contribute to surveillance of the UN blockade of Serbia and Montenegro in operation 'Sharp Vigilance' from July 1992. In late 1992 Owen and Vance offered a proposal to settle the conflict, which having been initially supported by the Americans was then rejected by the Clinton administration as being unduly harsh on the Bosnian Muslims. This rejection caused considerable anger in European capitals, not least because the UN was now providing peacekeepers, largely from Britain and France, to help with humanitarian aid in Croatia and Bosnia. This appeared to mock the Americans' claim that they were keen that the EU find a European settlement to a European crisis, but by 1993 it was evident that the EU's internal bickering was going to render 'joint action' impossible. The lack of an EU military 'option' effectively made it useless, and ultimately the UN and NATO, through I-FOR (Implementation Force) had to intervene in Bosnia as it was recognised that the Serbians would only yield to force. In November 1995 the US-brokered Dayton peace settlement demonstrated still further the limitations of EU foreign and defence capabilities. There was also a sense in Brussels of frustration that ultimately Dayton was not that significantly different to the original Owen–Vance plan of 1992. Yet the EU got to play only a supporting role in the Dayton talks, with the warring parties having been brought to the table by the might of American military power. Nevertheless the EU would be obliged to play a significant role in implementing the peace and overseeing the reconstruction of the region.[52]

Nor were economic events helping the Major government. On 16 September 1992 Britain experienced 'Black Wednesday' as the chancellor, Norman Lamont, was forced to withdraw the pound from the ERM, less than two years after joining. The government had spent over £10 billion trying to defend the pound against the currency speculators, and even a huge hike in interest rates to 15 per cent failed to control the money markets as the value of the pound crashed out of its exchange control parameters. Shortly the lira and the franc were under attack and the whole European monetary system was in chaos. The British blamed the French and, particularly, the Germans for artificially inflating the strength of the Deutschmark. Some critics suggest that it was disastrous that Britain made the maintenance of parity a 'badge of pride'.[53] The longer-term implication was to reinforce a latent Treasury Euroscepticism and sense that retaining economic sovereignty was paramount.[54] Hindsight shows that the economic consequences of German reunification and the subsequent high German interest rates placed unsustainable pressure on the pound's ERM parities, at a time when the UK economy really required lower interest rates to help it emerge from recession. The problem had been exacerbated because Britain's economic imperatives were increasingly diverting from those of Germany, the dominant country in the ERM. The British Treasury was hoping to ease monetary policy as British businesses and homeowners were struggling in the downturn, whilst in Germany the Bundesbank was seeking to use interest rate rises as a means of squeezing the inflationary pressures in the recently reunified German economy.[55]

Despite this economic calamity Major persevered with seeking Parliament's ratification of Maastricht. A series of narrow parliamentary majorities and a vote of confidence in Major gradually saw the bill work its way through Parliament before final approval on 2 August 1993. The whole process had not reflected well on the Conservative party, which appeared to be openly at war as its Eurosceptics sought to scupper the process. In July 1993 they had combined with Labour to defeat the government over the Social Chapter. Major had immediately responded with a confidence motion, which he won with a majority of thirty-nine. Following the ERM fiasco and the torturous experience Europe-wide of ratifying the Maastricht Treaty, many in the British government were hoping the Community would delay the implementation of the single currency and instead concentrate on a period of reflection and consolidation. This was not to prove the case. Whilst the Maastricht legislative process was potentially divisive for the Conservatives, it must be said that even Labour was not immune to intra-party divisions on the issue. The legislation ratifying the treaty provoked the most instances of Labour parliamentary rebellion in the 1992–97 Parliament.[56]

The 1994 Copenhagen European Council had offered eastern and central European countries the opportunity to apply for full membership. The Essen European Council agreed that applicants needed to demonstrate that they were developing free market economics and had stable democracies. The goal of EMU membership and the associated convergence criteria also needed to be demonstrated and it was agreed that existing opt-outs would not be open to new applicants. That the GDP of many of these applicant nations was only 40 per cent of the EU average posed particular problems for the development of the EU. In 1994 Major accepted the Ioannina compromise on the blocking minority in the EU Council of Ministers. Major did this because of the need to reform the voting system of the Council of Ministers given the impending enlargement. Major was strongly favourable to enlargement, believing that widening not deepening the EU integration process was the way forward. With Norway, Sweden, Finland and Austria due to join in January 1995, the EU needed to revise its voting systems if it was to make the management of business possible. At this point Britain had ten out of seventy-six votes on the Council, with twenty-three being required for a blocking minority. The changes would increase the total number of votes to ninety and raise the veto threshold to twenty-seven. However, only weeks before Major promised the

House of Commons that Britain would 'fight for them, we have fought for them, and we have achieved' keeping the blocking vote at twenty-three. Enlargement would be vetoed until the other states accepted the British view.[57] The British argument (supported by the Spanish) was that an increase in the size of the blocking minority would make it harder for groups of countries to exercise a veto and thus prevent the introduction of legislation to which a small number were substantially opposed. The u-turn was not only embarrassing for Major, but it also plunged his domestic political leadership into fresh crisis with backbencher Tony Marlow calling for his resignation, the first time a Conservative backbencher had openly called in the House of Commons for the resignation of a prime minister since 1963.[58] In fact, academic research has shown that Britain's voting position within the Council of Ministers would actually be strengthened by the changes.[59]

Domestic political faultlines

The intertwining of domestic politics with European matters and the scale of the controversy attached is starkly borne out by observing that the majority of senior ministerial resignations experienced by Thatcher and Major between 1986 and 1996 were directly related to European issues: Michael Heseltine and Leon Brittan (1986), Nigel Lawson (1989), Nicholas Ridley (1990), Geoffrey Howe (1990) and Derek Heathcote Amory (1996). This then multiplied itself at the lower levels after 1995 as the Conservatives were rocked by a succession of political defections specifically because of the European issue.[60] Domestically 1994–95 proved problematic for Major, with European matters continuing to provide a flashpoint. In November 1994 the government survived a confidence vote on the European Communities (Finance) bill by 330 to 303 votes. The eight Conservative MPs who had abstained on one or other of the votes found themselves stripped of the party whip the following day, and when joined by another MP in solidarity, the government lost its official majority in the House of Commons. The constant Eurosceptic attacks gradually wore Major down and in June 1995 he initiated a leadership contest to try and settle the matter once and for all. Although he defeated John Redwood, the contest showed that one-third of the parliamentary party did not support him. Then in December the government was defeated on the EU fisheries 'take note' motion.

Throughout all of this there was continued debate about the European single currency. After the currency crises around Black Wednesday, those European currencies which had managed to remain in the ERM found that by early 1994 most were trading within their old narrow or wide 6 per cent bandwidths. This led some to consider that the timetable for monetary union, as outlined at Maastricht, was now back on course. In Paris and Berlin there was a growing sense that a core group within the EU was going to have to act upon its integrationist interests, and if countries such as Britain and Denmark wished to remain outside then they would in turn be denied the opportunity to shape the future of the EU. Major was increasingly alert to this danger of exclusion and began presenting an image of a 'multi-track, multi-speed' EU, in which different member states could choose to progress along the integration path on different matters at different speeds.[61]

Meanwhile, another opportunity arose for John Major to placate his Eurorebels. The June 1994 Corfu summit was due to nominate Jean Luc Dehaene, the Belgian prime minister, as Commission President; however, Major decided to veto the nomination. The eventual replacement was Jacques Santer, appointed in 1995. That Santer's views on federalism were remarkably close to Dehaene's were glossed over by Major's government, which claimed it had stood up for British interests.[62] At least, though, there was no repeat of the 'line in the sand' that caused such embarrassment over QMV earlier in the year. The nomination of Santer also illustrated the difficulties of the new arrangements brought in following Maastricht whereby approval for the Commission was sought from the European Parliament *en bloc* rather than as individual commissioners. The European Parliament, anxious to flex its new powers, then only narrowly endorsed Santer's commission by 260 votes to 238.

Major was not solely placating the Eurosceptics; he also had to juggle the demands of the pro-Europeans, particularly his chancellor, Ken Clarke. To this end Major agreed to Clarke seeking to give Britain some economic room for manoeuvre over monetary union. This effectively meant seeking to engineer the economy into a position whereby it fulfilled the convergence criteria of the European Commission and gave Britain the opportunity of 'opting-in' to the single currency. To this end in November Clarke's budget made £24 billion of cuts in public expenditure, ensuring that Britain's debt now fell within the convergence criteria. Of course, sterling remained outside the ERM, and thereby Britain still failed to fulfil the criteria for exchange rate and interest rate convergence, but it was hoped in some quarters that if sterling remained stable outside the ERM that the EU would not seek to debar Britain if she asked to join the single currency. The responses from Berlin and Paris suggested otherwise, and the idea of a 'hard core' of EU states pushing ahead with monetary union following a Franco–German agenda appeared to be gathering momentum.

Britain's agricultural relations with the EU were thrown into crisis by the Commission's ban in March 1996 of British cattle and beef product exports. This followed the announcement of a possible link between the cattle disease bovine spongiform encephalopathy (BSE) and its human strain Creutzfeldt–Jakob disease (CJD). Although John Gummer, the minister for agriculture, was happy to pose for the media feeding beefburgers to his children, the European ban, and the subsequent crisis in consumer confidence, was considerable. It is estimated that it cost the sector 1,000 jobs, and given that previously the export beef trade had been worth £594 million annually, it was no surprise that the British government took the Commission to the Court of Justice, a case it lost in May 1996. For the British media this was evidence that the EU was not prepared to act for British interests, and the result was that some newspapers were to deny that BSE was an exclusively British problem and were seeking to highlight cases from France and Germany, thereby suggesting that Britain was being punished for her honesty.[63] The ban remained in place until June 1998, although the French would not resume importing British beef until October 2002. For many Eurosceptics this French self-interest is seen as further justification of the problem with European agricultural policy. The response of Major's government was retaliation in the form of boycotting European business, something that alienated still further Britain's European counterparts. This reinforced a sense that the French are the principle hindrance to reforming CAP. The 1999 Berlin summit postponed discussion of reforming CAP until after the 2001 French presidential elections, only for President Chirac and the centre-right government to then resist radical changes after 2002.

With the EU forging ahead in order to launch the euro on 1 January 1999, Major's stance became one of wait and see. He admitted to Parliament that membership was 'a matter of practice not principle', but recognised that there would be significant constitutional issues if Britain joined.[64] It now appeared that Major was holding up the possibility of a referendum on the single currency. The problem was that Major's 'sit on the fence' position satisfied few: the Eurosceptics felt he should be more explicit and reject the possibility of Britain joining outright, whilst the Europhiles were dissatisfied because of his lack of commitment. On 7 December 1995 the Franco–German 'Baden-Baden pact' sealed agreement to achieve a single currency before 2000. This prompted Major to warn the Madrid summit that the EU could not launch a single currency 'like lemmings over a cliff'. It should be remembered that Britain was not alone in having doubts about the single currency. Denmark, Sweden and Greece did not automatically sign up to adopting the euro, although Greece would subsequently join in 2001. The suggestion of a British referendum on the issue prompted the relaunch of the European Movement in Britain and there was a flurry of activity as both sides of the argument sought to provide evidence of the support (or lack of) for the currency. In November 1995 a CBI/Chambers of Commerce survey of 1,700 UK firms suggested the majority of businesses supported the single currency, were scornful of suggestions about withdrawing from the EU with only 7 per cent favouring that option, and the majority believed that domestic political squabbling over Europe was undermining British interests in the EU. Former Conservative party grandees including Edward Heath, Willie Whitelaw and Geoffrey Howe entered the fray, urging Major to adopt a Churchillian vision for Europe and warning that abstaining from involvement in the euro weakened Britain's position. For them,

> The tragedy of Churchill's Zurich speech was that, for too long, it did not inform Britain's post-war policy. We have sought to distance ourselves from Europe rather than decisively shape it ... we have been working to catch up ever since.[65]

The Cabinet though, deeply divided as it was, was gradually hardening its stance and agreed that EMU entry for Britain in 1999 was 'unlikely'. In the six months prior to the 1997 general election, analysis of the BBC and ITN news bulletins showed that positive stories about Conservative economic successes were countered by stories of Conservative European divisions and positive stories about Labour policy initiatives.[66] Nevertheless, the Conservative 1997 general election manifesto kept the official position at negotiate and then decide.[67] It mattered little; the electoral tide had turned back to Labour, and Major and the Conservatives were subjected to the party's worst electoral defeat since 1906. The question now was whether Tony Blair's 'New Labour' would adopt a different stance to Europe?

Some concluding thoughts

During the 1990s it became a familiar cry amongst Eurosceptics that the modern-day EU had developed in a manner (economically, politically and constitutionally) that went beyond that which had been accepted by the 1975 referendum. Indeed, the pace of integration since the 1986 Single European Act appeared relentless, especially given the expectation that the SEA marked a point for consolidation. The idea that the EU should only ever be an economic trading bloc was a misconception; a wider vision of political and economic union had been apparent from the 1960s, and it had set ambitious targets to achieve these goals by the early 1980s, so in a sense the pace post-1986 was in essence a balancing act for the 'barren' decade experienced after UK accession. Policy makers and parliamentarians from the outset have discussed the developmental expectations for closer unity. It was accepted that the EU was a 'dynamic' organisation whereby decisions were often taken that extended the authority of the Community's institutions into areas previously solely the preserve of national interest. It was realised that national economic policy decisions would 'be further restricted' as closer integration occurred.[68] The difficulty was that there now existed a generation of politicians who conveniently suffered amnesia or who could be selective in their reading of history.

5   Europe and New Labour 1997–2010

When Tony Blair's Labour government was elected in 1997 it came to power promising a more constructive European policy that would distinguish it from previous British, and especially Conservative, administrations. In common with predecessor governments there was talk of British 'leadership' within the EU. The purpose of this chapter is to consider whether indeed New Labour succeeded in convincing Europe that Britain was now a willing European; to consider the extent to which the Labour administrations of Blair, and then Brown, were able to shape and influence the EU in a British vein; and to question whether Labour has succeeded in shifting a reluctant British public towards greater approval for the European Union. From the outset Blair had one significant advantage over his recent predecessors, namely the relative Labour party unity on Europe, which left him in a stronger position to pursue the twin strategy of protecting Britain's national interest in Europe whilst pursing a British agenda in Europe. Yet at the point New Labour came to power it inherited a situation in which it appeared as though Britain's world influence had collapsed: Major's government had ended up carrying no real credibility with the Clinton administration in Washington whilst in Europe Britain's impotence was typified by the Major tactic of non-co-operation in response to the ban on BSE-infected beef whilst the EU deliberately delayed the final rounds of the Treaty of Amsterdam negotiations until after the British general election, hopeful that this would bring a new more amenable Labour administration to the table.

1997 general election

During the general election that brought Blair to power Europe had been prominent in the media coverage of the campaign, but not for positive reasons.[1] Rather, it was used by the Conservative-dominated press to lambaste John Major's unwillingness to rule out membership of the single currency, and to emphasise the impression of a growing rebellion from within the party. Nor was there much positivity from some of the party political campaigning. The Conservatives infamously produced a poster advertisement 'The ventriloquist's dummy' showing Blair sitting on the knee of Germany's

Chancellor Kohl. It was widely denounced by pro-European Conservatives, once more emphasising Conservative divisions, and the poster was then bastardised by the Referendum Party to show Major sitting on Kohl's other knee.[2] Nor were matters helped by Jacques Santer's speech in April, as president of the European Commission, during which he labelled Eurosceptics as 'doom merchants'.[3] The intervention was unwelcome to all British party leaders, even Tony Blair, and he found himself increasingly needing to take a tougher stance, emphasising his commitment to a referendum on the single currency and pledging that if he were representing Britain at the forthcoming Amsterdam inter-governmental negotiations he would use a veto on fishing quotas.[4]

Yet in terms of how the British public viewed Europe, the May 1997 general election was significant because it challenged the notion of the electoral viability of Euroscepticism. The presence of two avowed Eurosceptic parties, the Referendum Party and United Kingdom Independence Party (UKIP), ensured that at cross-party meetings European matters received a disproportionate amount of coverage, thereby skewing the impression that 'Europe' as an issue mattered. The natural sentiments of John Major ensured that Conservative policy whilst leaning towards a Eurosceptic position was reluctant to embrace the wholesale opposition favoured by some of its parliamentary party and activist membership. Labour, for the sake of electoral success, had succeeded in papering over its own divisions and only the Liberal Democrats appeared wholly committed to Europe. The Referendum Party contested 547 seats gaining 810,778 votes, but only 3.1 per cent of the vote in the constituencies it challenged. It is estimated that its leader Sir James Goldsmith spent £20 million. They overshadowed UKIP, who only managed to contest 194 seats and secured 1.2 per cent of the vote. These two Eurosceptic parties failed to win a single seat. Yet it has been suggested that they added to the scale of the Conservative losses, as for example in Putney where Goldsmith himself stood against David Mellor, and contributed to Labour's victory. However, psephological analysis of the results concludes that from their perspective 'it must largely deemed to have been a failure'.[5] Furthermore, it appeared that those Conservatives who themselves took an avowed opposition to the single currency gained no apparent advantage, suffering as badly at the hands of the electorate as their erstwhile colleagues who endorsed the official 'wait and see' position.[6] However, after this stillbirth of electoral Euroscepticism events subsequently were going to suggest that there remained some electoral potency in the message.

So the anointment of New Labour, with a landslide victory and a majority of 179, appeared to promise a new era in Britain's Europeanism. Some commentators saw in Blair an instinctive pro-European, and likened his enthusiasm on the issue to Edward Heath's.[7] As ever Blair faced the dual challenge of both making Britain work in Europe as well as making Europe work in Britain. The scale of Labour's majority suggested that these challenges would be easier than those faced by his immediate predecessor. Still Blair's background on Europe suggested a possible ambiguity. He had voted 'Yes' in the 1975 referendum and yet been elected in 1983 as a candidate for a party committed to withdrawal from the EEC. It's also worth observing that Blair was part of the newer generation of politician without personal experience of the Second World War and the privations associated with it, suggesting that the ability to empathise with the EU's founding fathers was now broken. The pragmatic answer would be that Blair's position in 1983 was one of convenience, and certainly through the passage of the Maastricht bill, he made his mark lambasting the Conservatives from the dispatch box in the House of Commons. Between 1994 and 1996 Blair increasingly proclaimed a positive European message, such as his April 1995 Chatham House speech.[8] However, this European policy was packaged not as the means to an end but rather as an integral necessity for achieving a wider range of objectives whether they were global influence or economic competitiveness. Yet the constraints of domestic concerns meant that Labour was forced to match the Conservatives' pledge for a referendum on the single currency in November 1996. Tactically such a pledge neutralised the issue in the electoral campaign, but it hardly chimed with pledges to lead reform in the EU, causing some to diagnose 'schizophrenia' in Labour's position.[9]

Since 1983 Labour had undergone a remarkable conversion on Europe, from advocating withdrawal to promoting active engagement.[10] The intellectual argument was that it appeared as though other member states had managed to make EU membership benefit their economic and social welfare systems in a manner that Britain had not. This 'social dimension' suggested that perhaps after all the EU was not the purely 'capitalist club' that many Labour supporters had assumed it to be in the 1970s and early 1980s. The trade union movement particularly thought Europe offered an opportunity to claw back many of the restrictions that the Thatcher governments had imposed upon it, especially in the field of employment legislation. The 1988 speech to the TUC annual conference by Commission president Jacques Delors, was symptomatic of this changing stance. The conversion to pro-Europeanism was also a strategic attempt to help reposition the party in the political centre ground, at a point when it appeared that the growing Euroscepticism of the Conservatives was moving it away from this territory. So whilst a few veterans from the 1980s remained opposed on economic and/or political grounds, the great majority of the parliamentary party was pro-euro and pro-European, especially amongst the large intake of young 97ers.[11] It is also noticeable that Labour had done repeatedly well in European parliamentary elections and as a result Labour MEPs had an increasingly influential role in the Strasbourg Parliament, were forging good relations with their centre-left European colleagues, and had a core of experienced politicians who had been 'Europeanised' in the EP before transferring to Westminster.[12] Amongst historians and political scientists there is little agreement about how to characterise these changes in Labour. Some would argue that after 1987 Labour was effectively adopting a neo-Thatcherite position on matters European whilst others would seek to portray these changes within a tradition of Labour party revisionism. Others have sought a halfway house in which they argue that it was only once Blair assumed the leadership that Labour was obliged to recognise the merits of the neo-Thatcherite position.[13]

Public opinion

Yet whilst Labour had become progressively more European this change was not reflected more widely in public opinion. The institutions of the EU have little recognition with British citizens, and this is symptomatic of the limited domestic support for Europe. Furthermore the British were significantly below the European average for having knowledge of the EU institutions. Whilst 86 per cent of respondents knew of the European Parliament only 36 per cent were aware of the Council of Ministers, compared to a European average of 63 per cent. Similarly British respondents showed considerably more scepticism about the trustworthiness of these institutions compared to their European counterparts.[14] As Lord Cockfield, the former British commissioner, observed, 'public relations about Europe has a very long way to go and perhaps more in the UK than most other countries.'[15] The issue of 'trust' can largely be explained by the attitude of the British media, which has not shied away from portraying Europe negatively: 'Up Yours Delors', the *Sun*'s notorious headline, being just one of many examples.[16] The increased Eurosceptic tone of the British press from the 1990s made it a significant pillar in the Eurosceptic cause, and contrasts very vividly with its virtual absence in the 1960s and 1970s (if the *Daily Express* is exempted). This hostility has been displayed from the level of individual journalists (like Simon Heffer, Matthew d'Ancona and Christopher Booker) to editors and proprietors, leaving Kenneth Clarke, the former Conservative chancellor, to lament that the 'Conservative press is almost without exception edited by way-out Eurosceptics'.[17] The negativity was not helped either by a succession of perceived injustices inflicted by the EU on the British nation, and the subsequent media portrayal of these.[18] In June 1998 the Commission recommended the lifting of the BSE-caused export ban on British beef, provided it was for meat deboned from animals between six and thirty months and provided the animal was born after 1 August 1996. Yet the French continued to block UK beef exports until October 2002 and the Commission appeared unwilling to enforce its mandate. Similarly Spanish fishermen operating in British waters whilst Cornish trawlers remained tied up in port or were being mothballed due to fishing quota restrictions, and the more recent allegations of fraud and mismanagement against the Commission and MEPs, have hardly instilled confidence.[19] The awareness issue is more problematic. It suggests the failing of successive British governments to communicate the methods of the EU's operations and implies a systemic unwillingness to ensure Britain feels a part of the EU. There have been tokenistic attempts to reverse these trends. In June 1995 the government released *Facts and Fairytales Revisited*, which aimed to dispel the myths associated with the EU.[20] In November 2004 the Foreign Office produced a fifty-page glossy brochure, *Guide to the European Union*, seeking to challenge misconceptions of the EU and to reassure the electorate that Britain was standing up for national interests. The extent to which such publications are actually read by the wider electorate must be questioned. It all confirms the longer-term view that the saliency of European matters fails to register with the British domestic electorate, and is perhaps a reflection that many of the policy making concerns of the EU institutions are technical procedures too complex and subtle to register.

However, gradually since 1997, there has been a noticeable depoliticisation of the European issue in domestic public discourse, and this represents a deliberate response of the Labour administration. Labour's strategy has been fourfold: it has claimed greater competency for defending British interests compared to the Conservatives; it has deliberately kept issues out of the parliamentary domain by promising a referendum (single currency, constitution); it has sought to depoliticise issues, as in the five tests for the euro; and it has used delaying tactics.[21] But also after 2001 the Conservatives, keen to heal their own internal rifts but also because of the need to appear as more than a 'single issue' party to the British electorate, have been relatively happy to downplay matters European.[22] These changes are borne out when comparing coverage of matters European in the media during the general election campaigns of 2001 and 2005. In 2001 the issue of Europe secured more media coverage than any other single issue; whereas it was almost a non-issue in 2005, and was similarly so in 2010.[23]

Nevertheless, early in the twenty-first century Britain continues to boast a vast array of Eurosceptic pressure groups with relatively few groups prepared to advocate the pro-European message. However, purely numerical totals would overly attribute strength when it is apparent that many groups have close links, have considerable overlaps in leadership and membership, and in many cases are insignificantly small. They also represent a plethora of objectives, some claiming to be pro-European, but anti-euro, and others championing a referendum.[24] The reality of the past twenty years has been the growing Eurosceptic confidence being less frequently moderated by a European movement made up of supporters of, but hardly enthusiasts for, Europeanism. There have nevertheless been spasmodic attempts to promote Europe. The campaign group Britain in Europe (BIE) was re-launched under the direction of Simon Buckby in 1999. This succeeded in prompting some cross-party unity on Europe.[25] Kenneth Clarke, ex-Conservative chancellor under John Major, let it be known that he was in 'broad agreement on the big issues of Europe' with Blair's Labour government.[26] Similarly Michael Heseltine (Conservative peer) and Charles Kennedy (Liberal Democrat leader) were willing to appear on BIE platforms. Neil Kinnock (former Labour leader), Chris Patten (Conservative) and Nick Clegg (Liberal Democrat) all agreed to join the board of BIE in 2004. Critics suggested BIE was too closely aligned with Number Ten and shied away from embarrassing the government over its failures to commit to the euro. In September 2003 Buckby resigned, frustrated at the government's failure to take the lead on euro entry and its unwillingness to push ahead with a referendum.[27] 'One speech every six months does not make a campaign' he complained.[28] In August 2005 BIE was wound up. At other points the Europeanists have tried to co-ordinate and promote their activities. In February 2000 more than 100 industrialists took out a full-page advertisement in the *Financial Times* calling for the UK to be 'at the heart of Europe'. The signatories include Chris Gent of Vodafone AirTouch, Unilever's Niall FitzGerald, Gerry Robinson of Granada and British Airways chairman Lord Marshall. They said there was a 'genuine risk' that Britain could be left with diminishing access to Europe, the 'world's largest consumer market'.[29] Again in 2003 these industrialists came out in favour of joining the euro, but it was clear that business was divided on the issue with an equally impressive range, such as Tim Martin (chair of J.D. Wetherspoon, the pub chain), David Lees (GKN Aerospace chairman), David Webster (chairman of the Safeway supermarket group) and John Clare (CEO of Dixon's), with the banks Barclays and Lloyds TSB maintaining a public neutrality.[30]

It should be remembered that the political landscape was significantly altered by New Labour, namely by the granting of devolution to the Scottish Parliament and the Welsh Assembly, with implications for the shaping of opinion. In many ways these regions had already developed distinctive political cultures, something Scotland underlined by the existence of separate legal and education systems, and an autonomous church. Although in the Scottish and Welsh cases the devolution settlement gave neither responsibility for European affairs, both devolved institutions were quick to realise the importance of European matters, both institutionally, and in impact with the various crises since 1999 in fishing and farming. As a consequence the expectation might be that the attitudes towards Europe within the devolved institutions would be distinct from the attitudes expressed at Westminster. Yet in reality the attitudes were broadly similar, with only minor deviations such as a more constrained form of Conservative Euroscepticism in Scotland.[31]

Amsterdam Treaty

One of Blair's almost immediate tasks upon election was to represent Britain at the Amsterdam inter-governmental EU conference of 16–17 June 1997. And whilst the EU had delayed this summit until after the conclusion of the British elections, not all in Europe seemed convinced that New Labour would represent much of a change. In May the Dutch minister of European affairs lamented that 'The New Labour government still seems to be afraid to move out of Mrs Thatcher's shadow' whilst his German counterpart similarly complained there was 'no substance' to Labour's supposed European credentials.[32] The challenge of the summit was to review the EU's institutional practices, which were considered too ineffectual following the 1995 expansion of the

Community to fifteen, with the accession of Austria, Finland and Sweden, and which were likely to come under even greater pressure with future enlargement plans. The Amsterdam summit is significant because Blair accepted the Social Chapter, thus reversing Britain's Maastricht opt-out. The summit also agreed the Pact for Stability and Growth, a German initiative, aimed at securing budgetary discipline within the Community as well as agreeing a new employment chapter to the Treaty and the inclusion of a new Article 13 that extended anti-discrimination measures. In comparison with past governments it seemed a much more positive and open response. Amsterdam also raised once again the possibility of a two-speed flexible Europe which accepted an 'agreement to disagree', and here Blair's government was conforming to past type of defending red lines. This can be seen in the British response to immigration and asylum. Amsterdam moved the Schengen agreement on immigration and asylum from the inter-governmental to the arena of community provision. In tandem with this emerged a growing awareness of the need for controls of population rather than borders. Schengen had been established in 1985 by France, Germany and the Benelux countries as a mechanism for enabling full free movement as part of the single market. However many other member states, including Britain, Ireland and Denmark, had refused to sign the agreement and continued to opt out of Title IV which ended passport controls. The British and Irish authorities have traditionally exploited their natural island geographical borders to exert firmer controls on immigration, and this explains their opt-out. The problem is that opt-outs and multi-speed arrangements make the decision making structure more complicated. What it all suggested was that New Labour still favoured intergovernmentalism, and still adhered to many of the 'niggle' areas of Britain's relationship with the EU.

The Amsterdam treaty extended the social provision of the EU to include employment with the expectation that this should be aspired to without damaging competitiveness. And whilst QMV was extended at Amsterdam, social security was kept as an issue for unanimity, and pay levels remained exempt from Community oversight. Blair had sided with Helmut Kohl of Germany to resist Lionel Jospin's attempts to revive former plans by Jacques Delors for more interventionist policies on growth and employment. Amsterdam also extended the remit of the Common Foreign and Security Policy (CFSP) pillar, creating a High Representative position to act as a roving ambassador for the EU whilst enhancing the peacekeeping and humanitarian roles of the EU. The Nice summit would then develop this by adding new provisions to create a European defence and security policy with a view of moving towards a common security policy. Key in all of this is the intergovernmental nature of the CFSP pillar with the emphasis on common strategies, positions and actions. The whole procedural experience of the IGC at Amsterdam left some frustrated as the Council meeting represented the final confirmatory stage of a year-long negotiation and the intergovernmental nature of the agreement process meant that some important issues were only agreed late at night and with last minute concessions that undermined the specialised longer-term negotiations. Further, critics bemoaned the failure to adopt institutional reforms ahead of enlargement: the matter of re-weighting the votes in the Council and the composition of the Commission showed the divisions between large and small states. The large states were opposed to any voting formula that gave the potential for a coalition of small states to outvote their more powerful neighbours. Amsterdam did increase the supranational oversight of the European Parliament but as a consequence the complex and fragmented nature of the Treaty 'reflects its status as a deal born from compromise, limited ambition and an inability to solve some of the central problems facing the Union'.[33] Ultimately many observers considered the Treaty of Amsterdam to have been little more than a 'damp squib'.[34] Not that the House of Commons was given this impression as Blair returned from the summit boasting that he had prevented the extension of QMV to the Social Chapter and that business would benefit because now that Britain was in the Chapter she could block further developments that might be detrimental to Britain.[35]

The single currency

Yet despite the apparent positiveness of the British European position, the schizophrenia was also quickly evident. In October 1997 Gordon Brown, the chancellor, announced that Britain would not enter the EMU during the current Parliament, but would look to join in the future if the single currency proved successful and fulfilled his five economic tests. The impression given was that Europe could still not work in Britain. Brown's Treasury tests would ascertain whether there was sustainable convergence between the British and 'euro' economies; whether there was flexibility to adapt to economic change; as well as the impact on investment, employment and the UK financial services industry.[36] Such a statement placed the Treasury at the heart of any future decision about joining the euro and implied that the verdict would be an economic rather than political one. However, the divisions that this statement revealed within the Blair cabinet were evidenced by the various counter-briefings on the matter that emerged from Number Ten, the Treasury, the Foreign Office and Blair's close ally, Peter Mandelson. Although the issue was eclipsed by the Iraq War, domestic opinion seemed to be hardening against the euro, with only 24 per cent viewing implementation as a priority, and significant elements within the trade union sector voicing hostility when previously they had been supportive. Within Westminster, the Commons Treasury Select Committee supported the Treasury view that reforms were required before Britain could join the euro, but it also warned that the ability of Britain to influence these reforms would diminish the longer the euro continued.[37] Furthermore, criticism was made that the 'tests' lacked precision, and although Brown did announce in June 2003 that the financial services 'test' had been passed, it rather suggested that the government was content to allow the euro experience to go it alone, not least because it avoided the need for a referendum which it could not be certain of winning. Ultimately 'globalisation' became the mantra, a threat to be both concerned for and embraced. As one academic characterised it, 'Britain has many supporters of the single currency but relatively few enthusiasts'.[38]

So without Britain, the EU pressed ahead with implementing the euro. In May 1998, a special European Council confirmed that the first wave of European states would join the single currency, although only four of these states (Finland, France, Luxembourg and Portugal) had actually met their convergence criteria. This incredibly significant moment for the European Union, also showed the limited significance of Britain in terms of the EU's policy agenda, because despite holding the presidency of the EU in the first half of 1998, Britain's non-participation in the euro emphasised her isolation. The euro came into being on 1 January 1999. Initially national banknotes would survive as denominations of the euro until new euro notes and coins were introduced on 1 January 2002 when 6 billion new banknotes and 37 billion new coins entered circulation. This became a very tangible and symbolic reminder of Europe's closer union. Concerns about the 'one glove fits all' nature of monetary union led the EU members to confirm at Amsterdam measures for budgetary discipline and reducing financial deficits. However, the governance of the EMU, and the independence of the European Central Bank, continued to cause friction between Germany and France, with the French displaying a greater reluctance to remove the voice of national finance ministers from EMU governance.

Defence and security

Away from the euro, Blair still appeared willing to be a good European. Bilateralism characterised Labour's approach to Europe in 1998. This 'step change' was a requirement that ministers, MPs and civil servants would seek to engage in regular contacts with their opposite numbers in other EU capitals, in order to establish a better understanding of matters European. Some considered that Labour was being too indiscriminate in its contacts, approaching a country or countries which had interests that coincided with Britain's on a particular issue. On the one hand this could be portrayed as a negative because Britain was using it as an exercise to block EU progress, yet Blair sought to characterise this as promoting British interests, sustaining a leadership role, and as a necessity with the expanding EU.

In late 1998 at St Malo Blair appeared to be seeking a positive bilateralism when he questioned the British association with NATO and the American alliance. In what some have termed 'a revolution in military affairs',[39] Blair suggested for the first time that Europe had a credible security and defence policy that was comparable, if not more important, than the NATO alliance.[40] This followed up a speech to the French National Assembly the previous March in which he foresaw the arenas of defence and security as ones in which the British and French were particularly well suited for co-operation.[41] It was a speech that his former spin doctor termed Blair's most important of the year.[42] Turning to defence matters as a means of seeking to establish British centrality, as a European policy maker, was not a new policy; the pedigree can be traced back to the end of the Second World War. The apparent reining back of the NATO alliance was a fresh departure, although again has a pedigree in the late 1940s when Labour figures were keen on the concept of a third force. The experience of Kosovo in 1999, where the Americans had been reluctant to commit military forces, appeared to justify this stance and a growing sense emerged that a form of rapid reaction force was increasingly necessary if the EU was to have a foreign policy of importance. Then alongside President Chirac he urged the speedy implementation of the Amsterdam security provisions. The inter-governmental nature of the CFSP explains the British enthusiasm, but some observers wondered whether the associated calls for greater co-operation in the arena stored up problems for the future, both in terms of expanding supranationalism and in terms of the Anglo–American relationship. In November 2000 Blair announced plans to commit British troops to Europe's rapid reaction force. He argued that it would strengthen NATO, rather than challenge it, and that it was more dangerous for European defence changes to occur without British involvement; furthermore, he claimed 'Every time I explain European defence to America, they understand it and end up supporting it.'[43] This was part of an EU-wide agreement whereby fourteen states agreed to provide 60,000 armed forces for a European rapid reaction force.

At the same time, emphasising Britain's importance in facilitating bilateral relationships, not least between Europe and the USA, was another traditional plank invoked by past British governments. Events following the attacks on the Twin Towers and American's post-9/11 'war on terror' would see Britain firmly reposition herself in the American camp, countering a period when it appeared as though much of Britain's foreign policy was being conducted within a EU context, whether seeking resolution to the Kosovo crisis or seeking to rein in the nuclear ambitions of North Korea and Iran. It has been estimated in the two months after 9/11 Blair covered more than 40,000 miles on thirty-one flights and held fifty-four meetings with foreign leaders.[44] Blair had hoped following the terrorist attacks that Europe could be made to matter to itself and its citizens as well as to the Americans, and that Britain could provide the conduit between the two. 'This is a moment to seize' he told the 2001 Labour conference. 'The kaleidoscope has been shaken. The pieces are in flux. Soon they will settle again. Before they do, let us reorder this world around us.'[45] Europe was less convinced. When Blair informed German chancellor Schröder in 2000 that Britain could act as a bridge across the Atlantic, the German response was sceptical: it was OK so long as the traffic was two-way.[46]

If Blair's foreign policy during his first term in office could be characterised as having been European, the emphasis of his second term was to be distinctly Atlanticist. Problems also arose in the vision Blair now found himself promoting of world affairs, and Britain's continued support for the Atlantic alliance. US–European relations hit a new low during and after the Iraq War, particularly with France and Germany. Blair positioned Britain as the USA's closest ally in Europe, and for some appeared to be the most pro-American prime minister to have been in Number Ten since 1945. It suggested that Britain looked to the USA rather than Europe, and that the pursuit of a common European foreign and security policy was a secondary concern. The limited impact of the EU on the international stage was a motivation behind the momentum for further reform of the structures adopted after Maastricht. This was enhanced by the reconfiguration of foreign and military priorities with the ending of the Cold War, the collapse of communism in the east and the reunification of Germany, and the recognised failure of the EU to act over civil war in the former Yugoslavia and then later with Kosovo. Despite the EU's unanimous condemnation of the 2001 terror attacks on the USA, the medium-term response of the USA over Afghanistan divided Europe between Britain, the new accession states and some of the Iberian countries and Germany and France. The rift then widened over Iraq because the EU was committed to multilateralism and respect for international law, making it increasingly difficult to accept the Bush administration's interpretation of United Nations resolutions and the subsequent military action to topple Saddam Hussein. The 2003 invasion of Iraq appeared to challenge these fundamentals. Perhaps the difficulty the EU has faced when trying to develop its international role is the perception that the EU is an economic as opposed to a military power. Ultimately what Blair was trying to do was balance the need for his perceived new internationalism that required America whilst positively engaging with Europe, but Iraq tested the very foundations of Blair's foreign policy. 'Old Europe', to borrow American secretary of defence Donald Rumsfeld's phrase, looked upon Blair's Atlanticism with considerable scepticism whilst his increasing alliance with conservatives in Spain and Italy, who similarly looked to America, suggested a betrayal to the European left. The invasion of Iraq did more than damage relations with Germany and France and thus adversely affect the British government's efforts to shape the EU agenda.[47] It impacted upon the domestic strand of its European strategy as the government's declining public popularity made it more defensive over how it presented European policy. Cue Chancellor Brown announcing in June 2003 that only one of the five tests for Britain's suitability to join the euro had been met. Similarly in April 2004, Blair immediately sought to neutralise the saliency of the EU's forthcoming constitutional treaty by pledging a referendum.

Budgetary reform

Alongside institutional reform it was recognised from 1998 that the means by which the EU was resourced required revision, not least because with the enlargement eastwards many of the applicant nations had GDPs 40 per cent below the EU average. The budgetary contributions of member states had always been a controversial issue, as Thatcher's clashes on the rebate in the early 1980s showed. The EU agreed that member states' share in the proportion of the total EU gross national product would attract a proportional contribution of 1.26 per cent. This levy had now become a significant contributory avenue to the EU, amounting to around 45 per cent of the budget in 2002. This was closely followed by VAT contributions which account for 35 per cent of the total EU budget, with 15 per cent coming from customs duty and the balance from agricultural trade levies. Initially the rate for the VAT contribution was 1 per cent of total tax, but the accession of Spain and Portugal obliged an increase to 1.4 per cent in 1986, before dropping back to 1 per cent in 1995. The 1999 Berlin summit then agreed that this should be reduced still further to 0.5 per cent from 2004. The EU acquired 100 billion euros from member nation contributions (£63 billion), which averages at 2.5 per cent of member states' public spending.[48]

Since membership Britain has frequently called for reforms of the Common Agricultural Policy (CAP), but secured only minor budgetary amendments. CAP used to account for 90 per cent of the EU budget, but this had fallen back to 45.5 per cent by 2001. CAP adversely costs the British taxpayer. Total CAP subsidies to farmers in 2000 amounted to £2,489 million whilst only £804 million was provided in the 2000 Comprehensive Spending Review for domestic subsidies.[49] The 2002 Curry Report on the future of British farming was highly critical of CAP, believing it distorted the market, inflated prices and masked inefficiencies. The report favoured removing market price support and associated production controls, and in line with British government thinking advocated a reallocation of resources away from subsidies to farmers towards support for rural development and environmental production. Curry also noted one significant problem for British agriculture. With Britain remaining outside the euro-zone, but with CAP operating as a 'euro' funded system, periods when sterling was high against the euro meant that British farmers were receiving depreciating subsidies.[50] The Commission presented plans in 2002 for a revision of CAP, which became know as the Fischler reforms. Britain, alongside Germany, the Netherlands, Denmark and Sweden were favourable to the ideas for decoupling the arrangement to produce agricultural good in exchange for direct support, for the proposal to redirect a fifth of CAP funds towards general development of agricultural areas; for proposed prices cuts for milk and grain; and for improved standards in animal welfare, food quality and environmental protection. However, the majority of member countries were opposed. In October 2002 Blair clashed with the French president Chirac at the Brussels summit, after attacking French efforts to preserve Europe's CAP as the leaders agreed plans to freeze farm spending from 2007. Aside from taking personal umbrage over the attack, Chirac retaliated by attacking Britain's annual £2 billion budget rebate and reminding his audience that without a Franco–German agenda the

EU would grind to a halt. By May 2003, negotiations and concessions had reduced the scale of opposition and left only France, Spain and Portugal objecting, but without a blocking minority in the Council of Ministers.[51] Ultimately the 2003 reforms were seriously moderated and retained the principle of subsidising farmers and protecting them from market forces and replaced price support with direct payments. In budgetary terms, it was predicted that the reforms were likely to increase the support for farmers. Margaret Beckett sold the reforms to the House of Commons as a reform with less bureaucracy,[52] yet academic analysis almost immediately cast doubt on this, suggesting it was only likely to increase the paperwork and require even greater numbers of officials to implement the scheme.[53]

Europe's impact

The legal impact of Europe can be felt through two different legal trajectories. The first is the human rights dimension that emanates from the Council of Europe and its European Court of Human Rights. The second is the EU's legal apparatus through the European Commission and the European Court of Justice (ECJ). The two systems are distinct from one another but are often confused. The human rights dimension took a fresh significance for Britain on 8 November 1998 when the Council of Europe's human rights convention was incorporated into UK law, 34 years after Harold Wilson had conceded to articles 25 and 46 and 47 years after Attlee's Labour government had opted out of granting British citizens the right of 'individual petition' to Strasbourg and the European Court of Human Rights. What the 1998 Human Rights Act did was enable British citizens to take the state and its agencies to court to defend basic human rights without having to seek the costly and time-consuming route of seeking the jurisdiction of the European Court of Human Rights as had been the case since 1966. The Act came into force in October 2000. The EU dimension potentially prejudices EU law over national law. It is one of the responsibilities of the Commission to ensure that the member nations implement the legal framework of the EU's treaties and laws. Formal notice is served on infringements once spotted, which become more vigorous if the Commission is obliged to issue a 'reasoned opinion'. Persistent failure to comply leads to the matter being referred to the European Court of Justice. Between 2000 and 2001 the Commission issued 2367 'infringement' notices, 989 'reasoned opinions' and passed 334 cases to the Courts of Justice (of which fourteen were against the British government in 2001).[54] Groups like Charter 88 have seen the European Courts as an indirect means of 'updating' the British constitution, and enabling individuals with a set of legally enforceable rights. Whilst some scholars consider that the ECJ 'has made a tremendous contribution to the development of European Community law and integration in Europe more generally'.[55]

Yet despite the growing legal oversight of its member states, the EU does appear weak over managing its internal affairs. Early in 1999 the EU was plunged into crisis over allegations of fraud and mismanagement. On 14 January 1999 the Santer Commission narrowly avoided a European Parliament censure motion as MEPs sought to establish some control over the Commission. Then on 15 March 1999 the entire Santer Commission resigned. This followed the First Report of the Committee of Independent Experts, which presented serious evidence of financial irregularities and fraud and showed that all twenty commissioners had been unaware of malpractice with the services they were running. It increased the calls for reform of the Commission's size and composition. The new Commission, headed by Romano Prodi, pledged zero tolerance; unfortunately this would prove an empty promise. The EU's Eurobarometer, an opinion polling mechanism that has been monitoring EU citizen opinion since the early 1970s, suggested that Europe-wide there was a significant improvement in satisfaction levels with the way democracy worked and attributed this to the resignation of Santer which 'served as proof that there were systems in place to ensure the EU works in a democratic way'. The people of the UK were the least satisfied (31 per cent) after the Swedish (28 per cent).[56]

The opportunity to express dissatisfaction with the EU arises with direct elections to the European Parliament. Low voter turnout suggests perhaps that the citizens of Europe do not perceive it in this manner, whilst the trend of Euro elections to follow national political fortunes suggests further difficulties with resolving the EU's democratic deficit. In Britain on 15 January 1999 the European Elections Act took a radical step and introduced proportional representation, in the form of a closed-list regional system. Each party contesting the election would rank its candidate in preference, by region. The number of seats won in a given region would be in proportion to the scale of vote received in that region. PR was potentially significant given that since 1979 British European elections have witnessed much bigger swings in seats than votes. It was expected that the new system would redress the balance away from over-representing the winning parties to providing breakthrough potential for the small parties. The list system did provide the large parties with fresh opportunities for managing their candidate selection, especially within the Conservative party where their MEPs have traditionally been seen as more pro-European than their Westminster colleagues. Consequently, William Hague used this as an opportunity to weed the candidates' list and ensure that those with Eurosceptic tendencies were more highly ranked. Polling day was 10 June across Europe. The Conservatives campaigned under the slogan 'In Europe, not run by Europe' arguing that Europe had to choose between becoming a 'superstate' or a more flexible Europe. Hague's interpretation was that all EU member states should accept the core components of a free market Europe, but that nation states should retain the right to opt out of non-core activities in order to purse policy at a national level. He advocated a Community whereby the member states should accept the core elements of the a free market, but have the opportunity to opt out of non-core activities where it was felt the pursuit of policy at the national level was in their interest, and that this right should be enshrined in a new treaty provision.[57] Labour reiterated their intention to join the euro only once the Treasury's five tests had been fulfilled, and campaigned upon a platform that pledged their intention to reform the EU: organisationally, financially and accountably. The Conservatives secured 35 per cent of the vote, but in a low-turnout election of below 25 per cent. Overall the Conservatives took thirty-six seats, Labour twenty-nine and the Liberal Democrats ten. However, amongst the nine others there were two each for the Greens and Scottish and Welsh nationalists as well as three UKIP successes, suggesting that in the space of two years the tide of electoral Euroscepticism had surged. If the same distribution of votes had occurred under the old single member, first-past-the-post system the Conservatives would have secured fifty seats, Labour twenty-nine and the Liberal Democrats none.[58]

Hague versus Blair

Opposing the euro became one of the centrepieces of the Conservatives' message under William Hague, who replaced John Major as leader in 1997. Hague decided to reject membership for ten years, and this policy position was consolidated with a party referendum in September 1998 endorsed by 84.4 per cent of the vote.[59] In February 2000 he launched the 'Keep the Pound' campaign as Conservatives counted down the number of days left to save the pound.[60] And this became the central theme of their 2001 general election campaign as they presented the election as the last chance to save sterling. By placing Europe so centrally in their campaign they risked presenting the Conservatives as a single-issue party, obsessed with Europe. It signalled the Conservatives' strategic dilemma of securing their core vote at a time when the UKIP had their electoral breakthrough and appeared to be winning over Conservative voters. Hague was able to limit dissent from candidates by allowing them to issue personal manifestos stating that they would vote to keep the pound without having to limit this pledge to a single Parliament.[61] When the party was duly defeated by Blair and Labour, Hague immediately resigned. Hague's successor Iain Duncan Smith, who had made his reputation as a Maastricht rebel, quickly sought to lower the prominence of Europe. The few public pronouncements that there were on the issue, such as saying 'never' to the euro, were intended both to emphasise the party's continued Eurosceptic tendencies whilst hoping that the categorical nature of such statements reduced their saliency, and deprived the media of opportunities to highlight the Conservatives' divisions.

For Labour, Europe was not a theoretical discussion point, but an actuality that required their government to participate in. As has often been the case, the idealism of opposition has to be tempered with pragmatism once the realities of government set in. The pragmatism in Blair's European policy can be seen through consideration of his changing stance on immigration and asylum. At Amsterdam Blair had secured an opt-out from the Schagen agreement, but as the numbers of asylum seekers began to rise rapidly a sense in Whitehall emerged that this issue might best be tackled in the national interest through a Europeanisation of the issue. In doing so it was hoped that this would oblige member states to play a greater role in absorbing the numbers of asylum seekers entering Europe who ultimately ended up in Britain. So in 1999 the British agreed to reverse part of its opt-out on Community immigration and asylum policies, whilst retaining as a 'non-negotiable' element Britain's right to maintain control at its national borders. It again returned to this issue during the discussion on a draft constitution and proposed the extension of QMV in asylum policy – a move Germany had previously sought to block.[62]

Blair's continued bilateralism was still evident in March 2000 when the European Council launched the Lisbon strategy to improve the competitiveness of the EU's economies and provide better employment and social cohesion by 2010. Blair, working alongside José Maria Aznar, the centre-right prime minister of Spain, had helped devise the agenda, which had the intention of adopting best practices via the 'open method of coordination' (OMC). Blair was keen on the 'new economy' agenda which aimed at making the EU the world's leading knowledge-based economy within a decade. He sought to liberalise trade and regulations in the EU in tandem with the Italians and Spanish, rather than the normal social democratic allies Labour have previously allied with, although by 2004 it was evident that this Lisbon strategy was stalling as first Romano Prodi declared it a 'failure' and then former Dutch prime minister Wim Kok bemoaned that a lack of political commitment on the part of member states had impeded progress.[63]

The Nice Treaty

The 2000 Nice intergovernmental conference was necessary to resolve the institutional issues that Amsterdam had failed to address, such as reform of the Commission's size, the Council vote re-weighting and the issue of QMV. Held over two days, 6–7 December 2000, the Nice summit agreed on how to reform the EU's structure and initiated another phase of enlargement, from mainly eastern European countries. Enlargement meant that the EU had to consider ways in which it could streamline its operations, and from the British perspective there were concerns that this would involve the extension of QMV into areas that were previously sacrosanct. Blair was aware that any apparent concessions in these areas would potentially provide the Conservative opposition, the Eurosceptic press and the numerous European lobby groups additional ammunition in what was widely expected to be an election year. In fact, Blair found himself in a rather unusual position of not being the bogeyman, with the French president instead coming under criticism for his handling of the negotiations. Ultimately Blair was able to present it as a safeguarding of Britain's immediate national interests, whereby he could argue that he had achieved his objectives on enlargement, encouraging flexible markets, keeping the veto on tax and social security and retaining the intergovernmental nature of the EU model, something he placed particular emphasis upon with his return to Britain. Nice was ratified in October 2002 after a second Irish referendum. Were their lessons for Blair and his own referendum pledges? It suggested that the larger the turnout the better the likelihood of success, and those who keep coming back to consult the people, with a strong and positive message, win the argument eventually. Under Nice the number of European Parliament seats was restricted, as was the size of the Commission, with the larger nations surrendering their second commissioners in exchange for a recalibration of the votes in the Council of Ministers. The matter of qualified majority voting was also complicated by insisting that any vote must fulfil three criteria. Aside from any decision needing to pass a voting threshold, QMV would require the support of at least half the member countries and the result also had to be shown to represent at least 62 per cent of the EU population, which ultimately meant that the 'big three' (Britain, France and Germany) could block virtually anything they all disagreed with as enlargement developed. Some of the Euro-elites saw Nice as a 'mediocre' treaty.[64] Academics have criticised the institutional voting framework that emerged from it, and argued that it slowed down the EU's decision-making process.[65] Others interpreted it as a 'triumph' for the 'big three', leaving the 'Commission and Parliament humiliated and frustrated'.[66] There was a significant decline in Commission activity post-enlargement and in the first year of the Nice rules. Legislative proposals (regulations, directives, decisions and recommendations) significantly declined in 2005 by 17.5 per cent compared to 2004 and 10.5 per cent on the 2003–4 average.[67] Nice did present possible problems for the future if Britain's attempts at bilateral diplomacy failed, in that the vote in the Council of Ministers of the six founder members was increased to 51 per cent, which meant they would have a potentially powerful majority were they to act together.

Towards a European constitution?

One of the outcomes of the Nice negotiations was that it presented the opportunity for discussions to take place on the future constitutional composition of the EU. There was concern within Whitehall that any new constitutional text might unravel all of Britain's carefully negotiated treaty clauses. Although Labour, in opposition, had been opposed to a written constitution, it seems that Blair's personal experience of the Nice negotiations, as the various European leaders bickered into the small hours over minute points, had given him cause to believe that a constitutional consolidation might enable future IGC to concentrate on the 'bigger picture' and possibly make the EU appear more relevant to its domestic populations. As a preliminary to these discussions, on 6 October 2000 in Warsaw, Blair proposed closer inter-governmental co-operation and a second Euro-parliamentary chamber of national MPs (although this was hardly a new idea, and it had a long pedigree in

Labour's thinking).[68] The British also began championing the idea of a fixed term president of the European Council elected by the heads of government, which it was felt would help limit the role of the European Commission's president and help drive the EU's agenda both at home and globally.

The discussions began in earnest in December 2001 with the Laeken Declaration creating a Convention on the Future of Europe, which met between February 2002 and July 2003. Chaired by former French president Giscard d'Estaing, the convention was charged with drafting a European constitution that would then go before an intergovernmental conference of the EU member states in 2003–4. The expectation was that a constitution would create a new European Union, separate from the member states, endowed with new powers and its own legal personality. New Labour appeared initially reluctant to embrace the Convention, but once it began gathering momentum, they became more active and sought to gain support for a Dashwood draft constitution (prepared by Alan Dashwood, professor of law at Cambridge) which characterised the EU as a group of sovereign states. Peter Hain was the government's representative, and he played a traditional British role of opposing suggestions that the EU should be endowed with wider powers, and objected to the idea of a elected European president, believing that this individual should be an administrator rather than a political leader. The question also arose as to whether a European constitution would actually diminish the 'democratic deficit' of the EU. Some scholars like Tsebelis were dismissive of this debate, not least because they were not certain what the discussion was about.[69] The government was also concerned that the federalists would use the constitutional discussions as an opportunity to enhance the role of the European Court of Justice by giving it scope to develop case law and enshrine the Charter of Fundamental Rights (which had been accepted at Nice as a non-binding political declaration). There was anxiety that this in particular would provide a vehicle by which the EU could expand social rights. Ultimately the British managed to prevent this from occurring. The draft constitutional treaty included three scales of policy co-ordination: 'competence', 'subsidiarity' and 'fundamental rights'. Competence meant the idea that the treaties provided the legal framework for the evolution of the policy co-ordination process. Subsidiarity was the decentralised method of policy implementation using regional and local actors as well as civil society partners, whilst fundamental rights was deemed to be the extension of the social values of the EU.

The initial intergovernmental conference failed to reach agreement; however, in March 2004 an EU conference in Brussels agreed that they should resolve the issue by June, and subsequently all twenty-five member states signed the draft. Blair's government presented the constitution as a tidying up exercise, arguing that it was creating a 'group of nations', not a 'superstate'. It was codification not innovation.[70] Essentially the constitutional treaty was a simplification and revision of existing treaties, with much of it already in practise. Nevertheless the public portrayal of it in Britain was of a radical new supranational order that would transform detrimentally Britain's relationship with the EU. Nine out of the twenty-five member states opted to hold a referendum on the constitution. However, the prospect of fighting a European election, at which the Conservatives would be promising a referendum on the matter, led the government to announce in April that they too would offer a referendum. The timing and the question would be the government's decision and many observers thought it would be unlikely to be conducted before autumn 2004 and more likely would be held over until a third Labour term in office at Westminster had been secured. In the event the French 'No' vote, 29 May 2005, and the Dutch rejection of the constitution on 2 June 2005, nullified the need for a British referendum and for the time being ended the prospects of an EU-wide constitution. One reason for the French rejection was a fear that France's 'social model' was being squeezed by the Lisbon treaty in preference for an Anglo-Saxon model of capitalism.[71] In June the European Council suspended ratification for a period of reflection whilst European Commission president Jose Manuel Barroso admitted, in September, that the EU would not have a constitution for 'at least three years'. The rejection of the constitution was seen to have once more plunged the EU into crisis, yet some academics like Moravcsik suggested that in fact this was evidence of the success and stability of the existing European settlement.[72] Others characterised the rejection as a procedural defeat, but saw the original agreement as a 'substantive victory'.[73]

From Blair to Brown

Domestically, the main parties had sought to use the constitution to gain electoral advantage over one another. A referendum on the European constitution was one of the central planks of Conservative strategy in the run up to the 2004 European elections, which were to be the first test of Michael Howard's leadership. However, in April Blair had acted quickly to neutralise this strategem by conceding to demands to hold one and the pledge was enough to diminish the power of the Conservative attack. Ultimately though the Conservatives succeeded in becoming the largest party for the first time since 1984, the victory was hollow as it only secured 27 per cent of the vote, its lowest ever share in a European election. The result also witnessed a surge in the UKIP vote from 7 per cent in 1999 to over 16 per cent. Blair sought to capitalise on this by portraying UKIP as the 'militant tendency' of the Conservatives.[74] Overall EU-wide the 2004 European elections produced a significant protest vote and a strong Eurosceptic showing. Turnout continued to shrink down to 44 per cent from 50 per cent in 1999. Only in Britain was turnout up, but still only registering at 38 per cent.[75]

With the failure of the constitution the EU appeared to be in disarray. In January 2005 the Council dropped excessive deficit proceedings against France and Germany after a European Court (ECJ) ruling declared the 3 per cent deficit limit was 'too severe'. Consequently in March 2005 the European

Council agreed to budget reform of the Stability and Growth Pact, which limits budget deficits to no more than 3 per cent of GDP and a maximum national debt of 60 per cent of gross domestic product. Further discussion in June at the next Council meeting saw agreement on reforms of CAP financing and formalised reform of the Stability and Growth pact. The summit also decided to have a two-year pause for reflection on the constitutional treaty after the French and Dutch rejection. In April 2005 the World Trade Organization found that the EU sugar regime flouted WTO rules, after complaints from Brazil, Australia and Thailand that EU farm subsidies to the sugar industry were unfair. Although this raised concerns that it would have an adverse effect on the British sugar industry, by 2006 the industry was actually buying up a larger proportion of the EU sugar quota and expanding production, particularly in East Anglia.

These issues mattered little to the Labour government, as all attention was now diverted towards the matter of winning a historic third term and determining the point at which Blair would relinquish leadership of the party to Gordon Brown.

Labour's 2005 manifesto packaged Europe in terms of internationalisation and globalisation, as it sought to balance external diplomatic needs with the internal domestic management strands that had been the hallmark of Blair's strategy. On 5 May 2005 he secured a third term in office with a much-reduced majority of sixty-five. The result showed the limited electoral viability that Blair had, with his popularity much reduced due to the Iraq War. But it also demonstrated the limited saliency of Europe in this contest, with an 'almost deafening political silence' on the matter.[76] Eventually, after considerable speculation, he announced in September 2006 his intention to step down the following year. Gordon Brown was scheduled to succeed him as prime minister on 27 June 2007.

In his last months as prime minister Blair oversaw Britain's presidency of the EU (July–December 2005), during which time he sought to press, with some German assistance, for greater economic, financial and social reform, and in exchange had to agree to accept a decline in its budget rebate that Thatcher had negotiated in 1984. In June 2006 the European Council in Brussels agreed to continue a two-track approach to institutional reform using existing treaties, followed in December by pledges to continue enlargement and make migration a key feature for 2007. Talks were also begun to consider Turkey and Croatia for membership. However, in May 2006 EU accession talks with Serbia were suspended until she gave full co-operation to the International Criminal Tribunal for Former Yugoslavia. But Britain's presidency was, undoubtedly, overshadowed by the 7 July 2005 terrorist bomb attacks on London's tube and bus network. There were, however, continuing differences with the USA, as well as amongst themselves, upon how best to tackle terrorism. In May 2006 the European Court annulled the passenger name records agreement with the USA. Generally Blair was fortunate in that external events played to his advantage, but he was also not afraid of challenging Europe in order to appeal to domestic audiences so that it appeared as if he were defending traditional British interests on the EU budget. In seeking to pursue a more deregulatory approach to the labour market and economic policy, whilst seeking to maintain control of border controls and calling for reforms of traditional British gripes such as the Common Agricultural Policy and championing enlargement there appears to have been considerable continuity between the EU policy priorities of New Labour and their Conservative predecessors.[77] However, the desire for doing so in the spirit of 'constructive engagement' would suggest a difference in approach even if ultimately there was continuity in the pragmatic pursuit of policy objectives.[78]

Observers were left wondering whether things would change under Brown's premiership. Prior to 1997 many had considered him to have been one of the most consistent of Labour's pro-Europeanists, but his apparent scepticism as Chancellor appeared to have come to the fore.[79] Under Brown's leadership it's clear that British enthusiasm for the single currency has diminished further, but also that Brown's personality (when compared with Blair) meant that he was less comfortable in the summit meeting environment and he had shown a willingness to allow his foreign secretary to take the lead in European policy. He also at times antagonised his fellow European counterparts by appearing to lecture them on apparent threats their reforms pose to the Anglo-Saxon economic model. He proved bullish over Lisbon, insisting that British national interests were defended and all its red lines maintained.[80]

Europe continued to trouble the Conservative party, but in a much less obvious manner than the Major years. David Cameron had succeeded Michael Howard in 2005 as the fifth Conservative leader in less than ten years. In July 2006 Cameron announced that from 2009, Conservative MEPs would ally with Czech Civic Democractic Party MEPs. He had pledged to leave the EPP-ED grouping during his leadership election campaign (in what was one of his few specific pledges), owing to their support for federalism. This commitment was electorally driven as Cameron was seeking to secure sufficient support from the right of his party. However, the pledge proved more difficult to fulfil as he found it difficult to persuade other mainstream parties to join a new group in 2006 and also because many of his MEPs were opposed to leaving the EPP-ED; consequently he quickly moderated his intentions and delayed the fulfilment until after the 2009 European elections. An interim measure was created with the Czechs and also the Bulgarian Union of Democratic Forces in the Movement for European Reform.[81] For some, the extension of the EU to include former Warsaw Pact countries has weakened the ideological resolve of the EU; these countries are concerned with economic liberalisation and preserving their own sovereignty. This has given Britain new allies in its 'offensive against the community' and encouraged its policy of 'red-lining everything that went beyond intergovernmentalism'.[82]

Lisbon Treaty

Early in 2007, the European Commission began revisiting the issue of the constitution and decided to proceed with a replacement treaty, which would merely amend existing treaties. For this reason the Blair government felt able to rule out a referendum on the basis that revisionism did not challenge the so-called 'red-line' position and was merely a modest repackaging, and Brown would subsequently adhere to this interpretation. In October 2007 an agreement was reached and the treaty was formally signed on 13 December. Brown, now prime minister, created some annoyance in European circles, by being unable to attend the formal signing ceremony, and arriving later in the day to add Britain's signature. Critics suggested this was down to embarrassment, and the government's resistance to a referendum was not helped by comments from former French president Giscard d'Estaing, the leading force behind the drafting of the original constitution, that the treaty differed only to the failed constitution 'in approach rather than content'. This comment merely confirmed the suspicions of critics that it was a European constitution by the back door.

Lisbon did indeed contain many of the elements of the failed European constitution. A new position of President of the European Council would be created once the treaty was ratified by all signatory member states, replacing the current system whereby countries took it in turns every six months to hold the presidency. An enhanced new foreign affairs position, the High Representative, would be created, whilst the Commission itself would be streamlined. A further redistribution of voting weights between member states will be implemented between 2014 and 2017, a reform delayed due to Polish objections. In addition the European Parliament would be reformed and this implemented in 2009, with the election of a President of the Parliament. The areas of justice and home affairs would come under the remit of the Community, whilst the removal of the national veto was to be extended. Blair did appear to achieve success at excluding any mention of the Charter of Fundamental Rights from the full treaty text or its annexes at the June European Council, whilst also securing a guarantee that the European Courts cannot use the charter to rule against British laws in the realms of labour law and social rights. Britain and Ireland continued to maintain their opt-out of the asylum, visa and immigration elements, and the concept of a two-speed Europe was emphasised with member states being given the right to opt in or out of policies in the entire field of justice and home affairs. Poland looked set to follow Britain's position on the fundamental rights, whilst Denmark opted out of the justice and home affairs policies.

Brown's challenge, having been able to side-step the referendum promise, was to safely guide the Treaty's ratification through Parliament. An increasingly rebellious parliamentary party meant this would be a relatively bruising if ultimately safe passage. At Westminster, parliamentary sceptics complained they had been restricted to only twelve days of debate, after the House of

Commons rejected a Conservative proposal to extend the Lisbon debate to eighteen days (supporters suggested this was more time than Nice, the Single European Act and Amsterdam combined). The method of debate was also criticised: morning sessions for general debate (dominated by front benches), short afternoon committee sessions, thereby preventing line-by-line scrutiny. Loyalists retorted that if the likes of Bill Cash, arch-Conservative Eurosceptic, did not take up so much time moving their amendments then more back-benchers would get an opportunity to speak. The position of the Liberal Democrats caused controversy on 26 February 2008 when frontbencher Ed Davey was ordered from the chamber of the House of Commons after protesting at the speaker's decision not to allow a debate on an amendment to consider whether a referendum should be conducted on British membership of the EU. The rest of the Liberal Democrats, including leader Nick Clegg, also left the chamber in protest. This Liberal Democrat position frustrated many Eurosceptics, because the party had refused to support calls for a referendum on the Lisbon Treaty itself, and some suspected this was little more that a cover for their uncertainty.[83] At the same time the 'I want a referendum' campaign was launched calling for a referendum on Lisbon and drawing cross-party support, including Labour backbenchers Frank Field and Kate Hoey. In a manner reminiscent of the 1970s they held a series of ten mini referenda conducted by postal vote in marginal Labour and Liberal Democrat seats. 420,000 ballot papers were sent to those names on the elec-toral register and 152,520 responded, with 88 per cent of respondents backing the calls for a referendum.[84]

On 5 March in a final opportunity to move amendments the Conservatives again tried to have a referendum on Lisbon called, but were defeated by 311–248 votes, after Nick Clegg ordered the Liberals to abstain. What the vote revealed was that all three main parties were divided on the issue. Twenty-nine Labour MPs rebelled and supported the amendment, as did thirteen Liberal Democrats, including three frontbench spokesmen who resigned their positions, whilst three well-known Conservative Europhiles opposed their party's amendment and a further two abstained.[85] The notice-able feature of the debate over the Lisbon Treaty was the relatively muted manner in which it was conducted and reported; perhaps because Brown's majority was never under threat, it failed to create the stir that had accompanied the Maastricht ratification process. On 19 June 2008 Brown's government successfully secured the parliamentary passage of the Lisbon treaty, although the wider European ratification process was in doubt owing to the Irish electorate's vote to reject it in a referendum on 12 June 2008.[86]

The credit crunch

2008 was to be a highly significant year economically, and proved to be one that not only challenged the national economic policies of the UK, but also European and global strategies, and it was a crisis that threatened the continued survival of the euro as a currency. A severe downturn in the American housing market led to a collapse in the sub-prime mortgage sector which resulted in a global loss of confidence in sub-prime, and other, markets globally. The international banking market suddenly became very reluctant to loan money amongst themselves and consequently the liquidity of the markets dried up. In Britain this led to the near collapse of several banks and required the Brown government to intervene either to nationalise (Northern Rock in February; Bradford and Bingley in September) or to broker rescue packages as with Alliance and Leicester, HBOS, Lloyds TSB and the Cheshire and Derbyshire Building Society. In October Brown announced a £400 billion bailout plan to restore financial stability, protect depositors and to add liquidity to the credit markets for businesses and individuals. The intervention became necessary as the continued slide in the share values of Britain's banks meant the entire banking system was in meltdown. Alongside this throughout 2008 the independent Bank of England repeatedly cut interest rates to a historic low of 0.5 per cent, the lowest level seen for fifty-four years, in an attempt to stave off recession and kick-start the economy.[87] But the banking crisis did not solely impact on Britain and in doing so tested the limits of the European integration experience and the EU's abilities to co-ordinate European action. By the beginning of October stock exchanges across Europe were down by 9 per cent whilst shares in some of Europe's leading banks were in free fall: HBOS down 41.5 per cent; Royal Bank of Scotland down 39 per cent; Germany's Commerzbank down 14 per cent and the Deutsche Bank down 8.9 per cent. This crisis led to the hasty arrangement of a summit of EU leaders convened in Paris to try and find a European solution, just as it appeared as though the crisis was to deepen still further with the collapse of the Icelandic banking system. President Sarkozy had been backing a multi-euro EU-wide government bailout plan along the lines of the United States Treasury's scheme. Germany, though, rejected this idea of a 'European shield', concerned at the implications for German taxpayers and wary of the backlash that might be experienced if Germany, as the largest net contributor to the EU, was seen to be paying more 'into a big pot where we do not have control and where we do not know where the German money might be used'.[88] What the credit crunch crisis did was demonstrate the limitations of European financial co-ordination and resulted instead in self-interested national-led responses. Ireland acted unilaterally in September to guarantee the deposits and debts of its six largest financial institutions, similarly the Greeks, and both in doing so offered guarantees that went well beyond the standard EU guarantee for the first 20,000 euros in a bank account. The Germans followed suit offering a 100 per cent guarantee of all private deposits and were followed by Denmark, Sweden and Austria. One of the problems facing the EU in trying to co-ordinate a Europe-wide response was the lack of an overall financial ministry, in the manner that national governments possess. As a consequence the only tool at its disposal to help manage the crisis was the European Central Bank and its interest rates. The Paris summit did agree to raise the EU's guaranteed deposit level, but otherwise it became evident that the co-ordination between European governments on fiscal and supervisory measures was to remain strictly voluntary.[89]

Further reformism

Within the EU 'constitutional' issues and 'governing' reforms have tended to be conceived and advanced in parallel. Some observers wish to see the two re-connected, observing the metaphor that 'Constitutionalism is the DOS or Windows of the European Community ... It is the operating system conditioning the process of governance itself.'[90] Attempts to explain this 'malaise' amongst Euro-elites produce a mixed narrative. Some incline to a view that the motivations for co-operation are no longer imperative, such as the end of war or curbing German expansion, and closer integration is no longer a necessary tool of domestic national statecraft. For Germany, reunification meant she had fewer reasons to ally with Europe; the end of the Cold War made it less obvious to build the EU as an alternative; furthermore France and Germany were no longer willing or able to underwrite the EU budget. Some suggested that enlargement had merely increased the size of the 'awkward squad', giving Britain key Nordic and eastern European allies. Matters have not been helped by a recognised lack of popular legitimacy, something that is aggravated by often hostile domestic media. The EU has itself failed to sell itself, whilst national governments are not unknown to use the EU as a means of bolstering their own domestic position, whether claiming credit for EU successes or heaping on the blame for failings. Finally shifting generational issues mean that few can appreciate the motivations behind the founding fathers' actions after the end of World War II. Mistakes play their part too. The French drew criticism for insisting on a referendum on the constitution, when parliamentary ratification was possible. Then bad luck played its role. The Dutch referendum, following so shortly after the French and at a point of heightened domestic political turmoil over immigration and multiculturalism, meant that the referendum was as much a domestic vote as one on the EU's future. Yet functionalists sense that it is these regular occurrences of the stop-start nature of the EU that make it the organisation that it is and which are eventually resolved by higher degrees of integration.[91] Should the Eurosclerosis of the early twenty-first century be blamed on the EU's organisational structure? Some observers point to the changed role of the Commission: it has merely 'become a big NGO that no longer defends the common interest ... websites, transparency and workshops are no substitute for thought and action'.[92] Enlargement has also made the work of the Commission harder, whilst recent Commission presidents Santer, Prodi and Barroso were seen as weak and imbued more with 'national' perspectives than 'Community' mission. At the same time changes to the European Council have been noted. A greater unwillingness of the Council of Ministers to make decisions and thereby pass matters upwards has clogged the European Council agenda and reduced opportunities for 'big ideas' thinking.

February 2008 saw fresh controversy over the activities of MEPs. Once more the accountability of European institutions was under scrutiny and particularly the financial credibility of the Santer Commission. This time claims appeared that MEPs were systematically misusing the expenses system and that these abuses were being covered up by the European Parliament despite being revealed in a secret audit. As a consequence all the main British political parties pledged to introduce systems that made the claims of their MEPs appear more transparent.[93] The abuses of the MEP system were to pale, at least in terms of registering with the British public, in comparison to the outrage that accompanied the reports about Westminster MPs' expenses claims in 2009; however, overall they did contribute to a growing sense that Britain's elected representatives were exploiting a system for their own profit and to the detriment of democracy. Nevertheless, these ongoing abuses must have contributed to the poor turnout in the June 2009 European election. Overall across Europe turnout was the lowest since elections began with only 43 per cent voting, in an election which in general saw the centre right benefit at the expense of the left. In Britain the Conservatives remained the largest party with twenty-two seats (27.7 per cent of the vote); followed by UKIP and Labour both with thirteen; the Liberal Democrats secured eleven whilst the Greens, BNP and SNP won two seats each. The results were significant because of the significant gains made by UKIP, despite all their internal problems, which had seen them become the second largest party, suggesting an expansion in the electoral appeal of Euroscepticism. The swing to the right was strongly and controversially emphasised by the success of the British National Party (BNP) which won two seats in the northeast of England. The electoral success of the minor parties since 1999 has been one of the noticeable features of the introduction of PR. The elections also saw the reduction of total European seats to 736 down from 785, a total that will be revised upward by the next elections to a total of 751.

Within the new Parliament there was some re-jigging of the political alliances. The Conservatives went ahead with their intention of leaving the EPP-ED to form the European Conservative and Reformist Groups (CRG) with MPs from seven other countries (including fifteen from Poland's Law and Justice party and nine from the Czech Civic Democrat Party) giving the CRG a bloc of fifty-five MEPs. UKIP also formed the Europe of Freedom and Democracy Group. The size of these new groupings is still dwarfed by the size of the Socialists (183 MEPs – and of which Labour is a member) and the EPP with 264. However, any pretence of unity within the Conservative MEP grouping was shattered by the actions of Macmillan Scott, their former leader, in July 2009, when he stood for election (and secured the nomination) as one of fourteen vice-presidents of the European Parliament against the officially sanctioned CRG candidate, the Polish MEP Michal Kaminski. On refusing to withdraw from the contest Macmillan Scott first endured the removal of the Conservative whip and then expulsion from the party.[94] Cameron's Polish allies were understandably furious and in an effort to try and hold the new CRG together, the Conservative MEP leader Timothy Kirkhope fell on his sword and offered the group leadership to Michal Kaminski. Macmillan Scott had regarded Kaminski as inappropriate and unfit to be leader of a group containing British Conservatives, not least because of allegations of a neo-fascist past and because of his views on homosexuals. Aside from weakening the CRG's unity, the loss of the group leadership for the Conservatives meant that they would get less exposure on the floor of the Parliament chamber, as the groups' leader is guaranteed speaking time in debates, and would potentially lose out when the various committee chairmanship positions were carved up.

Away from the domestic political wrangling, the EU has continued to be drawn towards further plans for enlargement. The enlargement discussions have tended to concentrate on issues of efficiency and utility, linked to arguments about extending the free market, and more recently, to reinforcing security. In the 1990s it was all about guaranteeing stability and avoiding the descent into authoritarianism (after communism) and doing so through the exporting of a capitalist model and the single market. Labelled as 'pragmatic discourse' by some political scientists, these arguments are being employed to favour the extension of EU membership to Turkey, or in some cases even Georgia and Ukraine, based on an assumption that the problems of trade and security are best solved by continuing to enlarge.[95] In December 1999 the EU indicated its willingness to consider Turkey for membership. Britain has been at the fore, since 2002, pushing for Turkey's full admission; but Turkey's refusal to extend a customs union deal to EU-member Cyprus partially froze the accession talks. Cyprus has been divided between Greek and Turkish areas since 1974 when Turkey invaded the north of the island in response to a Greek-backed military coup on the island. In the early stages of the European integration process Turkey secured membership of a number of the organisations including OECD (1948), Council of Europe (1949) and NATO (1952). Turkey has actually been trying to join the EU since 1959 when she was granted associate membership with the promise of full membership at a point in future when, European Commission President Hallstein declared, 'Turkey is part of Europe'.[96] Many Europeans fear that allowing the poor, populous, Muslim state to join the EU will flood Europe with poorly educated immigrants. Furthermore concerns over Turkey's human rights record have hindered matters. Concerns exist too over the location of Turkey, which borders Iraq, and the ongoing problems with the rights of Turkey's Kurdish minority. Similarly, security concerns abound over the possible accession of Georgia, which found itself invaded by and at war with Russia in August 2008. For many observers there is a sense that the EU is in danger of over-extending itself having failed to properly consolidate its business model, in the manner of a shop or restaurant franchise that over-expands and saturates its market, resulting in diminishing returns and ultimately ending up in administration.

Confirmation of Lisbon

On 2 October 2009 the Irish returned to the polls to again vote on Lisbon, seventeen months after 33 of her 43 parliamentary constituencies had rejected the Treaty. This time the result was a significant 'Yes' with 64 per cent of the electorate backing the Treaty, an increase of 20 per cent on the previous referendum, and all bar two constituencies supporting it.[97] This was followed on 3 November by the Czechs ratifying the treaty, and with that Lisbon came into force on 1 December 2009. Almost immediately David Cameron retreated from his pledge to hold a referendum, and speculation began as to who would occupy the new European posts. After Lisbon, Tony Blair's name was frequently mooted as a potential president of the Council, with it rumoured that President Sarkozy of France was favourable to such an appointment and Glenys Kinnock, Brown's Europe minister, admitting in July 2009 that the government would be supporting Blair's candidature. However, it was thought that Germany was less enthusiastic, and appeared to favour the candidature of ex-Austrian chancellor Wolfgang Schüssel, whilst Luxembourg's prime minister Jean-Claude Junker was spoken of as another possible choice. Blair's supporters found themselves also having to convince many of the smaller EU member states who were concerned about the implication of a European president hailing from a country that remained outside both the euro and the Schengen free-movement pact, and who was openly championing the cause of Turkey for membership.[98] Although Blair's candidature secured a lot of press coverage it was clear that the member states were divided between those who favoured a consensual leadership style and those who favoured a 'director'. European Commission president, Jose Manuel Barroso, likened the selection process to solving a Rubik's Cube puzzle. What emerged though surprised many, not least in Britain. Herman van Rompuy, the centre-right Belgian prime minister, was anointed as the unanimous choice of the twenty-seven member states for President of the Council in November, with the little known Euro-technocrat, Baroness Catherine Ashton (a Labour peer who had previously been an EU Trade commissioner, but had only served one year), emerging as the foreign affairs chief. Certainly amongst the British political press this latter appointment was greeted with much incredulity as journalists scrabbled to establish her relevant credentials and wondered whether she possessed sufficient foreign policy experience. Labour insiders argued that she was an ideal choice, not least because of her past close working relationship with Barroso. Since her appointment it appears that disquiet has spread amongst other member nations, with dissatisfaction arising over her choice of EU ambassador to Washington and her response to the Haiti earthquake.[99] Rompuy's election, whilst unanimous, did raise concerns in some quarters that he lacked a sufficiently high profile for representing the EU on the world stage, and also those favouring the cause of Turkish EU entry were troubled by past comments attributed to him which indicated his concern about the admission of an Islamic state.

Almost immediately Rompuy's skills were tested by the crisis threatening the entire euro zone arising from Greece's financial meltdown. It is by no means clear that Greece will be able to remain in the euro and that despite the substantial cuts in public sector expenditure intended to reduce the nation's huge deficit, economists are concerned that Greece's need to restructure her debt payments in the near future would meet with failure. Greece had to raise 11 billion euros by the end of May 2010 and a total of 54 billion euros by the end of the year. Some economists were speculating about the knock-on effects for the Iberian and British economies. The EU's willingness to bail out Greece was initally unclear. Germany was reluctant whilst Britain as a non-euro member believed it was under no obligation to assist. Agreement was reached that could allow Greece to call upon EU and IMF financial loans, but these are being held as an option of last resort. Whilst some Eurosceptics are predicting that this will lead to the collapse of the euro, the doom merchants have all too often predicted the imminent death of the European project, only for it to cheat and appear to sustain a new lease of life. What is more, it is becoming evident that Rompuy is quite a skilled political manoeuvrer behind the scenes. He is a 'quiet assassin', warned Nigel Farage of UKIP, and Rompuy has already begun to suggest that he intends to exercise his power to the full, provoking some concern in European capitals.[100]

Conclusion

Under New Labour Britain witnessed a level of Europeanism of the policy process not previously seen. Following Nice the government spent an estimated £23.5 million in designing euro-compatibility into governmental computer contracts (Inland Revenue, Customs and Excise, Social Security).[101] These patterns of governance increasingly mirror European experiences. Devolution means that the UK now experiences a multi-levelled system of government. The landscape has been transformed: the adoption of proportional representation for elections to the European parliament and the devolved assemblies; an independent Bank of England and the incorporation of the European Convention on Human Rights. Speaking in Aachen in 1999 Blair had declared his expectation that 'over the next few years Britain resolves once and for all its ambivalence towards Europe. I want to end the uncertainty, the lack of confidence, the Europhobia.'[102] Yet over a decade later Europe's relevance to public opinion still remains a problem, and this suggests that Labour failed, intentionally or not, to explain its European policies. It is clear that few regard it as an issue to determine voter choice (except perhaps in European elections). In 2005, for example, Europe features no higher than eighth on a list of voters' 'most important issues facing the country'.[103] It ought to be remembered that no matter how enthusiastically New Labour was committed to the European Union, ultimately the desire to retain power nationally proved even more powerful.

Notes

Introduction

1 For the historic lineage of the 'idea of Europe' see A. Pagden (ed.) *The Idea of Europe: From Antiquity to European Union* Cambridge: Cambridge University Press, 2002; P. Rietbergen *Europe: A Cultural History* London: Routledge, 1998.

2 Conservative Central Office press release: Michael Ancram speech 'Building true partnerships', 9 May 2002 www.conservatives.com/news. Accessed 22 October 2005.

3 P. Coupland *Britannia, Europa and Christendom: British Christians and European Integration* Basingstoke: Palgrave, 2006; M. Haller *European Integration as an Elite Process: The Failure of a Dream?* London: Routledge, 2008, pp. 243–44.

4 Conservative Party Archive [hereafter CPA]: J.A. Messop to R. Horton 11 May 1962, CCO500/31/2; 'Report and analysis of the state of the party' n.d. [February 1971] CCO20/32/28.

5 N.P. Ludlow 'Us or them? The meanings of 'Europe' in British political discourse' in M. Malmborg, and B. Strath (eds) *The Meaning of Europe: Variety and Contention within and among Nations* London: Berg Publishing, 2002.

6 For example *Daily Telegraph* B. Johnson 'This lunacy about Latin makes me want to weep with rage' 15 March 2010 www.telegraph.co.uk/comment/columnists/borisjohnson/7445850/This-lunacy-about-Latin-makes-me-want-to-weep-with-rage.html accessed 6 April 2010, see the 'comments' and the correspondence this prompted to the letters page.

7 R. Evans *Cosmopolitan Islanders: British Historians and the European Continent* Cambridge: Cambridge University Press, 2009.

8 H. Young *This Blessed Plot: Britain and Europe from Churchill to Blair* London: Macmillan, 1998 p. 499.

9 Sir Kenneth Clarke attributed this to the fact that during the First World War 'all the best elements of German culture and science were still in Germany and were supporting the German cause, whereas now they are outside Germany and supporting us.' I. McLaine *Ministry of Morale: Home Front Morale and the Ministry of Information in World War Two* London: Allen and Unwin, 1979 p. 156. See S. Hynes *A War Imagined: The First World War and English Culture* London: Bodley Head, 1990; J. Mander *Our German Cousins: Anglo–German Relations in the 19th and 20th Centuries* London: John Murray, 1974.

10 Avon Mss: Kenneth Chance to Anthony Eden 5 February 1937 AP13/1/51T.

11 R. Broad *Labour's European Dilemma: From Bevin to Blair* Basingstoke: Palgrave, 2001 p. 2.

12 M. Blackwell *Clinging to Grandeur: British Attitudes and Foreign Policy in the Aftermath of the Second World War* London: Greenwood Press, 1993.

13 Broad *European Dilemma* p. 34.
14 CPA: V.B. Petherick to COO, 6 September 1962, CCO500/31/4; Horton to COO, 23 August 1962, CCO500/31/2.
15 A. Milward *The UK and the EC volume 1: The Rise and Fall of a National Strategy 1945–63* London: Frank Cass, 2002 p. 272.
16 Broad *European Dilemma* p. 11.
17 J.W. Young 'Churchill's "no" to Europe: The "rejection" of European Union by Churchill's post-war government' *Historical Journal* 28, 4 (1985) p. 924.
18 M. Gehler cited O. Daddow (ed.) *Harold Wilson and European Integration: Britain's Second Application to Join the EEC* London: Frank Cass, 2003 p. 4.
19 *The Times* A. Meyer to editor, 11 October 1996, p. 21; C. Lord *British Entry to the European Community under the Heath Government* Aldershot: Dartmouth, 1993 p. 38.
20 N. Henderson *Water Under the Bridges* London: Hodder and Stoughton, 1945 p. 49.
21 P. Kennedy 'The tradition of appeasement in British foreign policy 1865–1939' *British Journal of International Studies* 2, 3 (1976) p. 214.
22 W.N. Medlicott *British Foreign Policy since Versailles* London: Methuen, 1967; S. Benn 'The uses of sovereignty' *Political Studies* 3, 2 (1955) pp. 109–22.
23 See for example, F.H. Hinsley *Sovereignty* Oxford: Alden Press, 1966; A. James *Sovereign Statehood* London: Allen and Unwin, 1986; A. Milward *et al. The Frontier of National Sovereignty: History and Theory* London: Routledge, 1993; S. Krasner *Sovereignty: Organised Hypocrisy* Princeton, NJ: Princeton University Press, 1999.
24 G. Howe *Conflict of Loyalty* London: Macmillan, 1994 p. 631; For further discussion of sovereignty see N.J. Crowson *The Conservative Party and European Integration* London: Routledge, 2006 pp. 83–89.
25 E.B. Haas *The Uniting of Europe: Political, Social, and Economic Forces, 1950–1957* Stanford, CA: Stanford University Press, 1958.
26 See Crowson *European Integration* pp. 188–200, 206–9; D. Butler and D. Marquand *European Elections and British Politics* London: Longman, 1981 pp. 27–28.
27 B. Rosamund 'The uniting of Europe and the foundation of EU studies: Revisiting the neofunctionalism of Ernest B. Haas' *Journal of European Public Policy* 12, 2 (2005) p. 238.
28 S. Hoffman 'Obstinate or obsolete? The fate of the nation-state and the case of Western Europe' *Daedalus* 95, 3 (1966) pp. 862–915.
29 M. Aspinall and G. Schneider (eds) *The Rules of Integration: Institutionalist Approaches to the Study of Europe* Manchester: Manchester University Press, 2001.
30 For further development of these theoretical approaches see B. Rosamund *Theories of European Integration* Basingstoke: Palgrave, 2000.
31 An exception here would be D.W. Unwin *The Community of Europe: A History of European Integration since 1945* Harlow: Longman, 1981.
32 Exceptions are P.M. Stirk (ed.) *European Unity in Context: The Inter-war Period* London: Pinter, 1989, C.H. Pegg *Evolution of the European Idea 1914–32* Chapel Hill: University of North Carolina Press, 1983 and P. Marsh *Bargaining on Europe: Britain and the First Common Market 1860–1892* London: Yale University Press, 1999.
33 For example: D.C. Watt *How War Came* London: Heinemann, 1989; J. Charmley *Chamberlain and the Lost Peace* London: Hodder and Stoughton, 1989; R.A.C. Parker *Chamberlain and Appeasement* London: Macmillan, 1993.
34 M. Gilbert *The Roots of Appeasement* London: Weidenfeld and Nicolson, 1966 p. 9.

35 Kennedy 'Traditions of appeasement'; P. Kennedy *Realities behind Diplomacy* London: Fontana, 1985, chs 5–6.

36 M. Cowling *The Impact of Hitler* Cambridge: Cambridge University Press, 1975.

37 P. Kennedy *The Realities Behind Diplomacy* London: Fontana, 1985 p. 229.

38 Austen Chamberlain Mss: Austen to King, 9 February 1925, AC52/378 cited R. Grayson *Austen Chamberlain and the Commitment to Europe: British Foreign Policy 1924–29* London: Cass, 1997 p. 41; D. Dutton *Austen Chamberlain: Gentleman in Politics* Bolton: Ross Anderson, 1985 p. 239.

39 Cited P. Catterall 'Macmillan and Europe' paper presented to Western Conference on British Studies, Houston, Texas, 2000.

40 Cited H. Macmillan *Tides of Fortune, 1945–55* London: Macmillan, 1969 p. 159.

41 M. Howard *The Continental Commitment: The Dilemma of British Defence Policy in the Era of Two World Wars* London: Temple Smith, 1972 p. 112; *Hansard* vol. 270, col. 632, 10 November 1932.

42 *The Times* 22 January 1998 p. 18 William Hague 'Why Tories should call Blair's bluff'.

43 Broad *European Dilemma* p. 3.

44 D. Dutton *Anthony Eden* London: Arnold, 1997 p. 301; Young *This Blessed Plot* p. 154; R. Ritchie *Enoch Powell on 1992* London: Anaya, 1989 p. 12.

45 J. McKay *Labour Party Attitudes to European Integration 1945–75* unpublished Ph.D. thesis, University of Birmingham 2006 p. 35, pp. 246–47 quote Peggy Crane, May 1974.

46 Ludlow 'All at sea' p. 5.

47 A. Shlaim *Britain and the Origins of European unity 1940–51*, Reading: University of Reading Graduate School of Contemporary European Studies, 1978 p. 8. A. Deighton *The Impossible Peace: Britain, the Division of Germany and the Origins of the Cold War*, Oxford: Clarendon Press, 1993.

48 For examples see D. Charlton *The Price of Victory* London: BBC, 1995; R. Denman *Missed Chances: Britain and Europe in the Twentieth Century* London: Cassell, 1996; E. Dell *The Schuman Plan and the British Abdication of Leadership in Europe* Oxford: Oxford University Press, 1995; R. Broad *Labour's European Dilemma* Basingstoke: Palgrave, 2001; A. Milward *The European Rescue of the Nation-State* London: Routledge, 1992, p. 433.

49 L. Brittan *A Diet of Brussels: The Changing Face of Europe* London: Little, Brown, 2000, p. 191; F. Pym *The Politics of Consent* London: Hamish Hamilton, 1984, p. 74; *The Independent* 19 September 1996, Heath, Howe, Hurd, Whitelaw et al. to editor; D. Healey *The Time of My Life* London: Michael Joseph, 1989 p. 115.

50 A. Seldon 'The Churchill administration 1951–55' in P. Hennessy and A. Seldon (eds) *Ruling Performance: British Governments from Attlee to Thatcher* Oxford: Blackwell, 1987 pp. 63–97.

51 www.number10.gov.uk/Page1510. Accessed 6 April 2010.

52 J.W. Young *Britain, France and the Unity of Europe* Leicester: Leicester University Press, 1988.

53 A. Milward *The Reconstruction of Western Europe 1945–51* London: Routledge, 1984.

54 Although these who coined it admit they are actually borrowing the term from historian Peter Marsh's 1978 study of Lord Salisbury *The Discipline of Popular Government: Lord Salisbury's Domestic Statecraft 1881–1902* London: Harvester, 1978.

55 Broad *European Dilemma*; N.J. Crowson *Facing Fascism: The Conservative Party and the European Dictators, 1935–40* London: Routledge, 1997; Crowson *European Integration*; W. Mulligan and B. Simms (eds) *The Primacy of Foreign Policy in British History* Basingstoke: Palgrave, 2010; A. Mullen *The British*

Left's 'Great Debate' on Europe London: Continuum, 2007; J. Turner *The Tories and Europe* Manchester: Manchester University Press, 2000; A. Forester *Euroscepticism*; J. Moon *European Integration in British Politics 1950–63* Aldershot: Gower, 1985; J. Toomey *Harold Wilson's EEC Application* Dublin: UCD Press, 2007; K. Featherstone *Socialist Parties and European Integration: A Comparative History* Manchester: Manchester University Press, 1988.

56 N. Beloff *The General Says No: Britain's Exclusion from Europe* Harmondsworth: Penguin, 1963; M. Camps *Britain and the European Community 1955–63* London: Oxford University Press, 1964; U. Kitzinger *Diplomacy and Persuasion: How Britain Joined the Common Market* London: Thames and Hudson, 1973; W. Kaiser *Using Europe, Abusing the Europeans: Britain and European Integration 1945–63* Basingstoke: Macmillan, 1996; J. Tratt *The Macmillan Government and Europe: A Study in the Process of Policy Development* Basingstoke: Macmillan, 1996; J. Ellison *Threatening Europe: Britain and the Creation of the European Community 1955–58* Basingstoke: Macmillan, 2000; H. Parr *British Policy towards the European Community: Harold Wilson and Britain's World Role 1964–67* London: Routledge, 2005; C. Hynes *The Year that Never Was: Heath, the Nixon Administration and the Year of Europe* Dublin: University College Dublin Press, 2009.

57 Daddow (ed.) *Harold Wilson and the EEC* p. 5.

58 CPA: Foreign Affairs Committee, 13 March 1963, 9 February 1965 CRD3/10/15.

59 U. Kitzwinger *The European Common Market and Community* London: Routledge, 1967; *Second Try* Oxford: Pergamon Press, 1968; *Diplomacy and Persuasion: How Britain Joined the Common Market* London: Thames and Hudson, 1973; and with D. Butler *The 1975 Referendum* London: Macmillan, 1976.

60 Amongst publications are: J. Pinder *Britain and the Common Market* London: Cresset Press, 1961; *The European Community's Policy towards Eastern Europe* London: Chatham House, 1975; *Federal Union* London: Macmillan, 1990; with R. Pryce *Europe After De Gaulle: Towards the United States of Europe* Harmondsworth: Penguin, 1969; with R. Pryce and A. Duff *Maastricht and Beyond: Building the European Union* London: Routledge, 1994; with S. Usherwood *The European Union: A Very Short Introduction* Oxford: Oxford University Press, 2007.

61 R. Broad *Community Europe: A Short Guide to the Common Market* 1969; R. Broad *Labour's European Dilemma* Basingstoke: Palgrave, 2001.

62 E. Windrich *British Labour's Foreign Policy* Palo Alto, CA: Stanford University Press, 1952; C.R. Attlee *As it Happened* London: Heinemann, 1954; E. Dell *The Schuman Plan and the British Abdication of Leadership in Europe* Oxford: Clarendon Press, 1995; McKay *Labour Party*; Broad *European Dilemma*.

63 A. Moravcsik *The Choice for Europe: Social Purpose and State Power from Messina to Maastricht* London: Routledge/UCL Press, 1998 pp. 164–76.

64 J.V.E. Ellison *Threatening Europe: Britain and the Creation of the European Community 1955–58* Basingstoke: Palgrave, 2000 pp. 178–86; N. Ashton *Kennedy, Macmillan and the Cold War* Basingstoke: Palgrave, 2002 p. 132.

65 Milward *Rise and Fall* pp. 310–51.

66 Milward *Rise and Fall* pp. 386–91, 415–17.

67 R.J. Leiber *British Politics and European Unity: Parties, Elites and Pressure Groups* California: University of California Press, 1970 p. 261.

68 Milward *Rise and Fall* pp. 466, 481.

69 S. Toschi 'Washington-London-Paris, an untenable triangle 1960–63' *Journal of European Integration History* 1, 2 (1995) p. 109.

70 N.P. Ludlow 'Challenging French leadership in Europe' *Contemporary European History* 8, 2 (1999) pp. 231–48; N.P. Ludlow *Dealing with Britain: The Six and the First UK Application to the EEC* Cambridge: Cambridge University Press, 1997 pp. 153–54.

71 Ludlow *Dealing with Britain*.

72 M. Schaad *Bullying Bonn: Anglo–German Diplomacy and European Integration 1955–61* Basingstoke: Macmillan, 2000 pp. 167–71; O. Bange *The EEC Crisis of 1963: Kennedy, Macmillan, De Gaulle and Adenauer in Conflict* Basingstoke: Palgrave, 2000 pp. 165–233.

73 H. Parr *British Policy towards the European Community: Harold Wilson and Britain's World Role 1964–67* London: Routledge, 2006 p. 9.

74 Tratt *The Macmillan Government* pp. 191–98, Crowson *European Integration*.

75 S. Bulmer 'Domestic politics and the European Community policymaking' *Journal of Common Market Studies* 21, 4 (1983) pp. 349–63; S. Bulmer and W. Patterson *The Federal Republic of Germany and the European Community* London: Allen Lane, 1987.

76 J. Bulpitt 'The European questions: Rules, national modernisation and the ambiguities of *Primat de Innenpolitik*' in D. Marquand and A. Seldon (eds) *The Ideas that Shaped Post-War Britain* London: Fontana, 1996, p. 215.

77 Cowling *The Impact of Hitler*.

78 A. Forster *Euroscepticism in Contemporary British Politics: Opposition to Europe in the British Conservative and Labour Parties since 1945* London: Routledge, 2002.

79 P. Norton *Conservative Dissidents: Dissent within the Parliamentary Conservative Party 1970–74* London: Temple Smith, 1978; R. Jackson *Rebels and Whips: Dissension and Cohesion in British Political Parties since 1945* London: Macmillan, 1968; D. Baker et al. 'Whips or scorpions? The Maastricht vote and the Conservative Party' *Parliamentary Affairs* 46, 2 (1993) pp. 151–66; and D. Baker et al. '1846 … 1906 … 1996? Conservative splits and European integration' *Political Quarterly* 64, 4 (1993) pp. 420–34.

80 J. McKay *Labour Party Attitudes to European Integration 1945–75* unpublished Ph.D. dissertation, University of Birmingham 2006, Broad *European Dilemma*.

81 P. Cowley. and P. Norton, 'Blair's bastards: Discontent within the PLP' *Centre for Legislative Studies Research Paper* 1/96 (1996).

82 N. Thompson *The Anti-Appeasers* Oxford: Clarendon Press, 1971.

83 L.J. Robins *The Reluctant Party: Labour and the EEC 1961–75* London: Hesketh, 1979 p. 4.

84 Crowson *European Integration* chs 4, 6.

85 Baker et al. '1846 … 1906 … 1996? Conservative splits and European integration'.

86 G. Garrett and G. Tsebelis 'More reasons to resist the temptation of power indices in the European Union' *Journal of Theoretical Politics* 11 (1999) pp. 331–38; 'Even more reasons to resist the power indices in the European Union' *Journal of Theoretical Politics* 13 (2001) pp. 99–105.

87 D. Wincott 'A community of law? "European" law and judicial politics: The Court of Justice and beyond' *Government and Opposition* 35, 1 (2000) pp. 3–26; M. Pollack, 'Representing diffuse interests in EC policy making' *Journal of European Public Policy* 4, 4 (1997) pp. 572–90.

88 J. Buller *National Statecraft and European Integration* London: Pinter, 2000.

89 H. Thompson *The British Conservative Government and the European Exchange Rate Mechanism 1979–1994* London: Pinter, 1996 pp. 172–73.

90 T. Börzel 'Pace-setting, foot-dragging, and fence-sitting: Member state responses to Europeanization' *Journal of Common Market Studies* 40, 2 (2002) pp. 196–208.

1 Inter-war years 1918–39

1 Viscount Grey *Twenty-Five Years 1892–1916* vol. 2, London: Hodder and Stoughton, 1925 p. 20.
2 M. Macmillan *Peacemakers: The Paris Peace Conference of 1919 and Its Attempts to End War* London: John Murray, 2003 pp. 72–73.
3 L.E. Ambrosius *Wilsonian Statecraft: Theory and Practice of Liberal Internationalism during World War One* Wilmington, DE: SR Books, 1991; K. Schwabe *Woodrow Wilson, Revolutionary Germany and Peacemaking 1918–19* Chapel Hill: University of North Carolina Press, 1985; A.S. Link *Woodrow Wilson: Revolution, War and Peace* Arlington Heights, IL: AHM Publishing, 1979.
4 A. Sharp *The Versailles Settlement: Peacemaking in Paris 1919* London: Macmillan, 1991 p. 13.
5 P.M. Bell *France and Britain, 1900–1940: Entente and Estrangement* Harlow: Longman, 1996 p. 114.
6 M. Trachtenberg *Reparations in World Politics: France and European Economic Diplomacy 1916–23* New York: Columbia University Press, 1980; W. McDougall *France's Rhineland Diplomacy 1914–24: The Last Bid for a Balance of Power in Europe* Princeton, NJ: Princeton University Press, 1978.
7 Macmillan *Peacemakers* pp. 63–64.
8 D. Weigall and P. Stirk (eds) *The Origins and Development of the European Community* Leicester: Leicester University Press, 1992 pp. 6–7.
9 J. Pinder 'Federalism in Britain and Italy: Radicals and the English liberal tradition' in P.M.R. Stirk *European Unity in Context: The Inter-war Period* London: Pinter, 1989 pp. 201–4.
10 S. Marks *The Illusion of Peace: International Relations in Europe, 1918–33* Basingstoke: Palgrave Macmillan, 2003.
11 J.M. Keynes *The Economic Consequences of the Peace* London: Macmillan, 1919; H. Nicolson *The Peacemakers 1919* London: Constable, 1933; R. Stannard Baker *Woodrow Wilson and the World Settlement* Garden City, NY: Doubleday, 1922.
12 Trachtenberg *Reparations in World Politics.*
13 P. Salmon 'Reluctant engagement: Britain and continental Europe 1890–1939' *Diplomacy and Statecraft* 8, 3 (1997) p. 146.
14 For example, Neville Chamberlain's House of Commons speech: *Hansard* vol. 333 cols 1399–1413, 24 March 1938.
15 Headlam Mss: diary 19 September 1938, D/He/34, Durham Record Office.
16 Bell *France and Britain* p. 126.
17 C. Fischer *The Ruhr Crisis 1923–1924* Oxford: Oxford University Press, 2003, p. 12.
18 S. Marks 'Myth of reparations' *Central European History* 11, 3 (1978) pp. 231–55.
19 B. McKercher *Transition of Power: Britain's Loss of Global Pre-eminence to the United States* Cambridge: Cambridge University Press, 1999, p. 77.
20 G. Johnson *The Berlin Embassy of Lord D'Aberdon 1920–26* Basingstoke: Palgrave, 2002 pp. 33–36, see chapter 2; see also A. Williams 'Sir John Bradbury and the Reparations Commission 1920–25' *Diplomacy and Statecraft* 13, 3 (2002) pp. 81–102.
21 Bell *France and Britain* p. 137.
22 Cited Fischer *Ruhr Crisis* p. 22.
23 S.C. Salazmann *Great Britain, Germany and the Soviet Union: Rapallo and After, 1922–34* Woodbridge: Boydell and RHS, 2003 pp. 172–78; K. Nielson *Britain, the Soviet Russia and the Collapse of the Versailles Order 1919–39* Cambridge: Cambridge University Press, 2006.
24 Salzmann *Great Britain, Germany.*

25 E. Goldstein, 'The British official mind and the Lausanne conference, 1922–23', *Diplomacy and Statecraft* 14, 2 (2003) pp. 185–206.
26 *Hansard House of Lords Debates* vol. 53, col. 785, 20 April 1923 (Curzon reading Bonar Law's statement).
27 R.C. Self *Britain, America and the War Debt Controversy: The Economic Diplomacy of an Unspecial Relationship 1917–1941* London: Routledge, 2006.
28 G. Johnson (ed.) *Locarno Revisited: European Diplomacy 1920–29* London: Routledge, 2004.
29 There were four Arbitration treaties between Germany, and respectively France, Belgium, Poland and Czechoslovakia as well as two Guarantee treaties between France and respectively Poland and Czechoslovakia.
30 Salmon 'Reluctant Agreement' p. 147.
31 Johnson *The Berlin Embassy.*
32 Austen Chamberlain to Hilda Chamberlain 11 October 1930, R.C. Self (ed.) *The Austen Chamberlain Diary Letters* Cambridge: Royal Historical Society Camden Series, 1995 p. 356.
33 D. Dutton *Austen Chamberlain: Gentleman in Politics* Bolton: Ross Anderson, 1985 p. 259.
34 F. Magee '"Limited liability"? Britain and the Treaty of Locarno' *Twentieth Century British History* 6, 1 (1995) pp. 1–22.
35 J. Wright *Gustav Stresemann: Weimar's Greatest Statesman* Oxford: Oxford University Press, 2002.
36 Johnson *The Berlin Embassy*, p. 161.
37 Salmon 'Reluctant engagement' p. 147.
38 R. Boyce 'British capitalism and the European unity between the wars' in P.M.R. Stirk (ed.) *European Unity in Context: The Inter-war Period* London: Pinter, 1989 p. 69.
39 Salmon 'Reluctant engagement' pp. 139–64.
40 P.M.R. Stirk 'Introduction: Crisis and continuity in interwar Europe' in P.M.R. Stirk (ed.) *European Unity in Context: The Interwar Period* London: Pinter, 1989, p. 2.
41 For FO response see E.L.Woodward and R. Butler (eds) *Documents on British Foreign Policy* second series, vol 1, London: HMSO, 1949 pp. 326, 330–31. See also C.H. Pegg *Evolution of the European Idea 1914–32* Chapel Hill: University of North Carolina Press, 1983; R. White 'Cordial caution: The British response to the French proposal for European federal union in 1930' in A. Bosco (ed.) *The Federal Idea: Volume 1: The History of Federalism from the Enlightenment to 1945* London: Lothian Foundation Press, 1991 pp. 237–62; R.W. Boyce 'Britain's first 'no' to Europe: Britain and the Briand Plan, 1929–30' *European History Quarterly* 10 (1980) pp. 17–45.
42 D. Dutton '"A nation of shopkeepers in search of a suitable Frenchman": Britain and Briand, 1915–30. 1930' *Modern and Contemporary France* 6, 4 (1988) p. 474.
43 D. Dutton 'A nation of shopkeepers' p. 475.
44 Bell *France and Britain* p. 166.
45 Boyce and Rolo take the view that Britain's negativity and delaying tactics destroyed what hope of success Briand had. Boyce 'Britain's first "no"' pp. 17–45; P.J.V. Rolo, *Britain and the Briand Plan: The Common Market That Never Was* Keele: University of Keele, 1972.
46 P. Salmon *Diplomacy and Statecraft* p. 148.
47 R. White 'The Europeanism of Coudenhove-Kalergi' and J. Pinder 'Federalism in Britain and Italy: Radicals and the English liberal tradition' in P.M.R. Stirk (ed.) *European Unity in Context: The Interwar Period* London: Pinter, 1989, pp. 23–40, 201–23.

48 Austen Chamberlain to Ida Chamberlain 9 March 1918 AC5/1/64 in R. Self (ed.) *The Austen Chamberlain Diary Letters* Cambridge: Royal Historical Society, 1995 pp. 79–80.
49 A. Chamberlain 'Great Britain as a European power' *Journal of the Royal Institute of International Affairs*, March 1930, pp. 180–89.
50 W. Churchill *Saturday Evening Post*, 15 February 1930.
51 Boyce 'British capitalism' pp. 79–80.
52 R. Broad *Labour's European Dilemma: From Bevin to Blair* Basingstoke: Palgrave, 2001 p. 1.
53 Broad *Labour's European Dilemma* p. 2.
54 Sir William Tyrell cited R Boyce 'British capitalism' pp. 66–67.
55 Bell *France and Britain* pp. 155–60. A. Sharp 'Britain and the Channel Tunnel 1919–20' *Australian Journal of Politics and History* 25, 1979 pp. 210–15; K. Wilson *Channel Tunnel Visions, 1850–1945: Dreams and Nightmares* London: Hambledon, 1994, ch. 5; R.S. Grayson, 'The British Government and the Channel Tunnel, 1919–39', *Journal of Contemporary History* 31, 1 (1996), pp. 125–44.
56 Cmnd 3484 p. 18 cited McKercher *Transition of Power* p. 72.
57 McKercher *Transition of Power* pp. 69–72, quote p. 72; see also D. Carlton *MacDonald versus Henderson: The Foreign Policy of the Second Labour Government* London: Macmillan, 1970.
58 F. Costigliola 'The United States and the reconstruction of Germany in the 1920s' *Business History Review* 50, 4 (1976) pp. 477–502.
59 McKercher *Transition of Power* p. 80.
60 Orme Sargent memo 18 March 1930 cited McKercher *Transition of Power* p. 99.
61 See P. Clavin *The Great Depression in Europe 1929–39* Basingstoke: Palgrave, 2000; Self *War Debt Controversy*.
62 G. Peden *British Rearmament and the Treasury 1932–1939* Edinburgh: Scottish Academic Press, 1979 p. 208.
63 McKercher *Transition of Power* pp. 100–101.
64 C. Kitching *Britain and the Problem of International Disarmament 1919–34* London: Routledge, 1999 p. 122. See also C. Kitching *Britain and the Geneva Disarmament Conference* London: Routledge, 2003.
65 Kitching *International Disarmament* p. 138.
66 Kitching *International Disarmament* p. 139.
67 TNA: Statement Relating to Defence, Cmnd 4827, White Paper March 1935, pp. 1–10 Cab24/254; Committee of Imperial Defence: Defence Requirements Sub-Committee 'Programme of the Defence Services 3rd Report' 21 November 1935 Cab 16/123; Pownall diary 27 March, 18 April, 6 May, 27 May, 8 July 1935 B. Bond (ed.) *Chief of Staff: The Diaries of Lt-Gen Sir Henry Pownall* London: Leo Cooper, 1972 pp. 66–67, 69, 71, 73, 74–75.
68 Headlam Mss: diary, 7, 10, 11 September 1937; A. Roberts *Holy Fox: A Biography of Edward Halifax* London: Weidenfeld and Nicolson, 1991 pp. 70–74; Leo Amery Diary 13 August 1935, J. Barnes and D. Nicholson (eds) *Empire At Bay: The Leo Amery Diaries* London: Hutchinson, 1990 p. 397.
69 D.S. Birn *League of Nations Union, 1918–45* Oxford: Clarendon Press, 1981.
70 J.A. Maiolo *The Royal Navy and Nazi Germany, 1933–39: A Study in Appeasement and the Origins of the Second World War* Basingstoke: Palgrave, 1998, chapter 1.
71 C. Bloch 'Great Britain, German rearmament and the naval agreement of 1935' in H.W. Gatzke (ed.) *European Diplomacy Between Two Wars, 1919–39* Chicago: Quadrangle Books, 1972 p. 149.
72 T. Hoerber 'Psychology and reasoning in the Anglo–German naval agreement 1935–39' *Historical Journal* 52, 1 (2009) pp. 153–74; C.M. Scammell 'The Royal

Navy and the strategic origins of the Anglo–German naval agreement of 1935' *Journal of Strategic Studies* 20, 2 (1997) pp. 92–118.

73 U. Bailer *Shadow of the Bomber: The Fear of Air Attack and British Politics* London: Royal Historical Society, 1981; M. Smith *British Air Strategy Between the Wars* Oxford: Clarendon Press, 1984.

74 Bell *France and Britain* pp. 161–62. In May 1922 Balfour suggested 75 tons of bombs per day indefinitely; in June 1923 the Salisbury Committee suggested 168 tons of bombs on London in first day before settling down to 84 tons per day.

75 Channon diary 17 December 1935 R.R. James (ed.) *Chips: The Diaries of Sir Henry Channon* London: Weidenfeld and Nicolson, 1969 pp. 48–49; Jones diary 14 January 1936 K. Middlemas (ed.) *Thomas Jones: Whitehall Diary vol 3* Oxford: Oxford University Press, 1969 p. 161; D. Waley *British Public Opinion and the Abyssinian War* London: Temple Smith, 1975 p. 65; J. Barnes and K. Middlemas *Baldwin: A Biography* London: Weidenfeld and Nicolson, 1969 p. 890.

76 Winterton Mss: diary 17 March 1936 1/41; Amery diary 17 March 1936 Barnes and Nicolson *Amery Diaries* p. 410; Bernays diary 17 March 1936 N. Smart (ed.) *The Diaries of Robert Bernays, 1932–39: An Insider's Account of the House of Commons* Lampeter: Edwin Mellon Press, 1996 p. 247; TNA CAB23/83(36) ff. 291–92 11 March 1936.

77 Austen Chamberlain to Hilda Chamberlain 15 March 1936 Self (ed.) *Austen Chamberlain Diary Letters* pp. 502–3.

78 *Hansard* vol. 309 col. 1492, 23 March 1936 (W.W. Astor).

79 TNA: Cab 23/83 24(36), 25 March 1936, ff. 380–81.

80 Chamberlain Mss: diary 17 June 1936. cited K. Feiling *Life of Neville Chamberlain* London: Macmillan, 1946 p. 296.

81 A. Crozier *Appeasement and Germany's Last Bid for Colonies* London: Macmillan, 1988.

82 TNA: Plymouth Report, Committee of Imperial Defence: Transfer of a Colonial Mandate to Germany: report of a sub-committee, 9 June 1936, CID paper no. 1236-B, Cab4/24.

83 K. Hildebrand *The Foreign Policy of the Third Reich* Berkeley: University of California Press, 1973 pp. 38–41.

84 T. Buchanan *The Spanish Civil War and the British Labour Movement* Cambridge: Cambridge University Press, 1991; T. Buchanan *Britain and the Spanish Civil War* Cambridge: Cambridge University Press, 1997; and N.J. Crowson *Facing Fascism: The Conservative Party and the European Dictators, 1935–40* London: Routledge, 1997, pp. 33–35, 77–80, 208–9.

85 D. Little 'Red scare, 1936: Anti-bolshevism and the origins of British non-intervention in the Spanish Civil War', *Journal of Contemporary History* 23 (1988), pp. 291–311.

86 Channon dairy 14 September 1936 James (ed.) *Chips*, p. 113.

87 G. Stone 'Britain, France and the Spanish problem 1936–39' in D. Richardson and G. Stone (eds) *Decisions and Diplomacy: Essays in Twentieth Century International History* London: Routledge, 1995 pp. 129–52; For impact in Britain see K. Watkin *Britain Divided: The Effect of the Spanish Civil War on British Public Opinion* London: Nelson, 1963; T. Buchanan *The Impact of the Spanish Civil War on Britain: War, Loss and Memory* Eastborne: Sussex Academic Press, 2007.

88 P. Dennis *Decision by Default: Peacetime Conscription and British Defence, 1919–39* London: Kegan Paul, 1972 p. 106.

89 Halifax in Cabinet 22 December 1937 cited G. Peden 'A matter of timing: The economic background to British foreign policy' *History* 69, 1 (1984) p. 26.

90 *Hansard* 7 March 1938 Neville Chamberlain.

91 P. Kennedy *Realities behind Diplomacy* 1981 p. 272.
92 P. Stafford 'Political autobiography and the art of the plausible: R.A. Butler at the Foreign Office 1938–39' *Historical Journal* 28, 4 (1985) p. 903.
93 For example Crozier *Germany's Last Bid* p. 225; A. R. Peters *Anthony Eden at the Foreign Office* Aldershot: Gower, 1986, pp. 285–95, suggests the rift had emerged between August and September 1937 over Chamberlain's attempt to restart talks with Italy.
94 On USA policy see R. Dallek *Franklin D. Roosevelt and American Foreign Policy* Oxford: Oxford University Press, 1979; C. MacDonald *The United States, Britain and Appeasement 1936–39* London: Macmillan, 1981; on Soviet policy see J. Haslam *The Soviet Union and the Struggle for Collective Security in Europe 1933–39* London: Macmillan, 1984.
95 Crowson *Facing Fascism* pp. 84–87; S. Ball *Guardsmen* London: HarperCollins, 2004 pp. 162–70.
96 Avon Mss: Mark Patrick to Anthony Eden 22 March 1938, AP14/1/796; Mark Patrick to Anthony Eden, 25 March 1938, AP14/1/797.
97 *Hansard* vol. 333 cols 1399–1413, 24 March 1938.
98 *Documents on British Foreign Policy* 3rd Series, I 349, 26–27 May 1938, 403–12.
99 Cuthbert Headlam Diaries September 1938 D/He/34; Chiefs of Staff assessment: see TNA: 'Note on the question of whether it would be in our military advantage to fight Germany now or to postpone the issue' Ismay to CID 20 September 1938 Cab21/544 14/2/51.
100 E.L. Woodward and R. Butler (eds) *Documents on British Foreign Policy* 3rd series, vol. II, London: HMSO, 1949 'Note of conversation between PM and Hitler, 30 September 1938' Dr Schmidt pp. 635–40.
101 R. Butler *The Art of the Possible* London: Hamish Hamilton, 1971 p. 73; see also Lord Templewood (Samuel Hoare) *Nine Troubled Years* London: Collins, 1954; E. Goldstein and I. Lukes (eds) *Munich 1938: Prelude to World War Two* Newbury: Cass, 1999.
102 Makins Mss: diary 6 October 1938.
103 *Daily Telegraph* 28 May 1992.
104 See Crowson *Facing Fascism* pp. 96–113.
105 Cited Hoerber 'Psychology and reasoning' p. 167.
106 TNA: Cabinet Committee on Foreign Policy, conclusions of meetings, 23, 26 January 1939, pp. 102, 109–15, 133–48, FP(36), Cab27/624.
107 Dennis *Decision by Default.*
108 D.C. Watt *How War Came: The Immediate Origins of the Second World War 1938–39* London: Heinemann, 1989, p. 166.
109 *Hansard* vol. 346 cols 1109–14, 26 April 1939 (Chamberlain).
110 See S. Newman *March 1939: The British Guarantee to Poland* Oxford: Clarendon Press, 1976; A. Prazmowska *Britain, Poland and the Eastern Front, 1939* Cambridge: Cambridge University Press, 1987.
111 Cited Stafford 'Political autobiography' p. 912.
112 Bell *France and Britain* p. 221.
113 Crowson *Facing Fascism* chapter 5.
114 Selborne Mss 'The relative situation in Sept. 1938 and Sept. 1939' MS.Eng.hist. c.1015 ff 13–27; Paul Emrys-Evans to Wolmer, 21 November 1939, MS.Eng.hist. c.1014 ff221–24.
115 W.S. Churchill *Arms and the Covenant* London: Cassell, 1938 p. 451.
116 Prazmowski *Britain, Poland* pp. 40–60.
117 Watt *How War Came* p. 331.
118 Neilson *Britain, Soviet Russia.*
119 Amery diary 19 May 1939 Barnes and Nicolson (eds) *Empire at Bay* p. 553; Channon diary 13 April, 5 May 1939 James (ed.) *Chips* pp. 193, 197.

120 Chamberlain Mss: Neville to Hilda, 28 May 1939, NC18/1/1101.
121 Avon Mss: Eden to Cranborne 12 July 1939 AP14/2/28.
122 Headlam Mss: Diary 17 August 1939, D/He/35.
123 C.A. MacDonald 'Economic appeasement and the German "moderates" 1937–39' *Past and Present* 56, 1 (1972) pp. 107–8, 115–16, 117.
124 B.J. Wendt ' "Economic appeasement" A crisis strategy' in W.J. Mommsen and L. Kettenacker (eds) *The Fascist Challenge and the Policy of Appeasement* London: Allen and Unwin, 1983 pp. 157–72.
125 S. Aster *1939: The Making of the Second World War* London: Simon and Schuster, 1974 pp. 243–59.
126 Stafford 'Political autobiography'.
127 Channon diary 22 August 1939 James (ed.) *Chips* p. 208.
128 A.M. Cienciala 'The Nazi-Soviet pact of August 23 1939: When did Stalin decide to align with Hitler and was Poland the culprit?' in Biskupski, M.B.B. (ed.) Ideology, Politics and Diplomacy in East Central Europe Rochester, NY: Rochester University Press, 2003 pp. 147–226.
129 Stafford 'R.A. Butler' p. 920.
130 R.A.C. Parker 'British government and the coming of war with Germany, 1939' in M.R.D. Foot (ed.) *War and Society: Historical Essays in Honour and Memory of J. R. Western, 1928–1971* London: Barnes and Noble, 1973 pp. 3–15.
131 *Hansard: House of Commons Debates 5th Series* vol. 350, col. 297, 3 Sept. 1939.
132 T.P.H. Beamish Mss: autobiographical notes, 2 September 1939, BEAM3/3, Churchill College Cambridge.
133 Brooks diary 4 September 1939 N.J. Crowson (ed.) *Fleet Street, Press Barons and Politics: The Journals of Collin Brooks* Cambridge: Royal Historical Society, 1998 p. 254.
134 A. Shlaim *Britain and the Origins of European Unity 1940–51* Reading: University of Reading Graduate School of Contemporary European Studies, 1978 p. 19.
135 See J. Charmley *Splendid Isolation: Britain and the Balance of Power 1874–1914* London: Hodder and Stoughton, 1999.
136 P. Kennedy 'The tradition of appeasement in British foreign policy 1895–1939' *British Journal of International Studies* 2, 3 (1976) pp. 195–215; P. Kennedy *The Realities Behind Diplomacy* London: Fontana, 1981 chs 5–6; see also P.W. Schroeder 'Munich and the British tradition' *Historical Journal* 19, 1 (1976) pp. 223–43.
137 This is developed further in Crowson *Facing Fascism*.
138 Chamberlain Mss: a pamphlet published by the *Bournemouth Guardian* called 'The vindication of Great Britain and strategic facts by Brigadier-General Sir Henry Page-Croft', NC 8/34/57. I am grateful to my MA student Jamie Perry for drawing my attention to this.

2 The post-war settlement 1940–61

1 Cadogan diary 2 August 1945 D. Dilks (ed.) *The Diaries of Sir Alexander Cadogan* London: Cassell, 1971 p. 778.
2 31 December 2006 Britain made last payment of $83 million. *Hansard* 3 May 2007, vol. 459 col. 1726 Ivan Lewis written answer; *Daily Telegraph* 'Business comment' 30 December 2006.
3 R. Bullen and M. Pelly (eds) *Documents on British Policy Overseas* 2nd series, vol II, London: HMSO, 1987 Document 33 p. 115.
4 For discussion of Britain's war aims see N.J. Crowson *Facing Fascism: The Conservative Party and the European Dictators 1935–40* London: Routledge, 1997 pp. 181–85, and of fall of Chamberlain pp. 185–97.

5 R.A.C. Parker *The Second World War: A Short History* Oxford: Oxford University Press, 2001; J.H. Bradley (series editor) *The Second World War: Asia and the Pacific* Garden City Park, NY: Square One, 2003; *The Second World War: Europe and the Mediterranean* Garden City Park, NY: Square One, 2002.

6 A.J. Lane and H. Temperley (eds) *The Rise and Fall of the Grand Alliance 1941–45* Basingstoke: Macmillan, 1995; D. Reynolds 'The "Big Three" and the division of Europe 1945–49' *Diplomacy and Statecraft* 1, 2 (1990) pp. 111–36; D. Reynolds *From World War to Cold War: Churchill, Roosevelt and the International History of the 1940s* Oxford: Oxford University Press, 2006.

7 V. Antonio and E. Calandri (eds) *The Failure of Peace in Europe 1943–48* Basingstoke: Palgrave, 2002; G.R. Hughes *Britain, Germany and the Cold War: The Search for a European Détente 1949–67* London: Routledge, 2007.

8 TNA: Joint Declaration by the President and Prime Minster 12 August 1941, PREM. The meeting with Roosevelt is described M. Gilbert *Winston S. Churchill VI 1939–1941* London: Heinemann, 1983 pp. 1154–68.

9 10 November 1942, Churchill's Guildhall speech, cited J. Charmley *Churchill: End of Glory: A Political Biography* London: Hodder and Stoughton, 1993, p. 431.

10 Dalton diary 23 February 1945 B. Pimlott (ed.) *The Second World War Diary of Hugh Dalton* London: Jonathan Cape, 1986 p. 836.

11 D. Reynolds *Summits: Six Meetings that Shaped the Twentieth Century* London: Allen Lane, 2007 pp. 103–62; A. Prazmowska *History of Poland* London: Palgrave Macmillan, 2006; M. Kitchen 'Winston Churchill and the Soviet Union during the Second World War' *Historical Journal* 30, 2 (1987) pp. 415–36.

12 Collin Brooks Mss: unpublished diary 8 May 1945.

13 P. Duignan and L.H. Gann *The United States and the New Europe 1945–93* Oxford: Blackwell, 1994 p. 38.

14 M. Lojko 'The failed handshake over the Danube: The story of Anglo–American involvement in the liberation of Central Europe at the end of the Second World War' *Hungarian Quarterly* 41 (2000) pp. 104–11; K. Salisbury 'British policy and German unity at the end of the Second World War' *English Historical Review* 94 (1979) pp. 786–804.

15 A. Deighton *The Impossible Peace: Britain, the Division of Germany and the Origins of the Cold War*, Oxford: Clarendon Press, 1993 p. 30.

16 T. Parrish *Berlin in the Balance 1945–49* Reading, MA: Perseus Books, 1998; M.D. Haydock *City under Seige: The Berlin Blockade and Airlift 1948–9* London: Brassey's, 1999.

17 Churchill's speech to Fulton College, Missouri, USA 5 March 1946.

18 L.H. Ismay *The Memoirs of Lord Ismay* London: Heinemann, 1960.

19 For British political reactions to civil war see A. Thorpe '"In a rather emotional state" The Labour Party and British intervention in Greece 1944–45' *English Historical Review* 21 (2006) pp. 1015–1105 and G.M. Alexander *The Prelude to the Truman Doctrine: British Policy in Greece 1944–47* Oxford: Clarendon Press, 1982.

20 M. P. Leffler *A Preponderance of Power: National Security, the Truman Administration and the Cold War* Stanford, CA: Stanford University Press, 1992.

21 T. Judt *Postwar: A History of Europe since 1945* London: William Heinemann, 2005 p. 85; see also S. Cox *The Strategic Air War Against Germany 1939–45: Report of the British Bombing Survey Unit* London: Frank Cass, 1997.

22 E. D. Nolfo 'The United States, Europe and the Marshall Plan' in A. Varsori and E. Calandri (eds) *The Failure of Peace in Europe 1943–48* Basingstoke: Palgrave, 2000, pp. 288–96; M. Schain (ed.) *The Marshall Plan: Fifty Years After* Basingstoke: Palgrave, 2001.

23 Duignan and Gann *The United States* p. 40.

24 *Foreign Relations of the United States (FRUS)* 1947, vol III (1972) p. 230, Memorandum by W. Clayton, Assistant Secretary of State, 'The European crisis' 27 May 1947.

25 Duignan and Gann *The United States* p. 41.

26 See A.S. Milward *The Reconstruction of Western Europe* London: Methuen, 1984 for OEEC.

27 'Market imperialism' borrowed from V. De Grazia *Irresistible Empire: America's Advance through 20th Century Europe* Cambridge, MA: Belknap Press, 2005; As for the impact of Marshall on the one hand Alan Milward is generally dismissive of the impact of America on Europe's recovery and economy, whereas Michael J. Hogan credits the US with some success at revitalising Europe's in its image. M.J. Hogan *The Marshall Plan: America, Britain and the Reconstruction of Western Europe 1947–52* Cambridge: Cambridge University Press, 1987.

28 W.M. Scammell *The International Economy since 1945* London: Macmillan, 2nd edn 1983 p. 120; J. Tomlinson 'Marshall Aid and the "shortage economy" in Britain in the 1940s' *Contemporary European History* 9, 1 (2000) pp. 137–55; T. Geiger and B. Kenner (eds) *Ireland, Europe and the Marshall Plan* Dublin: Four Courts, 2004.

29 A.S. Milward *The Rise and Fall of a National Strategy 1945–63* vol. 1 London: Frank Cass, 2002 p. 23.

30 Milward *Rise and Fall* vol. 1 p. 37.

31 Dalton diary 13 June 1947 B. Pimlott (ed.) *Political Diary of Hugh Dalton* London: Cape, 1986 p. 394.

32 For example Headlam diary 11 February 1947 S. Ball (ed.) *Parliament and Politics in the Age of Churchill and Attlee: The Headlam Diaries 1935–1951* Cambridge: Cambridge University Press/RHS, 1999, p. 487.

33 Similarly the Bretton Woods agreements had provided parliamentary hostility with 47 Conservatives opposing the first reading and 74 the second, S. Onslow *Backbench Debate within the Conservative Party and its Influence on British Foreign Policy* Basingstoke: Macmillan, 1997 p. 243.

34 C.R. Schenk *Britain and the Sterling Area: From Devaluation to Convertibility in the 1950s* London: Routledge, 1994.

35 D.W. Urwin *The Community of Europe: A History of European Integration since 1945* Harlow: Longman, 1991 pp. 7–12; A.J. Zurcher *The Struggle to Unite Europe 1940–58* New York: New York University Press, 1958.

36 Avi Shlaim characterises this offer as 'an utterly exceptional incident born of intense crisis.' p. 31 *Britain and the Origins of European Unity 1940–51* Reading: University of Reading Graduate School of Contemporary European Studies, 1978, see also A. Shlaim 'Prelude to downfall: The British offer of union to France, June 1940' *Journal of Contemporary History* 9, 3 (1974) pp. 26–63.

37 A. Eden [Lord Avon] *The Reckoning*, London: Cassell, 1965 p. 74.

38 Dodds-Parker Mss: Dodds-Parker to Edward Heath, 29 November 1967, MC: P2/7/3C/1 Magdalen College Archive, Oxford; BOAPAH: Maclay interview, LSE; another example would be Percy Grieve MP for Solihull *Daily Telegraph* obituary, August 1998.

39 M. Beloff 'Churchill and Europe' in R. Blake and Wm R. Louis (eds) *Churchill* Oxford: Oxford University Press, 1993, pp. 446–47.

40 R.R. James (ed.) *Complete Speeches of Winston Churchill 1897–1963* vol. VII, New York: Chelsea House, 1974.

41 M. Beloff 'Churchill and Europe' pp. 444–45, e.g. *Marlborough: His Life and Times, The World Crisis* London: George Harrap, 1933.

42 Conservative Party Archive: Foreign affairs committee, 3 June 1948, CRD2/43/1.

43 *Hansard*, vol. 468, col. 2204, 17 November 1949, Bevin.

44 H. Macmillan *Riding the Storm* London: Macmillan, 1971, p. 65.

45   A. Bullock *Ernest Bevin: Foreign Secretary 1945–51* vol. 3 London: Heinemann, 1983.
46   *Hansard* vol. 446, cols 398–99, 22 January 1948, Bevin.
47   Cooper diary 22 September 1947 J.J. Norwich (ed.) *The Duff Cooper Diaries* London: Weidenfeld and Nicolson, 2005 p. 449.
48   P.H. Spaak *The Continuing Battle: Memoirs of a European 1936–66* London: Weidenfeld and Nicolson, 1971 pp. 143, 145.
49   Woolton Mss: Woolton to Churchill n.d. July 1948 box 2.
50   J. Schnear 'Hopes deferred or shattered: The British Labour left and the Third Force Movement 1945–49' *Journal of Modern History* 56, 2 (1984) pp. 197–226.
51   D. Reynolds *Britannia Overruled: British Policy and World Power in the 20th Century* London: Longman, 1991 p. 195.
52   S. Greenwood *Britain and European Cooperation since 1945* Oxford: Blackwell, 1992, p. 24.
53   J. McKay *Labour Party Attitudes to European Integration 1945–75* unpublished Ph.D. University of Birmingham 2006 p. 52.
54   Milward *Rise and Fall* p. 33.
55   Milward *Rise and Fall* p. 34.
56   Broad *Labour's Dilemma* pp. 12–13.
57   Onslow *Backbench* p. 42.
58   Broad *Labour's Dilemma* p. 17.
59   Bullock *Ernest Bevin* p. 659; for Labour views of the delegations see H. Morrison *An Autobiography* London: Odhams, 1960 p. 279.
60   N.J. Crowson *The Conservative Party and European Integration* London: Routledge, 1996 p. 198.
61   Macmillan Mss: Harold to Dorothy, 22 August 1949, letter 2 MS.Macmillan. dep.c.11./1ff37–38.
62   R.M. Douglas *The Labour Party, Nationalism and Internationalism, 1939–51* London: Routledge, 2004 p. 252 fn 145.
63   Onslow *Backbench* pp. 46–47, 247.
64   C. Archer *Organizing Europe: The Institutions of Integration* London: Arnold, 1994 p. 64.
65   Bevin had vetoed Spaak's appointment as chair of OEEC, Spaak *Continuing Battle* p. 196.
66   Douglas *Labour Party* p. 252 fn 144.
67   J. Pinder and R. Mayne *Federal Union: The Pioneers: A History of Federal Union* Basingstoke: Macmillan, 1990 p. 103.
68   J. Monnet *Memoirs* London: Collins, 1978 pp. 325–26.
69   Spaak *Continuing Battle* pp. 219–25.
70   Lord Birkenhead cited in Onslow *Backbenchers* p. 71.
71   J. Grahl 'A fateful decision? Labour and the Schuman Plan' in J. Fyrth (ed.) *Labour's High Noon: The Government and the Economy 1945–51* London: Lawrence and Wishart, 1993 pp. 148–62; J.W. Young 'The Schuman Plan and the British Association' in J. Young (ed.) *The Foreign Policy of Churchill's Peacetime Administration* Leicester: Leicester University Press, 1988 pp. 109–34; A.W. Lovett 'The United States and the Schuman Plan: A study in French diplomacy 1950–52' *The Historical Journal* 39, 2 (1996) pp. 425–55.
72   Cited in E. Dell *The Schuman Plan and the British Abdication of Leadership in Europe* Oxford: Clarendon Press, 1995 p. 23.
73   Unfortunately there is still no biography of Schuman in English.
74   Dell *Schuman Plan* p. 4.
75   Reynolds *Britannia Overruled* p. 194.
76   S. Greenwood 'Bevin, France and Western union' *European History Quarterly* 14 (1984) pp. 332–33.

77　Milward *Rescue of Nation State* pp. 401–4.
78　Onslow *Backbench* pp. 57–69.
79　Crowson *European Integration* p. 20.
80　Monnet *Memoirs* pp. 325–26.
81　C. Lord *Absent at the Creation: Britain and the Formation of the European Community 1950–52* Aldershot: Dartmouth, 1996 p. 147.
82　W. Wallace 'Defence: The defence of sovereignty or the defence of Germany?' in R. Moran and C. Bray (eds) *Partners and Rivals in Western Europe: Britain, France and Germany* Aldershot: Gower, 1986 pp. 230–32.
83　Crowson *European Integration* p. 22.
84　Maxwell Fyfe quote from H. Macmillan *Tides of Fortune: 1945–55* London: Macmillan, 1969 p. 463; Lord Kilmuir *Political Adventure* London: Weidenfeld and Nicolson, 1964 p. 187.
85　Lord *Absent at the Creation* pp. 148–49.
86　O. Daddow (ed.) *Harold Wilson and European Integration* London: Frank Cass, 2003 p. 4.
87　Onslow *Backbench* p. 82; Macmillan diary 24 October 1954 P. Catterall (ed.) *Macmillan Diaries: The Cabinet Years 1950–57* London: Macmillan, 2003 p. 363; N. Piers Ludlow *Dealing With Britain* Cambridge: Cambridge University Press, 1997 p. 19.
88　H.P. Spaak *The Continuing Battle: Memoirs of a European* London: Little, Brown, 1971; M. Charlton *Price of Victory* London: BBC Books, 1983.
89　Catterall *Macmillan Diaries* p. 517n. For a possible explanation see P. Catterall 'Macmillan and Europe 1950–56: The Cold War, the American context and the British approaches to European integration' *Cercles* 5 (2002) pp. 103–6.
90　W. Kaiser *Using Europe, Abusing the Europeans* Basingstoke: Macmillan, 1996 p. 35.
91　Kaiser *Using Europe* pp. 30–31, 43 (quote), 48, 59.
92　Macmillan Mss: diary, 14 December 1955, MS.Macmillan.dep.d.20.
93　Wm R. Louis and R. Owen (eds) *Suez 1956: The Crisis and its Consequences* Oxford: Clarendon Press, 1989; W.S. Lucas *Divided We Stand: Britain, the United States and the Suez Crisis* London: Hodder and Stoughton, 1991.
94　W. Kaiser and G. Staerck　*British Foreign Policy 1955–64* Basingstoke: Macmillan, 1989; Kaiser *Using Europe* pp. 48–49.
95　Kaiser *Using Europe* pp. 51–53.
96　Macmillan Mss: diary, 14 December 1955, MS.Macmillan.dep.d.20.
97　Kaiser, *Using Europe* p. 53, see Macmillan's actions as 'logical'.
98　J. Ellision *Threatening Europe: Britain and the Creation of the European Community 1955–58* Basingstoke: Macmillan, 2000 p. 8.
99　J. Ellision 'A grand design? Selwyn Lloyd, the Foreign Office and the question of Europe 1955–57' paper presented to Twentieth Century History seminar, University of Birmingham, 9 December 1998.
100　H. Macmillan *Riding the Storm 1956–59* London: Macmillan, 1971 p. 246.
101　L. Baston *Reggie: The Life of Reginald Maudling* Stroud: Sutton, 2004.
102　M. Camps *Britain and the European Community 1955–1963* Oxford: Oxford University Press, 1964 pp. 509–10, 517.
103　Ellision *Threatening Europe.*
104　Camps *European Community* p. 172.
105　Kaiser *Using Europe* pp. 72–87; Young *Britain and European Unity* p. 171; Milward *The European Rescue of the Nation State* London: Routledge, 1992 p. 433.
106　Ellison *Threatening Europe.*
107　R. Griffiths 'A slow one hunderd and eight degree turn: British policy towards the Common Market, 1955–60' in G. Wiles (ed.) *Britain's Failure to Enter the*

European Community 1961–63 London: Frank Cass, 1997; R. Lamb *The Macmillan Years 1957–63* London: John Murray, 1995 p. 102.

108 Charlton *The Price of Victory.*
109 Crowson *European Integration* p. 26.
110 A detailed narrative of these negotiations can be found in M. Camps *Britain and the European Community* chapter 7.
111 *Hansard* House of Commons vol. 599 cols 1368–1494 12 February 1959.
112 *Hansard* House of Commons vol. 615 cols 1055–1180 14 December 1959.
113 Camps *Britain and the European Community* pp. 184–209.
114 Camps *Britain and the European Community* p. 278.
115 *Hansard* House of Lords, vol. 224 cols 855–67, quote col. 867 (Boothby) 30 June 1960.

3 The application phase 1961–75

1 E.g. A. Sked and C. Cook *Post-war Britain: A Political History* Harmondsworth: Penguin, 1990 pp. 168–69.
2 *Hansard* House of Lords 3 August 1961, vol. 234 cols 246–54 (Chando – who was making his maiden speech), rest of debate cols 217–80. Miriam Camps considered Chando's contribution to be the 'one of the best speeches made on the subject' of supporting entry, *Britain and the European Community 1955–63* Oxford: Oxford University Press, 1964 p. 365.
3 G. Wilson *Special Interests and Policy Making: Agricultural Politics and Politics in Britain and the United States of America* London: Wiley, 1977 pp. 22, 27.
4 Macmillan Mss: diary, 21 August 1962; Macmillan Ministerial Mss: Butler to Macmillan, 1 September [1961] MS. Macmillan.dep.c.310 ff. 226–27.
5 Kaiser suggests the EEC application was tactical to secure US support for a UK independent nuclear role. W. Kaiser *Using Europe, Abusing the Europeans* Basingstoke: Macmillan, 1996.
6 O. Daddow (ed.) *Harold Wilson and European Integration: Britain's Second Application to Join the EEC* London: Frank Cass, 2003 p. 3.
7 Kaiser *Using Europe* p. 110.
8 Camps, *European Community* p. 231.
9 P. Walker *Staying Power: An Autobiography* London: Bloomsbury, 1991, pp. 30–31. A. May (ed.) *Britain, the Commonwealth and Europe* Basingstoke: Palgrave, 2001.
10 C. Lord *British Entry to the European Community under the Heath Government of 1970–1974* Aldershot: Dartmouth, 1993 p. 16.
11 R. Aldous and S. Lee (eds) *Harold Macmillan and Britain's World Role* London: Macmillan, 1996 p. 142.
12 R. Broad *Labour's European Dilemma* p. 35.
13 E.g. view offered by S. Greenwood *Britain and European Co-operation since 1945* Oxford: Blackwell, 1992 pp. 82–83.
14 Selwyn Lloyd to Council of Europe Consultative Assembly January 1960; and John Profumo to WEU Assembly June 1960.
15 Camps *European Community* p. 281.
16 Macmillan Cabinet Papers on-line CAB 128/35 21 July 1961 ff 262–65; 24 July 1961 ff 274–75.
17 Kaiser *Using Europe* pp. 138–39.
18 *Hansard* vol. 645 cols 928–42, 31 July 1961 (Macmillan).
19 S. George *An Awkward Partner: Britain in the European Community* Oxford: Oxford University Press, 2nd edn, 1994 p. 33 citing the *Guardian.*
20 J. Moon *European Integration in British Politics 1950–63: A Study in Issue Change* Aldershot: Gower, 1985 pp. 59, 155, 165.

21 *Hansard* 5th series vol. 645 cols 1477–1606, 1651–1786, 2–3 August 1961.
22 Hinchingbrooke Mss: 'Note of conversation with PM in Smoking Room of House of Commons 18 July 1961', D/MAP265.
23 J. McKay *Labour Party Attitudes to European Integration 1945–1975* unpublished Ph.D., University of Birmingham, 2006; R. Broad *Labour's European Dilemma: From Bevin to Blair* Basingstoke: Palgrave, 2001; and N.J. Crowson *Conservative Party and European Integration since 1945* London: Routledge, 2006.
24 See R. Broad *Labour's European Dilemma* pp. 40–47.
25 See Crowson, *European Integration* chapter 4 'The Conservative Europeanist'; see also A. Forester *Euroscepticism in Contemporary British Politics: Opposition to Europe in the British Conservative and Labour Parties since 1945* London: Routledge, 2002.
26 Hinchingbrooke Mss: Common Market Committee D/MAP283.
27 Macmillan Mss: diary, 5 August 1961, MS. Macmillan.dep.d.43 f. 17.
28 See Avon Mss: Avon to Turton, 20 June 1960, AP23/64/25A; see also D. Dutton *Anthony Eden: A Life and Reputation* London: Arnold, 1997 chapter 10 'Eden and Europe'.
29 Camps *European Community* p. 368.
30 McKay *Labour Party Attitudes* pp. 102–3.
31 For example Kaiser, *Using Europe*; N.P. Ludlow *Dealing with Britain: The Six and the First UK Application to the EEC* Cambridge: Cambridge University Press, 1997.
32 McKay *Labour Party Attitudes* p. 146.
33 *Conservative Party Conference Report* 1962, p. 53, *Archives of British Conservative Party* Harvester, card no. 24.
34 D. Dutton 'Anticipating Maastricht: The Conservative Party and Britain's first application to join the European Community' *Contemporary Record* 7, 3 (1993) pp. 527–28.
35 N.J. Crowson 'Lord Hinchingbrooke, Europe and the November 1962 South Dorset by-election' *Contemporary British History* 17, 3 (2003) pp. 43–64.
36 Polling data derived from A. King and R. Wybrow (eds) *British Political Opinion: The Gallup Polls* London: Politicos, 2001, ch. 15; R.J. Leiber *British Politics and European Unity: Parties, Elites and Pressure Groups* Berkeley: University of California Press, 1970 p. 207; Dutton 'Anticipating Maastricht' pp. 527–28.
37 Macmillan Ministerial Papers: Macmillan to Wyndham, 21 October 1962, MS. Macmillan.dep.c.353 ff337–38.
38 Camps *European Community*.
39 J.A. Ramsden *The Winds of Change: Macmillan to Heath 1957–1975*, London: Longman, 1995 p. 170.
40 Macmillan Ministerial Mss: Macmillan to Wyndham, 21 October 1962, MS.Macmillan.dep.c.353 ff. 337–38.
41 J. Lacouture *De Gaulle: The Ruler 1945–70* London: Collins Harvill, 1991, English trans. pp. 357, 376.
42 U. Kitzinger (ed.) *The European Common Market and Community* London: Routledge, 1967 pp. 182–94; U. Kitzinger *Second Try* Oxford: Pergamon Press, 1968 pp. 311–17.
43 *Conservative Campaign Guide 1964* p. 469, Archives of British Conservative Party microfiche card 463; Conservative Party Report 1963 p. 88 (Meyer) ABCP microfiche card 27.
44 Macmillan Mss: diary 16 July 1963 MS.Macmillan dep.d.49; TNA: Cab128/37 CC59, 8 October 1963, FO371/169, memo Paris Embassy to FO, 11 June 1963.

45 W. Wallace 'Defence: The defence of sovereignty, or the defence of Germany?' in R. Morgan and C. Bray (eds) *Partners and Rivals in Western Europe: Britain, France and Germany* Aldershot: Gower, 1986 pp. 230–32.

46 P. Ludlow 'Challenging French leadership in Europe: Germany, Italy and the Netherlands and the outbreak of the Empty Chair crisis 1965–66' *Contemporary European History* 8, 2 (1999) pp. 231–48.

47 N. Rollings 'British industry and European integration 1961–73: From first application to final membership' *Business and Economic History* 27, 2 (1998) pp. 444–54.

48 Moon *European Integration* pp. 189–93; Leiber *British Politics and European Unity* pp. 52–54; T. Bromund 'Whitehall, the National Farmers' Union and Plan G 1956–57' *Contemporary British History* 15, 2 (2001) pp. 76–97.

49 R.J. Leiber 'Interest groups and political integration: British entry into Europe' *The American Political Science Review* 66, 1 (1972) pp. 53–67; A. McKinlay, H. Mercer and N. Rollings 'Reluctant Europeans? The Federation of British Industries and European Integration' *Business History* 42, 4 (2000) pp. 91–116.

50 R. Broad *Labour's European Dilemma* pp. 59–61; C. Archer *Organizing Europe: The Institutions of Integration* London: Edward Arnold, 1994 p. 66.

51 K. Middlemas *Orchestrating Europe: The Informal Politics of European Union 1973–1995* London: Fontana, 1997 p. 723.

52 D. Butler and A. King *The British General Election of 1966* London: Macmillan, 1966 p. 103.

53 *Hansard* vol. 735 col. 1539 10 November 1966 (Wilson).

54 Cited P. Gliddon 'The British Foreign Office and domestic propaganda on the European Community, 1960–72' *Contemporary British History* 23, 2 (2009) p. 161.

55 D. Jay *Change and Fortune* London: Hutchinson, 1980 pp. 360–70; D. Evans *While Britain Slept: The Selling of the Common Market* London: Gollancz, 1975 pp. 59–71.

56 W. Wallace *Foreign Policy Process in Britain* London: RIIA, 1975 pp. 345–48.

57 Recent works on the 1967 application include H. Parr *Britain's Policy towards the European Community: Harold Wilson and Britain's World Role 1964–67* London: Routledge, 2005; and J. Toomey *Harold Wilson's EEC Application* Dublin: UCD Press, 2007.

58 Crossman diary 2 May 1967 R. Crossman *Diaries of A Cabinet Minister 2* London: Hamish Hamilton, 1976 pp. 336, 340.

59 Crossman diary 9 May 1967 Crossman *Diaries 2* p. 349.

60 Gliddon 'British Foreign Office' p. 162.

61 Broad *Labour's European Dilemma* pp. 65–66.

62 The 'mediocrity and parochialism' of Commonwealth leaders is said to have hastened Wilson's conversion, Broad *Labour's European Dilemma* p. 59.

63 Parr suggests July 1966 after the sterling crisis; Young suggests before the March 1966 election, whilst biographer Ziegler believes the autumn of 1966 is the most plausible point. H. Parr 'Gone native: The Foreign Office and Harold Wilson's policy' in O. Daddow (ed.) *Harold Wilson and European Integration* London: Cass, 2003 p. 82; S. Fielding and J. Young *The Labour Governments 1964–70 Vol 2: International Policy* London: Macmillan, 1989 p. 146; P. Zeigler *Harold Wilson: The Authorized Life* London: Weidenfeld and Nicolson, 1993 p. 332.

64 J. Young *Britain and European Unity* pp. 90–91.

65 *Hansard* vol. 748 col. 1418 20 June 1967 (Wilson), rest of statement cols 1418–27.

66 For the text of De Gaulle's press conference see F. Nicholson and R. East (eds) *From the Six to the Twelve: The Enlargement of the European Communities* Harlow: Longman, 1987 pp. 52–54.

67 C. O'Neill *Britain's Entry into the European Community: Report on the Negotiations of 1970–72* London: Cass, 2000 ch. 33, para. 19 p. 337.
68 H. Wilson *The Labour Government 1964–70: A Personal Record* London: Weidenfeld and Nicolson, 1971, pp. 334–41, 407–18, quote p. 409.
69 Wallace 'Defence'.
70 D. Butler and M. Pinto-Duschinsky *The British General Election of 1970* London: Macmillan, 1970 pp. ix, 134–36.
71 All post-1945 manifestos for the main parties can be accessed online www.psr. keele.ac.uk/area/uk/man.htm. Accessed 23 January 2008. Butler and Pinto-Duschinsky *General Election of 1970*, London: Macmillan, 1971 pp. 440, 444.
72 Marten Mss: press release of Heath Speech, Paris, 5 May 1970, M.S.Eng.hist. c.1138 ff 22–31.
73 C. Lord *British Entry to the European Community* Aldershot: Dartmouth, 1993 p. 40.
74 Transcript of this meeting can be accessed www.margaretthatcher.org/archive/ heath-eec.asp. Accessed 22 April 2008.
75 For a detailed explanation of the negotiation see U. Kitzinger *Diplomacy and Persuasion: How Britain Joined the Common Market* London: Thames and Hudson, 1973.
76 Crowson *European Integration* pp. 75–76.
77 Heath's Godkin lecture cited in K. Stoddart 'Nuclear weapons in Britain's policy towards France 1960–74' *Diplomacy and Statecraft* 18, 4 (2007) pp. 719–44.
78 C. Hynes *The Year That Never Was: Heath, the Nixon Administration and the Year of Europe* Dublin: UCD Press, 2009.
79 Crowson *European Integration* p. 39.
80 Reynolds *Britannia Overruled* p. 243.
81 CPA: ORC poll 17–21 February 1971 CCO180/13/1/3; ORC poll, 30 June–4 July 1971, CCO180/13/1/6.
82 *Hansard* vol. 831 col. 650 (Howe), cols 743–52 (Heath), 17 February 1972.
83 *Daily Telegraph* Teddy Taylor to editor, 21 January 1997.
84 M. Shapiro 'The European Court of Justice' in A.M. Sbragia (ed.) *Euro-politics: Institutions and Policymaking in the 'New' European Community* Washington, DC: Brookings Institution Press, 1992 p. 123.
85 King (ed.) *British Political Opinion* p. 301.
86 R. Jowell and J.D. Spence *The Grudging Europeans* London: SCPR, 1975.
87 J. Spence 'Movements in the public mood 1961–75' in R. Jowell and G. Hoinville (eds) *Britain into Europe: Public Opinion and the EEC 1961–75* London: Croom Helm, 1976 p. 31.
88 Crowson *European Integration* pp. 40, 100.
89 Boyle Mss: memo 'Common added-value tax system' Gordon Pears CRD, 17 February 1969; CPA: B. Reading to E. Heath 15 July 1969, CRD3/7/8/1.
90 A. Geddes *The European Union and British Politics* Basingstoke: Palgrave, 2004 p. 75.
91 D. Butler and U. Kitzinger *The 1975 Referendum* London: Macmillan, 1976; Crowson *European Integration* pp. 41–44.
92 A. Forster 'Anti-Europeans, Anti-Marketeers and Eurosceptics' *Political Quarterly* 73, 3 (2002) p. 304.

4 Britain in Europe: from EEC to EU, 1975–97

1 C. Bray 'National images, the media and public opinion' in R. Morgan and C. Bray (eds) *Partners and Rivals in Western Europe: Britain, France and Germany* Aldershot: Gower, 1986 pp. 54–77.

2 S. George *Britain and European Integration since 1945* Oxford: Blackwell, 1991 p. 23.

3 W.F.W. Vanthoor *A Chronological History of the European Union* Cheltenham: Edward Elgar, 1999 p. xv.

4 The Latin translates as 'it was thought capable of command, until it commanded' and is Tacitus on Roman Emperor Galba. Thank you to my colleagues Simon Yarrow and Caterina Bruschi for the translation and source identification. *The Economist* 22 March 1982. www.coverbrowser.com/image/economist/1381-85.jpg. Accessed 15 February 2010.

5 G. Marks 'Structural policy in the European Community' in A.M. Sbragia (ed.) *Euro-politics: Institutions and Policymaking in the 'New' European Community* Washington, DC: Brookings Institution Press, 1992 p. 194n.

6 C. Archer *Organising Europe: The Institutions of Integration* London: Arnold, 1994 pp. 149–51; K. Middlemas *Orchestrating Europe: The Informal Politics of European Union 1973–1995* London: Fontana, 1995 p. 84.

7 B. Laffan *Integration and Co-operation in Europe* London: Routledge, 1992 p. 55.

8 George *European Integration* p. 24; a view concurred with by Middlemas *Orchestrating Europe* p. 71.

9 D. Healey *The Time of My Life* London: Penguin, 1990 pp. 438–39.

10 K. Burke and A. Cairncross *'Goodbye, Great Britain': The 1976 IMF Crisis* London: Yale University Press, 1992.

11 G. Howe *Conflict of Loyalty* London: Macmillan, 1994 p. 111.

12 Thatcher Foundation online archive: Nigel Lawson to Thatcher, 30 October 1978, www.margaretthatcher.org.

13 D. Butler and G. Butler (eds) *Twentieth Century British Political Facts* Basingstoke: Macmillan, 2000 p. 512.

14 J. Young *Britain and European Unity, 1945–92* Basingstoke: Macmillan, 1993 p. 130.

15 Peter Middleton, Treasury civil servant cited in H. Young *One of Us* London: Pan, 1990 pp. 185–87.

16 Middlemas *Orchestrating Europe* p. 119.

17 C. Pickering '"Sir Douglas in Euroland". Treasury officials and the European Union 1977–2001' *Public Management* 80, 3 (2002) p. 592.

18 H. Young *This Blessed Plot: Britain and Europe from Churchill to Blair* London: Macmillan, 1998 p. 314.

19 F. Pym *The Politics of Consent* London: Hamish Hamilton, 1984.

20 I. Gilmour *Dancing with Dogma* London: Simon and Schuster, 1992 p. 240.

21 M. Thatcher *Downing Street Years* London: HarperCollins, 1993 pp. 309–10.

22 D. Kavanagh *Thatcherism and British Politics* London: Macmillan, 1990 p. 268.

23 P. Lange 'Politics of the social dimension' in A.M. Sbragia (ed.) *Euro-politics: Institutions and Policymaking in the 'New' European Community* Washington, DC: Brookings Institution Press, 1992 p. 246.

24 Young *This Blessed Plot* p. 311.

25 Harold Macmillan's phrase criticising Thatcher's privatisation plans.

26 *Hansard* vol. 21 col. 1148 14 April 1982 (Thatcher).

27 L.L. Martin 'Institutions and cooperation: Sanctions during the Falklands Islands conflict' *International Security* 4, 16 (1992) pp. 143–78.

28 Thatcher *Downing Street Years* p. 548.

29 Hinchingbrooke Mss: Hinch to Robin Williams, 14 February 1983, D/MAP86 Dorset Record Office

30 Cited in R. Broad *Labour's European Dilemma: From Bevin to Blair* Basingstoke: Palgrave, 2001 p. 142.

31 S. George *Politics and Policy within the European Community* Oxford: Oxford University Press, 1985 pp. 154–66.Greece was under military dictatorship from April 1967 until July 1974; democracy only returned to Spain after the death of Franco in November 1975, although instability continued with a failed coup in 1981; Portugal remained under military rule following the death of Salazar in 1970 and only returned to democracy in 1975.

32 *Economist* 'Well heeled dwarf beside the giant', 6 December 1986, p. 62.

33 J. Lodge (ed.) *European Union: The European Community in Search of a Future* London: Macmillan, 1986.

34 *Financial Times* 20 June 1984.

35 Howe *Conflict* p. 456.

36 Votes Council of Ministers: 1981 increased to 63 (45 QMV); 1986 76 (54 QMV). Commissioners: 1981, 14; 1986, 17; European Parliament: 1979, 410 (UK, 81 same as with Ireland, France, Germany); 1981, 434 (same distribution); 1986, 518 (same distribution).

37 *Hansard* 6th series vol. 82, cols 185, 189, 190 2 July 1985 (Thatcher).

38 B. Laffan *Integraton and Co-operation in Europe* London: Routledge, 1992 p. 153.

39 Laffan *Integration* pp. 157–58.

40 *Hansard* 6th series, vol. 93, col. 346 (Anthony Kershaw), 5 March 1986.

41 C. Pickering 'Sir Douglas in Euroland' p. 586.

42 Howe *Conflict* p. 533.

43 Thatcher Foundation: speech to College of Europe, Bruges, 20 September 1988, www.margaretthatcher.org. Accessed 28 January 2008.

44 For development of this argument see S. George *An Awkward Partner: Britain in the European Community* Oxford: Oxford University Press, 1990 p. 195.

45 G. Urban *Diplomacy and Illusion in the Court of Margaret Thatcher: An Insider's View* London: I.B. Tauris, 1996 p. 151; *Spectator* 12 July 1990.

46 K. Larres 'Margaret Thatcher, the Foreign Office and German reunification' *Cercles* 5 (2002) pp. 175–82; see also Urban *Diplomacy and Illusion*.

47 *Hansard* vol. 178 col. 869, 30 October 1989 (Thatcher).

48 A. Seldon *Major: A Political Life* London: Weidenfeld and Nicolson, 1997 pp. 166–68.

49 *Hansard* vol. 199 col. 275 20 November 1991 (Major).

50 D. Hurd *Memoirs* London: Little, Brown, 2003 p. 424.

51 For further detail see Archer *Organizing Europe* pp. 239–51.

52 F. Cameron *The Foreign and Security Policy of the European Union: Past, Present and Future* Sheffield: Sheffield Academic Press, 1999 pp. 27–32; D. Owen *Balkan Odyssey* New York: Harcourt Brace, 1995; R. Holbrooke *To End a War* New York: Random House, 1998.

53 Stephens *Politics and the Pound* p. 259.

54 K. Dyson *The Politics of the Euro-Zone: Stability or Breakdown?* Oxford: Oxford University Press, 2000.

55 J. Buller 'Contesting Europeanisation: Agents, institutions and narratives in British monetary policy' *West European Politics* 29, 3 (2006) pp. 389–409.

56 P. Cowley and P. Norton 'Blair's bastards: Discontent within the PLP' *Centre for Legislative Studies Research Paper* 1/96 (1996) pp. 21–22.

57 *Hansard* vol. 240 col. 803, 29 March 1994 (Major); *Economist* 'Raise your eyes, there is a land beyond' 25 September 1993.

58 *Hansard* vol. 240 col. 802 29 March 1994 (Marlow).

59 R.J. Johnson 'The conflict over qualified majority voting in the European Union Council of Ministers' *British Journal of Political Science* 25, 2 (1995) pp. 245–54.

60 Crowson *European Integration* p. 63.

61 See also his Leiden speech September 1995 Seldon *Major* p. 486.

62 *Hansard* vol. 245 col. 944, 30 June 1994; vol. 252, col. 579, 17 January 1995.

63 R. Brookes 'Newspapers and national identity: the BSE/CJD crisis and the British press' *Media, Culture, Society* 21 (1999) pp. 259–60.
64 *Hansard* vol. 255, cols 1060–74, quote col. 1068 (Major) 1 March 1995.
65 *Independent* letter to the editor, 19 September 1996.
66 N. Gavin and D. Sanders 'The economy and voting' *Parliamentary Affairs* 50, 4 (1997) pp. 631–40.
67 www.psr.keele.ac.uk/area/uk/man.htm. Accessed 20 April 2006.
68 CPA: 'Thinking European' Michael Niblock 4 February 1972, CRD3/10/14.

5 Europe and New Labour 1997–2010

1 In the second half of the 1997 campaign 15 per cent of all media reporting on the election was about European policy, more so than any other issue. J. Turner *The Tories and Europe* Manchester: Manchester University Press, 2000 p. 209.
2 D. Butler and D. Kavanagh, *The British General Election of 1997* Basingstoke: Macmillan, 1997 plate 1.
3 *Independent* 22 April 1997 S. Helm, 'Santer scorns the "Prophets of Doom"' p. 14.
4 For an overview of the campaign see Butler and Kavanagh *General Election of 1997* pp. 105–8.
5 J. Curtice and M. Steed, 'The results analysed' in D. Butler and D. Kavanagh *The British General Election of 1997* p. 308.
6 Curtice and Steed 'The results analysed' p. 308.
7 P. Stephens, 'The Blair Government and Europe', *Political Quarterly* 2001 p. 67; J. Smith 'A missed opportunity? New Labour's European policy 1997–2005' *International Affairs* 81, 4 (2005) p. 707.
8 *Independent* 6 April 1995 P. Wynn Davies and R. Dowden 'Blair takes high ground on Europe'.
9 S. Bulmer 'New Labour, New European policy? Blair, Brown and utilitarian supranationalism' *Parliamentary Affairs* 61, 4 (2008) pp. 597–620.
10 R. Holden *The Making of New Labour's European Policy* Basingstoke: Palgrave, 2002; see also S. Fella 'New Labour, same old Britain? The Blair government and European Treaty reform' *Parliamentary Affairs* 59, 4 (2006) pp. 622–25.
11 D. Baker 'Britain and Europe: The argument continues' *Parliamentary History* 54 (2001) pp. 281–82.
12 J. Smith 'A missed opportunity? New Labour's European policy 1997–2005' *International Affairs* 81, 4 (2005) p. 706.
13 C. Hay *The Political Economy of New Labour: Labouring under False Pretences* Manchester: Manchester University Press, 1999; R. Hefferrnan *New Labour and Thatcherism: Political Change in Britain* Basingstoke: Palgrave, 2001; S. Fielding *The Labour Party: Continuity and Change in the Making of New Labour* Basingstoke: Palgrave, 2003; S. Fella *New Labour and the European Union: Political Strategy, Political Transition and the Amsterdam Treaty Negotiations* Aldershot: Ashgate, 2002.
14 A. Geddes *The European Union and British Politics* Basingstoke: Palgrave, 2004 p. 95.
15 N.J. Crowson *The Conservative Party and European Integration* London: Routledge, 2006 p. 127.
16 *Sun* 1 November 1990 front page. http://sunheadlines.blogspot.com/2008/11/classics-up-yours-delors.html. Accessed 15 February 2010.
17 P. Stephens *Politics and the Pound* London: Macmillan, 1996 p. 330.
18 R. Brookes 'Newspapers and national identity: The BSE/CJD crisis and the British press' *Media, Culture and Society* 21 (1999) pp. 247–63.

19 *Independent* N. Schoon 'Spanish allowed to fish British waters' 23 December 1994; *Independent* S. Goodman 'Empire blood proves thicker than EU water than fishing water' 14 March 1995; *Independent* S. Helm 'Belgium fraud squad lifts lid on EU corruption' 15 January 1996; *Sun* 'Clean up EUR act' 26 May 2009.
20 Likewise in March 1971 the Heath government had released a series of twelve free 'factsheets', echoing the Treasury 'broadsheets' issued in 1961–63. Crowson *European Integration* p. 145.
21 K. Oppermann 'The Blair government and Europe: The policy of containing the salience of European integration' *Parliamentary Affairs* 3 (2008) pp. 156–82.
22 Crowson *European Integration* pp. 68–70.
23 A. Geddes 'In Europe, not interested in Europe' in A. Geddes and J. Tonge (eds) *Labour's Second Landslide: The British General Election 2001* Manchester: Manchester University Press, 2002 p. 151; P. Whiteley, P. Stewart, M. Sanders and H. Clarke 'The issue agenda and voting in 2005' in P. Norris and C. Wlezien (eds) *Britain Votes 2005* Oxford: Oxford University Press, 2005 pp. 146–61.
24 D. Baker 'Britain and Europe: The argument continues' pp. 278–79; D. Baker 'Britain and Europe: More blood on the Euro-carpet' *Parliamentary Affairs* 55, 2 (2002) p. 320.
25 BBC online Brian Wheeler 'Euro campaign urges Blair to act' 8 May 2002 http://news.bbc.co.uk/1/hi/uk_politics/1895199.stm. Accessed 8 May 2002.
26 *The Times*, 28 July 1998 p. 18.
27 *Independent on Sunday* 24 August 2003 'Pro-Euro group in crisis after staff exodus'.
28 *Guardian* 10 September 2003.
29 *Financial Times* February 2000.
30 D. Baker and P. Sherrington 'Britain and Europe: Europe and/or America?' *Parliamentary Affairs* 57, 2 (2004) p. 350.
31 D. Baker, N. Randall and D. Seawright 'Celtic exceptionalism? Scottish and Welsh parliamentarians' attitudes to Europe' *Political Quarterly* (2002) pp. 211–26.
32 J. Smith 'Missed Opportunity?' p. 708.
33 P. Lynch, N. Neuwahl and W. Rees 'Conclusions: Maastricht, Amsterdam and Beyond' in P. Lynch, N. Neuwahl, and W. Rees (eds) *Reforming the European Union from Maastricht to Amsterdam* Harlow: Longman, 2000 p. 242.
34 Stephens 'The Blair government' p. 69.
35 *Hansard* vol. 296 cols 313–16 18 June 1997 www.publications.parliament.uk. Accessed 15 February 2010.
36 *Hansard* vol. 299, col. 583–84 27 October 1997. See also D. Howarth 'The domestic politics of British policy on the euro' *Journal of European Integration* 29, 1 (2007) pp. 47–68.
37 House of Commons Treasury Committee 5th Report, 22 April 1998: www.publications.parliament.uk/pa/cm199798/cmselect/cmtreasy/503v/ts0502.htm. Accessed 15 February 2010.
38 Baker 'More blood' p. 318; Baker and Sherrington 'Europe and/or America?' pp. 348–51.
39 Jolyon Howorth cited in S. Bulmer 'New Labour, New European policy?' p. 609.
40 Text of Joint Declaration on European Defence, UK-French summit 3–4 December 1998 St Malo www.parliament.uk/commons/lib/research/rp2000/rp00-020.pdf, pp. 42–43. Accessed 15 February 2010.
41 *Guardian* M. White 'EU must change, Blair tells French' 25 March 1998 p. 10; *Independent* J. Lichfield 'French right salutes "Le Blairisme"' 25 March 1998.
42 *Observer* P. Mandelson 'Blair's first birthday: Best times, worst times: Memoirs of a spin doctor' 26 April 1998 p. 25.

43   *Daily Telegraph* Blair interview, J. Murphy 'US launches attack on Euro Army' 18 March 2001.
44   W. Wallace 'The collapse of British foreign policy' *International Affairs* 82, 1 (2005) p. 53.
45   *Financial Times* 4 November 2001.
46   Stephens 'Blair government' p. 70.
47   C. Schweiger 'British-German relations in the European Union after the war on Iraq' *German Politics* 13, 1 (2004) pp. 35–55.
48   Statistics drawn from Geddes *European Union* pp. 127–30.
49   C. Pickering 'Sir Douglas in Euroland: Treasury officials and the European Union 1977–2001' *Public Administration* 80, 3 (2002) pp. 588, 597.
50   Cabinet Office *Farming and Food: A Sustainable Future* January 2002 http://archive.cabinetoffice.gov.uk/farming/pdf/PC%20Report2.pdf. Accessed 15 February 2010.
51   K. Lynggaard and P. Nedergaard 'The logic of policy development: Lessons learned from reform and routine within the CAP 1980–2003' *Journal of European Integration* 31, 3 (2009) pp. 291–309; Peter Nedergaard 'The 2003 reform of the Common Agricultural Policy: Against all the odds or rational explanations?' *Journal of European Integration* 28, 3 (2006) pp. 203–23.
52   *Hansard* vol. 407 cols 1220–35 26 June 2003.
53   Nedergaard 'The 2003 reform' p. 219.
54   Figures from Geddes *European Union* p. 105.
55   D. Wincott 'A community of law? "European" law and judicial politics: The Court of Justice and beyond' *Government and Opposition* 35, 1 (2000) p. 10.
56   *Standard Eurobarometer* 52 (April 2000) pp. 12–13, http://ec.europa.eu/public_opinion/archives/eb/eb52/eb52_en.htm accessed 4 June 2008.
57   Conservative Central Office press release, 24 May 2001 'Our vision for Europe', Francis Maude, www.conservatives.com/news accessed 2 April 2006.
58   A.L. Teasdale 'The politics of the 1999 European elections' *Government and Opposition* 34, 4 (1999) p. 445; D. Butler and M. Westlake *British Politics and the European Elections 1999* Basingstoke: Macmillan, 2000.
59   *Daily Telegraph*, 6 October 1998.
60   Conservative Central Office press release, 26 May 2001 'Six days to save the pound', www.conservatives.com/news accessed 2 April 2006.
61   P. Lynch 'The Conservatives and Europe 1997–2001' in M. Garnet and P. Lynch (eds) *The Conservatives in Crisis* Manchester: Manchester University Press, 2003 p. 158.
62   S. Fella 'New Labour, same old Britain? The Blair government and European Treaty reform' *Parliamentary Affairs* 59, 4 (2006) pp. 629, 634.
63   Smith 'Missed opportunity' pp. 710–11.
64   G. Ross 'What do "Europeans" think? Analyses of the European Union's current crisis by European elites' *Journal of Common Market Studies* 46, 2 (2008) p. 402.
65   G. Garrett and G. Tsebelis 'More reasons to resist the temptation of power indices in the European Union' *Journal of Theoretical Politics* 11 (1999) pp. 331–38; G. Garrett and G. Tsebelis 'Even more reasons to resist the power indices in the European Union' *Journal of Theoretical Politics* 13 (2001) pp. 99–105.
66   Baker 'Argument continues' p. 287.
67   G. Tsebelis 'Thinking about the recent past and the future of the EU' *Journal of Common Market Studies* 46, 2 (2008) p. 273.
68   Full text can be found at www.ena.lu/address_given_tony_blair_polish_stock_exchange_warsaw_october_2000-020005648.html. Accessed 26 February 2010.
69   Tsebelis 'Thinking about the recent past' pp. 270–73.
70   C. Lord 'Two constitutionalisms? A comparison of British and French government attempts to justify the Constitutional Treaty' *Journal of European Public*

Policy 15, 7 (2008) p. 1007. This article also compares the saliency of aspects of the treaty between the French and British and shows how each government attributes different meanings to the treaty to legitimise and justify.

71 B. Rosamond and D. Wincott 'Constitutionalism, European integration and British political economy' *British Journal of Politics and International Relations* 8 (2006) p. 2.

72 A. Moravcsik 'What can we learn from the collapse of the European constitutional project?' *Politische Vierteljahresschrift* 47, 2 (2006) pp. 219–41.

73 Tsebelis 'Thinking about the recent past' pp. 265–92.

74 D. Baker and P. Sherrington 'Britain and Europe: The dog that didn't bark' *Parliamentary Affairs* 58, 2 (2005) p. 310.

75 D. Butler and M. Westlake *British Politics and the European Elections 2004* Basingstoke: Palgrave, 2005.

76 P. Sherrington 'Confronting Europe: UK political parties and the EU 2000–2005' *British Journal of Politics and International Relations* 8 (2006) p. 69.

77 See J.W. Young *Britain and European Unity 1945–99* Basingstoke: Macmillan, 2000 p. 179.

78 S. Fella 'New Labour, same old Britain?' p. 628.

79 C.M. O'Donnell and R. Whitman 'European policy under Gordon Brown: Perspectives on a future prime minister' *International Affairs* 83, 1 (2007) pp. 253–72.

80 *Hansard* vol. 465 col. 288 11 October 2007 (Brown); vol. 407 cols 1220–35 22 October 2007 (Brown).

81 P. Lynch and R. Whitaker 'A loveless marriage: The Conservatives and the European People's Party' *Parliamentary Affairs* 61, 1 (2008) pp. 31–51.

82 Ross 'What do "Europeans" think?' p. 404.

83 *Hansard* vol. 472 col. 923 26 February 2008 www.publications.parliament.uk/pa/cm200708/cmhansrd/cm080226/debtext/80226-0007.htm#0802264. Accessed 15 February 2010.

84 *Daily Telegraph* P. Johnson 'MPs face mass lobby for EU referendum' 12 April 2008; see also www.iwantareferendum.com/yourarea.aspx. Accessed 15 February 2010 for the referenda results.

85 *Hansard* vol. 472 cols 1749–1864 5 March 2008. www.publications.parliament.uk/pa/cm200708/cmhansrd/cm080305/debtext/80305-0004.htm#08030572000001. Accessed 15 February 2010.

86 C.M. Brugha 'Why Ireland rejected the Lisbon Treaty' *Journal of Public Affairs* 8 (2008) pp. 303–8; J. O'Brennan 'Ireland say No (again): The 12 June 2008 referendum on the Lisbon Treaty' *Parliamentary Affairs* 62, 2 (2009) pp. 258–77.

87 M.J. Hall 'The sub-prime crisis, the credit crunch and bank "failure": An assessment of the UK authorities' response' Loughborough University Department of Economics Discussion Paper WP2008-14 (2008).

88 German finance minister Peer Steinbruck cited *Time* 'Europe struggles for a response to the bank crisis' 7 October 2008.

89 *New York Times* 'Facing a financial crisis, European nations put self-interest first' 8 October 2008. For Brown's defence of his policy see the *Independent* 'Brown defends response to banking crisis' 16 July 2009.

90 J.H.M. Weiler 'The reformation of European constitutionalism' *Journal of Common Market Studies* 35, 1 (1997) pp. 97–98.

91 Based upon Ross 'What do "Europeans" think?' pp. 389–412.

92 Ross 'What do "Europeans" think?' p. 400.

93 BBC news online http://news.bbc.co.uk/1/hi/programmes/the_daily_politics/8058100.stm 'Daily politics on MEPs' expenses' 20 May 2009. Accessed 14 July 2009.

94 *Daily Telegraph* 15 July 2009.

95 V.A. Schmidt 'European elites on the European Union: What vision for the future?' in A. Gamble and D. Lane (eds) *European Union and World Politics: Consensus and Division* Basingstoke: Palgrave, 2009.

96 J. Redmond *The Next Mediterranean Enlargement of the EC: Turkey, Cyprus and Malta?* Aldershot: Dartmouth, 1993 p. 23.

97 *The Observer* H. McDonald 'Ireland votes in favour of Lisbon Treaty' 4 October 2009 p. 1; O'Brennan 'Ireland say No' pp. 258–77.

98 *Guardian* 'I'll be president of Europe if you give me the power – Blair' 2 February 2008; *Independent* 'Tony Blair backed to be Europe's first president' 15 July 2009.

99 *The Telegraph* B. Waterfield 'Baroness Ashton, the fall guy of Europe' www.telegraph.co.uk/news/worldnews/europe/belgium/7332870/Baroness-Ashton-the-fall-guy-of-Europe.html. Accessed 28 February 2010; *Guardian* 'Lady Ashton needs to work some magic' 2 March 2010 www.guardian.co.uk/commentisfree/2010/mar/02/lady-ashton-european-commission-disenchanted. Accessed 2 March 2010; BBC news online 'Lady Ashton takes flak in EU diplomatic battle' 3 March 2010 http://news.bbc.co.uk/1/hi/world/europe/8546108.stm. Accessed 3 March 2010.

100 *Daily Telegraph* B. Waterfield 'War in the EU as Herman Van Rompuy makes "power grab"' 26 February 2010 www.telegraph.co.uk/news/worldnews/europe/eu/7326640/War-in-the-EU-as-Herman-Van-Rompuy-makes-power-grab.html. Accessed 26 February 2010.

101 Baker 'More blood' p. 317.

102 Cited Stephens 'Blair government' p. 67.

103 P. Webb 'The attitudinal assimilation of Europe by the Conservative Parliamentary Party' *British Politics* 3 (2008) p. 431.

Bibliography

Aldous, R. and Lee, S. (eds) *Harold Macmillan and Britain's World Role* London: Macmillan, 1996.

Alexander, G.M. *The Prelude to the Truman Doctrine: British Policy in Greece 1944–47* Oxford: Clarendon Press, 1982.

Ambrosius, L.E. *Wilsonian Statecraft: Theory and Practice of Liberal Internationalism during World War One* Wilmington, DE: SR Books, 1991.

Antonio, V. and Calandri, E. (eds) *The Failure of Peace in Europe 1943–48* Basingstoke: Palgrave, 2002.

Archer, C. *Organizing Europe: The Institutions of Integration* London: Arnold, 1994.

Ashford, N. 'The EEC' In Layton-Henry, Z. (ed.) *Conservative Party Politics* London: Longman, 1980 pp. 95–125.

Ashton, N. *Kennedy, Macmillan and the Cold War* Basingstoke: Palgrave, 2002.

Aspinall, M. and Schneider, G. (eds) *The Rules of Integration: Institutionalist Approaches to the Study of Europe* Manchester: Manchester University Press, 2001.

Aster, S. *1939: The Making of the Second World War* London: Simon and Schuster, 1974.

Attlee, C.R. *As it Happened* London: Heineman, 1954.

Bailer, U. *Shadow of the Bomber: The Fear of Air Attack and British Politics* London: Royal Historical Society, 1981.

Baker, D. 'Britain and Europe: The argument continues' *Parliamentary History* 54, 2 (2001) pp. 276–88.

——'Britain and Europe: More blood on the Euro-carpet' *Parliamentary Affairs* 55, 2 (2002) pp. 317–30.

Baker, D., Gamble, A. and Ludlam, S. 'Whips or scorpions? The Maastricht vote and the Conservative Party' *Parliamentary Affairs* 46, 2 (1993) pp. 151–66.

——'1846 … 1906 … 1996? Conservative splits and European integration' *Political Quarterly* 64, 4 (1993) pp. 420–34.

——'MPs and Europe' *British Elections and Parties Review* 9 (1999) pp. 170–85.

Baker, D., Randall, N., and Seawright, D. 'Celtic Exceptionalism? Scottish and Welsh Parliamentarians' Attitudes to Europe' *Political Quarterly* (2002) pp. 211–26.

Baker, D. and Sherrington, P. 'Britain and Europe: Europe and/or America?' *Parliamentary Affairs* 57, 2 (2004) pp. 347–65.

——'Britain and Europe: The dog that didn't bark' *Parliamentary Affairs* 58, 2 (2005) pp. 303–17.

Baker, K. *Turbulent Years* London: Faber and Faber, 1993.

Ball, M. *The Conservative Conference and Eurosceptical Motions, 1992–5* London: Bruges Group Occasional Paper no 23.

Ball, S. *Guardsmen* London: HarperCollins, 2004.

Ball, S. (ed.) *In the Age of Attlee and Churchill: The Diaries of Cuthbert Headlam 1935–51* Cambridge: Royal Historical Society Camden Series, 1999.

Ball, S. and Seldon, A. (eds) *The Heath Government: A Reappraisal* London: Longman, 1996.

Bange, O. *The EEC Crisis of 1963: Kennedy, Macmillan, De Gaulle and Adenauer in Conflict* Basingstoke: Palgrave, 2000.

Barnes, J. and Middlemas, K. *Baldwin: A Biography* London: Weidenfeld and Nicolson, 1969.

Barnes, J. and Nicholson, D. (eds) *Empire At Bay: The Leo Amery Diaries* London: Hutchinson, 1980.

Baston, L. *Reggie: The Life of Reginald Maudling* Stroud: Sutton, 2004.

Bayliss, J. *The Diplomacy of Pragmatism: Britain and the Formation of NATO* Basingstoke: Macmillan, 1993.

Beamish, T.P.H. and St John Stevas, N. *Sovereignty: Substance or Shadow* London: CPC, 1971.

Bell, P.M. *France and Britain, 1900–1940: Entente and Estrangement* Harlow: Longman, 1996.

Beloff, M. 'Churchill and Europe' In Blake, R. and Louis, Wm R. (eds) *Churchill* Oxford: Oxford University Press, 1993 pp. 443–56.

Beloff, N. *The General Says No: Britain's Exclusion from Europe* Harmondsworth: Penguin, 1973.

Benn, S. 'The uses of sovereignty' *Political Studies* 3, 2 (1955) pp. 109–22.

Birn, D.S. *League of Nations Union, 1918–45* Oxford: Clarendon Press, 1981.

Blackwell, M. *Clinging to Grandeur: British Attitudes and Foreign Policy in the Aftermath of the Second World War* London: Greenwood Press, 1993.

Bloch, C. 'Great Britain, German rearmament and the naval agreement of 1935' In Gatzke, H.W. (ed.) *European Diplomacy Between Two Wars, 1919–39* Chicago: Quadrangle Books, 1972 pp. 121–51.

Blondel, J. 'United Kingdom' In Lindsay, K. (ed.) *European Assemblies: The Experimental Period 1949–59* London: Stevens and Sons, 1960.

Body, R. *The Breakdown of Europe* London: NEP, 1989.

——*Europe of Many Circles: Constructing a Wider Europe* London: NEP, 1990.

Bond, B. (ed.) *Chief of Staff: The Diaries of Lt-Gen Sir Henry Pownall* London: Leo Cooper, 1972.

Boothby, R. *Recollections of a Rebel* London: Hutchinson, 1978.

Boyce, R. 'Britain's first "no" to Europe: Britain and the Briand plan, 1929–30' *European History Quarterly* 10 (1980) pp. 17–45.

——'British capitalism and the European unity between the wars' In Stirk, P.M.R. (ed.) *European Unity in Context: The Inter-war Period* London: Pinter, 1989 pp. 65–83.

Boyson, R. *Speaking My Mind* London: Peter Owen, 1994.

Bradley, J.H. (series editor) *The Second World War: Europe and the Mediterranean* Garden City Park, NY: Square One, 2002.

——*The Second World War: Asia and the Pacific* Garden City Park, NY: Square One, 2003.

Brandreth, G. *Breaking the Code: Westminster Diaries 1990–1997* London: Weidenfeld and Nicolson, 1999.

Branston, U. *Britain and European Unity* London: CPC, 1953.

Bray, C. 'National Images, the Media and Public Opinion' In Morgan, R. and Bray, C. (eds) *Partners and Rivals in Western Europe: Britain, France and Germany* Aldershot: Gower, 1986 pp. 54–77.

Brittan, L. *Europe: The Europe We Need* London: Hamish Hamilton, 1994.

——*A Diet of Brussels: The Changing Face of Europe* London: Little, Brown, 2000.

Broad, R. *Labour's European Dilemma: From Bevin to Blair* Basingstoke: Palgrave, 2001.

Broad, R. and Preston, V. (eds) *Moored to the Continent? Britain and European Integration* London: Institute of Historical Research, 2001.

Bromund, T. 'Whitehall, the National Farmers' Union and Plan G 1956–57' *Contemporary British History* 15, 2 (2001) pp. 76–97.

Brookes, R. 'Newspapers and national identity: The BSE/CJD crisis and the British press' *Media, Culture, Society* 21, 2 (1999) pp. 247–63.

Brugha, C.M. 'Why Ireland rejected the Lisbon Treaty' *Journal of Public Affairs* 8 (2008) pp. 303–8.

Brunson, M. *A Ringside Seat: The Autobiography* London: Hodder and Stoughton, 2000.

Buchanan, T. *The Spanish Civil War and the British Labour Movement* Cambridge: Cambridge University Press, 1991.

——*Britain and the Spanish Civil War* Cambridge: Cambridge University Press, 1997.

——*The Impact of the Spanish Civil War on Britain: War, Loss and Memory* Eastbourne: Sussex Academic Press, 2007.

Bullen, R. and Pelly, M. (eds) *Documents on British Policy Overseas* 2nd series, vol. II, London: HMSO, 1987.

Buller, J. *National Statecraft and European Integration* London: Pinter, 2000.

——'Contesting Europeanisation: Agents, institutions and narratives in British monetary policy' *West European Politics* 29, 3 (2006) pp. 389–409.

Bullock, A. *Ernest Bevin: Foreign Secretary 1945–51* vol. 3, London: Heinemann, 1983.

Bulmer, S. 'Domestic politics and the European Community policymaking' *Journal of Common Market Studies* 21, 4 (1983) pp. 349–63.

——'New Labour, new European policy? Blair, Brown and utilitarian supranationalism' *Parliamentary Affairs* 61, 4 (2008) pp. 597–620.

Bulmer, S. and Patterson, W. *The Federal Republic of Germany and the European Community* London: Allen Lane, 1987.

Bulpitt, J. 'The European questions: Rules, national modernisation and the ambiguities of *Primat de Innenpolitik*' In Marquand, D. and Seldon, A. (eds) *The Ideas That Shaped Post-War Britain* London: Fontana, 1996.

Burke, K. and Cairncross, A. *'Goodbye, Great Britain': The 1976 IMF Crisis* London: Yale University Press, 1992.

Butler, D. and Butler, G. (eds) *Twentieth Century British Political Facts* Basingstoke: Macmillan, 2000.

Butler, D. and Jowett, P. *Party Strategies in Britain: A Study of the 1984 European Elections*, Basingstoke: Macmillan, 1985.

Butler, D. and Kavanagh, D. *The British General Election of 1987* Basingstoke: Macmillan, 1988.

——*The British General Election of 1997* Basingstoke: Macmillan, 1997.

——*The British General Election of 2001* Basingstoke: Palgrave, 2002.

Butler, D. and King, A. *The British General Election of 1964* London: Macmillan, 1965.

——*The British General Election of 1966* London: Macmillan, 1966.

Butler, D. and Kitzinger, U. *The 1975 Referendum* London: Macmillan, 1976.

Butler, D. and Marquand, D. *European Elections and British Politics* London: Longman, 1981.

Butler, D. and Pinto-Duschinsky, M. *The British General Election of 1970* London: Macmillan, 1970.

Butler, D. and Rose, R. *The British General Election of 1959* London: Macmillan, 1960.

Butler, D. and Westlake, M. *British Politics and the European Elections 1994* Basingstoke: Macmillan, 1994.

——*British Politics and the European Elections 1999* Basingstoke: Macmillan, 2000.

——*British Politics and the European Elections 2004*, Basingstoke: Palgrave, 2005.

Butler, R.A. *The Art of the Possible* London: Hamish Hamilton, 1971.

Butt, R. 'The Common Market and Conservative Party politics 1961–62' *Government and Opposition* 2, 3 (1967) pp. 372–86.

Cabinet Office *Farming and Food: A Sustainable Future* January 2002.

Cameron, F. *The Foreign and Security Policy of the European Union: Past, Present and Future* Sheffield: Sheffield Academic Press, 1999.

Campbell, J. *Edward Heath: A Biography* London: Pimlico, 1994.

——*Margaret Thatcher: Grocer's Daughter, Volume 1* London: Jonathan Cape, 2000.

——*Margaret Thatcher: Iron Lady, Volume 2* London: Jonathan Cape, 2002.

Camps, M. *Britain and the European Community 1955–1963* Oxford: Oxford University Press, 1964.

Carlton, D. *MacDonald versus Henderson: The Foreign Policy of the Second Labour Government* London: Macmillan, 1970.

Carrington, Lord. *Reflect on Things Past* London: Collins, 1988.

Cash, B. *Against a Federal Europe: The Battle for Britain* London: Duckworth, 1991.

Castle, B. *The Castle Diaries 1964–70* London: Weidenfeld and Nicolson, 1980.

Catterall, P. 'Macmillan and Europe 1950–56: The Cold War, the American context and the British approaches to European integration' *Cercles* 5 (2002) pp. 93–108.

Catterall, P. (ed.) *Macmillan Diaries: The Cabinet Years 1950–57* London: Macmillan, 2003.

Chamberlain, A. 'Great Britain as a European power' *Journal of the Royal Institute of International Affairs*, March 1930, pp. 180–89.

Charlton, D. *The Price of Victory* London: BBC, 1983.

Charmley, J. *Churchill: End of Glory: A Political Biography* London: Hodder and Stoughton, 1993.

——*Splendid Isolation: Britain and the Balance of Power 1874–1914* London: Hodder and Stoughton, 1999.

Chatham House *Britain in Western Europe: WEU and the Atlantic Alliance* London: RIIA, 1955.

Churchill, R. (ed.) *Europe Unite: Speeches 1947 and 1948 by Winston Churchill* London: Cassell, 1950.

Churchill, W.S. *Marlborough: His Life and Times, The World Crisis* London: George Harrap, 1933.

——*Arms and the Covenant* London: Cassell, 1938.

Cienciala, A.M. 'The Nazi-Soviet pact of August 23 1939: When did Stalin decide to align with Hitler and was Poland the culprit?' In Biskupski, M.B.B. (ed.) Ideology, Politics and Diplomacy in East Central Europe Rochester, NY: Rochester University Press, 2003 pp. 147–226.

Clarke, A. *Diaries* London: Weidenfeld and Nicolson, 1993.

Clavin, P. *The Great Depression in Europe 1929–39* Basingstoke: Palgrave, 2000.

Cockfield, Lord. *The European Union: Creating the Single Market* London: Wiley Chancery Law, 1994.

Cole, J. *As It Seemed to Me* London: Weidenfeld and Nicolson, 1995.

Conservative Political Centre *Our Voice in Europe* London: CPC, 1976.

Costigliola, F. 'The United States and the reconstruction of Germany in the 1920s' *Business History Review* 50, 4 (1976) pp. 477–502.

Coupland, P. *Britannia, Europa and Christendom: British Christians and European Integration* Basingstoke: Palgrave, 2006.

Cowley, P. and Norton, P. 'Blair's bastards: Discontent within the PLP' *Centre for Legislative Studies Research Paper* 1/96 (1996).

Cox, S. *The Strategic Air War Against Germany 1939–45: Report of the British Bombing Survey Unit* London: Frank Cass, 1997.

Critchley, J. and Halcrow, M. *Collapse of the Stout Party: The Decline and Fall of the Tories* London: Gollancz, 1997.

Crossman, R. *Diaries of a Cabinet Minister 2* London: Hamish Hamilton, 1976.

Crowson, N.J. *The Conservative Party and European Integration* London: Routledge, 1996.

——*Facing the Dictators: The Conservative Party and the European Dictators, 1935–40* London: Routledge, 1997.

——(ed.) *Fleet Street, Press Barons and Politics: The Journals of Collin Brooks* Cambridge: Royal Historical Society, 1998.

——'Lord Hinchingbrooke, Europe and the November 1962 South Dorset by-election' *Contemporary British History* 17, 3 (2003) pp. 43–64.

Crozier, A. *Appeasement and Germany's Last Bid for Colonies* London: Macmillan, 1988.

Currie, E. *Diaries 1987–1992* London: Little, Brown, 2000.

Curtis, S. (ed.) *Journals of Woodrow Wyatt: Thatcher's Fall and Major's Rise*, vol. 2, London: Macmillan, 1992.

Daddow, O. (ed.) *Harold Wilson and European Integration: Britain's Second Application to Join the EEC* London: Frank Cass, 2003.

——*Britain and Europe since 1945: Historiographical Perspectives on Integration* Manchester: Manchester University Press, 2004.

Dallek, R. *Franklin D. Roosevelt and American Foreign Policy* Oxford: Oxford University Press, 1979.

De Grazia, V. *Irresistible Empire: America's Advance through 20th Century Europe* Cambridge, MA: Belknap Press, 2005.

Deighton, A. *The Impossible Peace: Britain, the Division of Germany and the Origins of the Cold War*, Oxford: Clarendon Press, 1993.

——'Last piece of the jigsaw: Britain and the creation of Western European Union 1954' *Contemporary European History* 7, 2 (1998) pp. 181–97.

Dell, E. *The Schuman Plan and the British Abdication of Leadership in Europe* Oxford: Clarendon Press, 1995.

Denman, R. *Missed Chances: Britain and Europe in the Twentieth Century* London: Cassell, 1996.

Dennis, P. *Decision by Default: Peacetime Conscription and British Defence, 1919–39* London: Kegan Paul, 1972.

Dickie, J. *Inside the Foreign Office* London: Chapmans, 1992.

Dilks, D. (ed.) *The Diaries of Sir Alexander Cadogan* London: Cassell, 1971.

Dockrill, S. *Britain's Policy for West German Rearmament 1950–55* Cambridge: Cambridge University Press, 1991.

Douglas, R.M. *The Labour Party, nationalism and internationalism 1939–51* London: Routledge, 2004.

Duignan, P. and Gann, L.H. *The United States and the New Europe 1945–93*, Oxford: Blackwell, 1994.

Dutton, D. *Austen Chamberlain: Gentleman in Politics* Bolton: Ross Anderson, 1985.

——'"A nation of shopkeepers in search of a suitable Frenchman": Britain and Briand, 1915–30', *Modern and Contemporary France* 6, 4 (1988) pp. 463–78.

——'Anticipating Maastricht: The Conservative Party and Britain's first application to join the European Community' *Contemporary Record* 7, 3 (1993) pp. 522–40.

——*Anthony Eden: A Life and Reputation* London: Arnold, 1997.

Dyson, K. *The Politics of the Euro-Zone: Stability or Breakdown?* Oxford: Oxford University Press, 2000.

Eden, A. (Lord Avon) *The Reckoning*, London: Cassell, 1965.

Ellison, J. *Threatening Europe: Britain and the Creation of the European Community 1955–58* Basingstoke: Macmillan, 2000.

European Movement *European Movement and Council of Europe* London: Hutchinson, n.d.

Evans, D. *While Britain Slept: The Selling of the Common Market* London: Gollancz, 1975.

Evans, H. *Downing Street Diary: Macmillan Years 1957–63* London: Hodder and Stoughton, 1981.

Evans, R. *Cosmopolitan Islanders: British Historians and the European Continent* Cambridge: Cambridge University Press, 2009.

Featherstone, K. *Socialist Parties and European Integration: A Comparative History* Manchester: Manchester University Press, 1988.

Feiling, K. *Life of Neville Chamberlain* London: Macmillan, 1946.

Fella, S. *New Labour and the European Union: Political Strategy, Political Transition and the Amsterdam Treaty Negotiations* Aldershot: Ashgate, 2002.

——'New Labour, same old Britain? The Blair government and European treaty reform' *Parliamentary Affairs* 59, 4 (2006) pp. 621–37.

Fielding, S. *The Labour Party: Continuity and Change in the Making of New Labour* Basingstoke: Palgrave, 2003.

Fielding, S. and Young, J.W. *The Labour Governments 1964–70 Vol 2: International Policy* London: Macmillan, 1989.

Fischer, C. *The Ruhr Crisis 1923–1924* Oxford: Oxford University Press, 2003.

Foreign Relations of the United States (FRUS) 1947, vol III, Washington, DC: Office of the Historian, 1972.

Forster, A. 'Anti-Europeans, anti-marketeers and Eurosceptics' *Political Quarterly* 73, 3 (2002) pp. 299–308.

——*Euroscepticism in Contemporary British Politics: Opposition to Europe in the British Conservative and Labour Parties since 1945* London: Routledge, 2002.

Fursdon, E. *The European Defence Community* London: Macmillan, 1980.

Garrett, G. and Tsebelis, G. 'More reasons to resist the temptation of power indices in the European Union' *Journal of Theoretical Politics* 11 (1999) pp. 331–38.

——'Even more reasons to resist the power indices in the European Union' *Journal of Theoretical Politics* 13 (2001) pp. 99–105.

Gavin, N. and Sanders, D. 'The economy and voting' *Parliamentary Affairs* 50, 4 (1997) pp. 631–40.

Geddes, A. 'In Europe, not interested in Europe' In Geddes, A. and Tonge, J. (eds) *Labour's Second Landslide: The British General Election 2001* Manchester: Manchester University Press, 2002.

——*The European Union and British Politics* Basingstoke: Palgrave, 2004.

Gehler, M. and Kaiser, W. 'Transnationalism and early European integration: the *Nouvelles Equipes Internationales* and the Geneva circle 1945–57' *Historical Journal* 44, 3 (2001) pp. 773–98.

Geiger, T. and Kenner, B. (eds) *Ireland, Europe and the Marshall Plan* Dublin: Four Courts, 2004.

George, S. *Politics and Policy within the European Community* Oxford: Oxford University Press, 1985.

George, S. (ed.) *Britain and the European Community: The Politics of Semi-Detachment* Oxford: Oxford University Press, 1992.

——*An Awkward Partner: Britain in the European Community*, 2nd edn, Oxford: Oxford University Press, 1994.

Gilbert, M. *The Roots of Appeasement* London: Weidenfeld and Nicolson, 1966.

——*Winston S. Churchill, VI: 1939–1941* London: Heinemann, 1983.

Gill, C. *Whips' Nightmare: Diary of a Maastricht Rebel*, Spennymoor: Memoir Club, 2003.

Gilmour, I. *Dancing with Dogma* London: Simon and Schuster, 1992.

Gliddon, P. 'The British Foreign Office and domestic propaganda on the European Community, 1960–72' *Contemporary British History* 23, 2 (2009) pp. 155–80.

Goldstein, E. 'The British official mind and the Lausanne conference, 1922–23' *Diplomacy and Statecraft* 14, 2 (2003) pp. 185–206.

Goldstein, E. and Lukes, I. (eds) *Munich 1938: Prelude to World War Two* Newbury: Cass, 1999.

Gowland, D. and Turner, A. *Reluctant Europeans: Britain and European Integration 1945–1988* Harlow: Pearson, 2000.

Grahl, J. 'A fateful decision? Labour and the Schuman Plan' In Fyrth, J. (ed.) *Labour's High Noon: The Government and the Economy 1945–51* London: Lawrence and Wishart, 1993 pp. 148–62.

Grayson, R.S. 'The British government and the Channel tunnel, 1919–39' *Journal of Contemporary History* 31, 1 (1996) pp. 125–44.

——*Austen Chamberlain and the Commitment to Europe: British Foreign Policy 1924–29* London: Cass, 1997.

Greenwood, S. 'Bevin, France and Western union' *European History Quarterly* 14 (1984) pp. 319–38.

——*Britain and European Co-operation since 1945* Oxford: Blackwell, 1992.

Grey, Viscount. *Twenty-Five Years 1892–1916*, vol. 2, London: Hodder and Stoughton, 1925.

Griffiths, R. 'A slow one hundred and eighty degree turn: British policy towards the Common Market, 1955–60' In Wilkes, G. (ed.) *Britain's Failure to Enter the European Community 1961–63* London: Frank Cass, 1997.

Haas, E.B. *The Uniting of Europe: Political, Social, and Economic Forces, 1950–1957* Stanford, CA: Stanford University Press, 1958.

Hall, M.J. 'The sub-prime crisis, the credit crunch and bank "failure": An assessment of the UK authorities' response' Loughborough University Department of Economics Discussion Paper WP2008–14 (2008).

Haller, M. *European Integration as an Elite Process: The Failure of a Dream?* London: Routledge, 2008.

Hansard: House of Commons Parliamentary Debates 5th and 6th series London: HMSO.

Hansard: House of Lords Parliamentary Debates London: HMSO.

Haslam, J. *The Soviet Union and the Struggle for Collective Security in Europe 1933–39* London: Macmillan, 1984.

Hay, C. *The Political Economy of New Labour: Labouring under False Pretences* Manchester: Manchester University Press, 1999.

Haydock, M.D. *City under Seige: The Berlin Blockade and Airlift 1948–9* London: Brassey's, 1999.

Healey, D. *The Time of My Life* London: Penguin 1990.

Heath, E. *Course of My Life: My Autobiography* London: Hodder and Stoughton, 1998.

Heathcoat Amory, D. *The European Constitution* London: CPS, June 2003.

Hefferrnan, R. *New Labour and Thatcherism: Political Change in Britain* Basingstoke: Palgrave, 2001.

Henderson, N. *Water Under the Bridges* London: Hodder and Stoughton, 1945.

Heseltine, M. *The Challenge of Europe: Can Britain Win?* London: Weidenfeld and Nicolson, 1989.

Hildebrand, K. *The Foreign Policy of the Third Reich* Berkeley: University of California Press, 1973.

Hinsley, F.H. *Sovereignty* Oxford: Alden Press, 1966.

Hoerber, T. 'Psychology and reasoning in the Anglo–German naval agreement 1935–39' *Historical Journal* 52, 1 (2009) pp. 153–74.

Hoffman, S. 'Obstinate or obsolete? The fate of the nation-state and the case of Western Europe' *Daedalus* 95, 3 (1966) pp. 862–915.

Hogan, M.J. *The Marshall Plan: America, Britain and the Reconstruction of Western Europe 1947–52* Cambridge: Cambridge University Press, 1987.

Holbrooke, R. *To End a War* New York: Random House, 1998.

Holden, R. *The Making of New Labour's European Policy* Basingstoke: Palgrave, 2002.

House of Commons *Minutes of Evidence to Select Committee on Direct Elections to the European Parliament* London: HMSO, 1976.

——*Select Committee on Direct Elections to the European Parliament 2nd Report* London: HMSO, 1976.

——*House of Commons Treasury Committee 5th Report* London: HMSO, 22 April 1998.

Howard, M. *The Continental Commitment: The Dilemma of British Defence Policy in the Era of Two World Wars* London: Temple Smith, 1972.

Howarth, D. 'The domestic politics of British policy on the euro' *Journal of European Integration* 29, 1 (2007) pp. 47–68.

Howe, G. *Conflict of Loyalty* London: Macmillan, 1994.

Hughes, G.R. *Britain, Germany and the Cold War: The Search for a European Détente 1949–67* London: Routledge, 2007.

Hurd, D. *An End to Promises: Sketch of Government 1970–74*, London: Collins, 1979.

——*Memoirs* London: Little, Brown, 2003.

Hynes, C. *The Year That Never Was: Heath, the Nixon Administration and the Year of Europe* Dublin: UCD Press, 2009.

Hynes, S. *A War Imagined: The First World War and English Culture* London: Bodley Head, 1990.

Ismay, L.H. *The Memoirs of Lord Ismay* London: Heinemann, 1960.

Jackson, R. *The Powers of the European Parliament* London: CPC, n.d. [1978].

Jackson, R.J. *Rebels and Whips: Dissension and Cohesion in British Political Parties since 1945* London: Macmillan, 1968.

James, A. *Sovereign Statehood* London: Allen and Unwin, 1986.

James, R.R. (ed.) *Chips: The Diaries of Sir Henry Channon* London: Weidenfeld and Nicolson, 1969.

——(ed.) *Complete Speeches of Winston Churchill 1897–1963*, vol. VII, New York: Chelsea House, 1974.

Jansen, T. *The European Peoples' Party*, Basingstoke: Macmillan, 1998.

Jay, D. *Change and Fortune* London: Hutchinson, 1980 pp. 360–70.

Johnson, G. *The Berlin Embassy of Lord D'Aberdon 1920–26* Basingstoke: Palgrave, 2002.

——(ed.) *Locarno Revisited: European Diplomacy 1920–29* London: Routledge, 2004.

Johnson, R.J. 'The conflict over qualified majority voting in the European Union Council of Ministers' *British Journal of Political Science* 25, 2 (1995) pp. 245–54.

Jowell, R. and Spence, J.D. *The Grudging Europeans* London: SCPR, 1975.

Judt, T. *Postwar: A History of Europe since 1945* London: Heinemann, 2005.

Kaiser, W. *Using Europe, Abusing the Europeans: Britain and European Integration 1945–63* Basingstoke: Macmillan, 1996.

Kandiah, M. 'British domestic politics, the Conservative party and foreign policy-making' In Kaiser, W. and Staerck, G. (eds) *British Foreign Policy 1955–64* Basingstoke: Macmillan, 1999 pp. 61–88.

Kavanagh, D. *Thatcherism and British Politics* London: Macmillan, 1990.

Kennedy, P. 'The tradition of appeasement in British foreign policy 1895–1939' *British Journal of International Studies* 2, 3 (1976), 195–215.

——*Realities Behind Diplomacy: Background Influences on British External Policy 1865–1980* London: Fontana, 1985.

Keynes, J.M. *The Economic Consequences of the Peace* London: Macmillan, 1919.

Kilmuir, Earl of. *Political Adventure: The Memoirs of the Earl of Kilmuir* London: Weidenfeld and Nicolson, 1964.

King, A. *Britain Says Yes: 1975 Referendum on the Common Market* Washington: AEI Press, 1977.

King, A. and Wybrow, R. (eds) *British Political Opinion: The Gallup Polls* London: Politicos, 2001.

King, C. *The Cecil King Diaries, 1965–1970* London: Cape, 1972.

——*The Cecil King Diaries, 1970–1974* London: Cape, 1975.

Kitchen, M. 'Winston Churchill and the Soviet Union during the Second World War' *Historical Journal* 30, 2 (1987) pp. 415–36.

Kitching, C. *Britain and the Problem of International Disarmament 1919–34* London: Routledge, 1999.

——*Britain and the Geneva Disarmament Conference* London: Routledge, 2003.

Kitzinger, U. *The European Common Market and Community* London: Routledge, 1967.

——*Second Try* Oxford: Pergamon Press, 1968.

——*Diplomacy and Persuasion: How Britain Joined the Common Market*, London: Thames and Hudson, 1973.

Krasner, S. *Sovereignty: Organised Hypocrisy* Princeton, NJ: Princeton University Press, 1999.

Lacouture, J. *De Gaulle: The Ruler 1945–70* London: Collins Harvill, 1991. English trans. Alan Sheridan.

Laffan, B. *Integration and Co-operation in Europe* London: Routledge, 1992.

Lamb, R. *The Macmillan Years 1957–63* London: John Murray, 1995.

Lamont, N. *Sovereign Britain* London: Duckworth, 1995.

——*In Office* London: Little, Brown, 1999.

Lane, A.J. and Temperley, H. (eds) *The Rise and Fall of the Grand Alliance 1941–45* Basingstoke: Macmillan, 1995.

Lange, P. 'Politics of the social dimension' In Sbragia, A.M. (ed.) *Euro-politics: Institutions and Policymaking in the 'New' European Community* Washington, DC: Brookings Institution Press, 1992 pp. 225–56.

Larres, K. 'Margaret Thatcher, the Foreign Office and German reunification' *Cercles* 5 (2002) pp. 175–82.

Lawson, N. *View from Number 11: Memoirs of a Tory Radical* London: Bantam Press, 1992.

Leffler, M.P. *A Preponderance of Power: National Security, the Truman Administration and the Cold War* Stanford, CA: Stanford University Press, 1992.

Leiber, R.J. *British Politics and European Unity: Parties, Elites and Pressure Groups* Berkeley: University of California Press, 1970.

——'Interest groups and political integration: British entry into Europe' *The American Political Science Review* 66, 1 (1972) pp. 53–67.

Link, A.S. *Woodrow Wilson: Revolution, War and Peace* Arlington Heights, IL: AHM Publishing, 1979.

Little, D. 'Red scare, 1936: Anti-Bolshevism and the origins of British non-intervention in the Spanish Civil War', *Journal of Contemporary History* 23 (1988) pp. 291–311.

Lodge, J. (ed.) *European Union: The European Community in Search of a Future* London: Macmillan, 1986.

——*The 1994 Elections to the European Parliament* London: Pinter, 1996.

Lojko, M. 'The failed handshake over the Danube: The story of Anglo–American involvement in the liberation of Central Europe at the end of the Second World War' *Hungarian Quarterly* 41 (2000) pp. 104–11.

Lord, C. *British Entry to the European Community under the Heath Government of 1970–1974* Aldershot: Dartmouth, 1993.

——*Absent at the Creation: Britain and the Formation of the European Community 1950–52* Aldershot: Dartmouth, 1996.

——'Two constitutionalisms? A comparison of British and French government attempts to justify the constitutional treaty' *Journal of European Public Policy* 15, 7 (2008) pp. 1001–18.

Louis, Wm R. and Owen, R. (eds) *Suez 1956: The Crisis and Its Consequences* Oxford: Clarendon Press, 1989.

Lovett, A.W. 'The United States and the Schuman Plan: A study in French diplomacy 1950–52' *The Historical Journal* 39, 2 (1996) pp. 425–55.

Lucas, W.S. *Divided We Stand: Britain, the United States and the Suez Crisis* London: Hodder and Stoughton, 1991.

Ludlow, N.P. *Dealing with Britain: The Six and the First UK Application to the EEC* Cambridge: Cambridge University Press, 1997.

——'Challenging French leadership in Europe: Germany, Italy and the Netherlands and the outbreak of the Empty Chair crisis 1965–66' *Contemporary European History* 8, 2 (1999) pp. 231–48.

——'Us or them? The meanings of "Europe" in British political discourse' In Malmborg, M. and Strath, B. (eds) *The Meaning of Europe: Variety and Contention within and among Nations* London: Berg Publishing, 2002.

Lynch, P. 'The Conservatives and Europe 1997–2001' In Garnet, M. and Lynch, P. (eds) *The Conservatives in Crisis* Manchester: Manchester University Press, 2003 pp. 146–63.

Lynch, P. and Whitaker, R. 'A loveless marriage: The Conservatives and the European People's Party' *Parliamentary Affairs* 61, 1 (2008) pp. 31–51.

Lynch, P., Neuwahl, N. and Rees, W. 'Conclusions: Maastricht, Amsterdam and beyond' In Lynch, P., Neuwahl, N. and Rees, W. (eds) *Reforming the European Union from Maastricht to Amsterdam* Harlow: Longman, 2000 pp. 235–48.

Lynggaard, K. and Nedergaard, P. 'The logic of policy development: Lessons learned from reform and routine within the CAP 1980–2003' *Journal of European Integration* 31, 3 (2009) pp. 291–309.

MacDonald, C. 'Economic appeasement and the German "moderates" 1937–39' *Past and Present* 56, 1 (1972) pp. 105–31.

——*The United States, Britain and Appeasement 1936–39* London: Macmillan, 1981.

Macmillan, H. *Tides of Fortune: 1945–55* London: Macmillan, 1969.

——*Riding the Storm 1956–59* London: Macmillan, 1971.

——*Pointing the Way 1959–61* London: Macmillan, 1972.

——*At the End of the Day 1961–63* London: Macmillan, 1973.

Macmillan, M. *Peacemakers: The Paris Peace Conference of 1919 and Its Attempts to End War* London: John Murray, 2003.

Magee, F. '"Limited liability"? Britain and the Treaty of Locarno' *Twentieth Century British History* 6, 1 (1995) pp. 1–22.

Maiolo, J. *The Royal Navy and Nazi Germany, 1933–39: A Study in Appeasement and the Origins of the Second World War* Basingstoke: Palgrave, 1998.

Mander, J. *Our German Cousins: Anglo–German Relations in the 19th and 20th Centuries* London: John Murray, 1974.

Marks, G. 'Structural policy in the European Community' In Sbragia, A.M. (ed.) *Euro-politics: Institutions and Policymaking in the "New" European Community* Washington DC: Brookings Institution Press, 1992 pp. 191–224.

Marks, S. 'Myth of reparations' *Central European History* 11, 3 (1978) pp. 231–55.

——*The Illusion of Peace: International Relations in Europe, 1918–33* Basingstoke: Palgrave Macmillan, 2003.

Marsh, P. *The Discipline of Popular Government: Lord Salisbury's Domestic Statecraft 1881–1902* London: Harvester, 1978.

——*Bargaining on Europe: Britain and the First Common Market 1860–1892* London: Yale University Press, 1999.

Martin, L.L. 'Institutions and cooperation: Sanctions during the Falklands Islands conflict' *International Security* 4, 16 (1992) pp. 143–78.

Mawby, S. *Containing Germany: Britain and the Arming of the Federal Republic* Basingstoke: Macmillan, 1999.

May, A. (ed.) *Britain, the Commonwealth and Europe* Basingstoke: Palgrave, 2001.

McDougall, W. *France's Rhineland Diplomacy 1914–24: The Last Bid for a Balance of Power in Europe* Princeton, NJ: Princeton University Press, 1978.

McKay, D. *Federalism and European Union: A Political Economy Perspective* Oxford: Oxford University Press, 1999.

McKay, J. *Labour Party Attitudes to European Integration 1945–75* Unpublished Ph.D. dissertation, University of Birmingham, 2006.

McKercher, B. *Transition of Power: Britain's Loss of Global Pre-eminence to the United States* Cambridge: Cambridge University Press, 1999.

McKinlay, A., Mercer, H. and Rollings, N. 'Reluctant Europeans? The Federation of British Industries and European integration' *Business History* 42, 4 (2000) pp. 91–116.

McLaine, I. *Ministry of Morale: Home Front Morale and the Ministry of Information in World War Two* London: Allen and Unwin, 1979.

Medlicott, W.N. *British Foreign Policy since Versailles* London: Methuen, 1967.

Meyer, A. *Stand Up and Be Counted* London: Heinemann, 1990.

Middlemas, K. (ed.) *Thomas Jones: Whitehall Diary vol 3* Oxford: Oxford University Press, 1969.

——*Orchestrating Europe: The Informal Politics of European Union 1973–1995* London: Fontana, 1997.

Milward A.S. *The Reconstruction of Western Europe* London: Methuen, 1984.

——*The European Rescue of the Nation-State* London: Routledge, 1992.

——*The UK and the EC Volume 1: The Rise and Fall of a National Strategy 1945–63* London: Frank Cass, 2002.

Milward, A.S., Lynch, F., Romero, F., Ranieri, R. and Sørensen, V. *The Frontier of National Sovereignty: History and Theory* London: Routledge, 1993.

Monnet, J. *Memoirs* London: Collins, 1978.

Moon, J. *European Integration in British Politics 1950–63: A Study in Issue Change* Aldershot: Gower, 1985.

Moravcsik, A. *The Choice for Europe: Social Purpose and State Power from Messina to Maastricht* London: Routledge/UCL Press, 1998.

——'What can we learn from the collapse of the European constitutional project?' *Politische Vierteljahresschrift* 47, 2 (2006) pp. 219–41.

Morrison, H. *An Autobiography* London: Odhams, 1960.

Mullen, A. *The British Left's 'Great Debate' on Europe* London: Continuum, 2007.

Mulligan, W. and Simms, B. (eds) *The Primacy of Foreign Policy in British History* Basingstoke: Palgrave, 2010.

Nedergaard, P. 'The 2003 reform of the Common Agricultural Policy: Against all the odds or rational explanations?' *Journal of European Integration* 28, 3 (2006) pp. 203–23.

Newman, S. *March 1939: The British Guarantee to Poland* Oxford: Clarendon Press, 1976.

Nicholson, F. and East, R. (eds) *From the Six to the Twelve: The enlargement of the European Communities* Harlow: Longman, 1987.

Nicolson, H. *The Peacemakers 1919* London: Constable, 1933.

Nicolson, N. (ed.) *Diaries and Letters of Harold Nicolson 1945–62* London: Collins, 1968.

Nielson, K. *Britain, Soviet Russia and the Collapse of the Versailles Order 1919–39* Cambridge: Cambridge University Press, 2006.

Nolfo, E.D. 'The United States, Europe and the Marshall Plan' In Varsori, A. and Calandri, E. (eds) *The Failure of Peace in Europe 1943–48* Basingstoke: Palgrave, 2000 pp. 288–96.

Norton, P. *Conservative Dissidents: Dissent within the Parliamentary Conservative Party 1970–74* London: Temple Smith, 1978.

Norwich, J.J. (ed.) *The Duff Cooper Diaries* London: Weidenfeld and Nicolson, 2005.

Nott, J. *Here Today Gone Tomorrow: Recollections of an Errant Politician* London: Politicos, 2002.

Nutting, A. *Europe Will Not Wait*, London: Hollis and Carter, 1960.

O'Brennan, J. 'Ireland say No (again): The 12 June 2008 referendum on the Lisbon Treaty' *Parliamentary Affairs* 62, 2 (2009) pp. 258–77.

O'Donnell, C.M. and Whitman, R. 'European policy under Gordon Brown: Perspectives on a future prime minister' *International Affairs* 83, 1 (2007) pp. 253–72.

O'Neill, C. *Britain's Entry into the European Community: Report on the Negotiations of 1970–72* London: Cass, 2000.

Onslow, S. *Backbench Debate within the Conservative Party and Its Influence on British Foreign Policy* Basingstoke: Macmillan, 1997.

Oppermann, K. 'The Blair government and Europe: The policy of containing the salience of European integration' *Parliamentary Affairs* 3 (2008) pp. 156–82.

Owen, D. *Balkan Odyssey* New York: Harcourt Bruce, 1995.

Pagden, A. (ed.) *The Idea of Europe: From Antiquity to European Union* Cambridge: Cambridge University Press, 2002.

Parker, R.A.C. 'British government and the coming of war with Germany, 1939' In Foot, M.R.D. (ed.) *War and Society: Historical Essays in Honour and Memory of J. R. Western, 1928–1971* London: Barnes and Noble, 1973, pp. 3–15.

——*Chamberlain and Appeasement* Basingstoke: Macmillan, 1994.

——*The Second World War: A Short History* Oxford: Oxford University Press, 2001.

Parr, H. 'Gone native: The Foreign Office and Harold Wilson's policy' In Daddow, O. (ed.) *Harold Wilson and European Integration* London: Cass, 2003 pp. 75–94.

——*Britain's Policy towards the European Community: Harold Wilson and Britain's World Role 1964–67* London: Routledge, 2005.

Parris, M. *Chance Witness: An Outsider's Life in Politics* London: Viking, 2002.

Parrish, T. *Berlin in the Balance 1945–49* Reading, MA: Perseus Books, 1998.

Patten, C. *Britain, Asia and Europe: A Conservative View* London: Conservative Political Centre, 1995.

Pearce, R. (ed.) *Patrick Gordon Walker: Political Diaries 1932–1971*, London: Historians' Press, 1991.

Peden, G. *British Rearmament and the Treasury 1932–1939* Edinburgh: Scottish Academic Press, 1979.

——'A matter of timing: The economic background to British foreign policy' *History* 69, 1 (1984) pp. 15–28.

Pegg, C.H. *Evolution of the European Idea 1914–32* Chapel Hill: University of North Carolina Press, 1983.

Peters, A.R. *Anthony Eden at the Foreign Office* Aldershot: Gower, 1986.

Pickering, C. ' "Sir Douglas in Euroland". Treasury officials and the European Union 1977–2001' *Public Management* 80, 3 (2002) pp. 583–99.

Pimlott, B. (ed.) *Political Diary of Hugh Dalton* London: Cape, 1986.

——(ed.) *The Second World War Diary of Hugh Dalton* London: Jonathan Cape, 1986.

Pinder, J. *Britain and the Common Market* London: Cresset Press, 1961.

——*The European Community's Policy towards Eastern Europe* London: Chatham House, 1975.

——'Federalism in Britain and Italy: Radicals and the English liberal tradition' In Stirk, P.M.R. (ed.) *European Unity in Context: The Inter-war Period* London: Pinter, 1989 pp. 201–43.

Pinder, J. and Mayne, R. *Federal Union: The Pioneers: A History of Federal Union* Basingstoke: Macmillan, 1990.

Pinder, J. and Pryce, R. *Europe After De Gaulle: Towards the United States of Europe* Harmondsworth: Penguin, 1969.

Pinder, J., Pryce, R. and Duff, A. *Maastricht and Beyond: Building the European Union* London: Routledge, 1994.

Pinder, J. and Usherwood, S. *The European Union: A Very Short Introduction* Oxford: Oxford University Press, 2007.

Pollack, M. 'Representing diffuse interests in EC policy making' *Journal of European Public Policy* 4, 4 (1997) pp. 572–90.

Prazmowska, A. *Britain, Poland and the Eastern Front, 1939* Cambridge: Cambridge University Press, 1987.

——*History of Poland* London: Palgrave Macmillan, 2006.

Pym, F. *The Politics of Consent* London: Hamish Hamilton, 1984.

Ramsden, J. *The Age of Churchill and Eden, 1940–1957* London: Longman, 1994.

——*Winds of Change: Macmillan to Heath, 1957–75* London: Longman, 1995.

Redmond, J. *The Next Mediterranean Enlargement of the EC: Turkey, Cyprus and Malta?* Aldershot: Dartmouth, 1993.

Redwood, J. *Our Currency, Our Country: The Dangers of European Monetary Union* Harmondsworth: Penguin, 1997.

——*Stars and Strife: The Coming Conflict between the USA and European Union* London: Palgrave, 2001.

Reynolds, D. 'The "Big Three" and the Division of Europe 1945–49' *Diplomacy and Statecraft* 1, 2 (1990) pp. 111–36.

——*Britannia Overruled: British Policy and World Power in the 20th Century* London: Longman, 1991.

——*From World War to Cold War: Churchill, Roosevelt and the International History of the 1940s* Oxford: Oxford University Press, 2006.

——*Summits: Six Meetings That Shaped the Twentieth Century* London: Allen Lane, 2007.

Ridley, N. *My Style of Government* London: Hutchinson, 1991.

Rietbergen, P. *Europe: A Cultural History* London: Routledge, 1998.

Ritchie, R. *Enoch Powell on 1992* London: Anaya, 1989.

Roberts, A. *Holy Fox: A Biography of Edward Halifax* London: Weidenfeld and Nicolson, 1991.

Robins, L.J. *The Reluctant Party: Labour and the EEC 1961–75* London: Hesketh, 1979.

Rollings, N. 'British Industry and European Integration 1961–73: From first application to final membership' *Business and Economic History* 27, 2 (1998) pp. 444–54.

Rosamund, B. 'The uniting of Europe and the foundation of EU studies: Revisiting the neofunctionalism of Ernest B. Haas' *Journal of European Public Policy* 12, 2 (2005) pp. 237–54.

——*Theories of European Integration* Basingstoke: Palgrave, 2000.

Rosamond, B. and Wincott, D. 'Constitutionalism, European Integration and British Political Economy' *British Journal of Politics and International Relations* 8, 1 (2006) pp. 1–14.

Ross, G. 'What do "Europeans" think? Analyses of the European Union's current crisis by European elites' *Journal of Common Market Studies* 46, 2 (2008) pp. 389–412.

Salazmann, S.C. *Great Britain, Germany and the Soviet Union: Rapallo and After, 1922–34* Woodbridge: Boydell and RHS, 2003.

Salisbury, K. 'British policy and German unity at the end of the Second World War' *English Historical Review* 94 (1979) pp. 786–804.

Salmon, P. 'Reluctant engagement: Britain and continental Europe 1890–1939' *Diplomacy and Statecraft* 8, 3 (1997) pp. 139–64.

Scammell, C.M. 'The Royal Navy and the strategic origins of the Anglo–German naval agreement of 1935' *Journal of Strategic Studies* 20, 2 (1997) pp. 92–118.

Scammell, W.M. *The International Economy since 1945*, 2nd edn, London: Macmillan, 1983.

Schaad, M. *Bullying Bonn: Anglo–German Diplomacy and European Integration 1955–61* Basingstoke: Macmillan, 2000.

Schain, M. (ed.) *The Marshall Plan: Fifty Years After* Basingstoke: Palgrave, 2001.

Schenk, C.R. *Britain and the Sterling Area: From Devaluation to Convertibility in the 1950s* London: Routledge, 1994.

Schmidt, V.A. 'European elites on the European Union: What vision for the future?' In Gamble, A. and Lane, D. (eds) *European Union and World Politics: Consensus and Division* Basingstoke: Palgrave, 2009 chapter 13.

Schnear, J. 'Hopes deferred or shattered: The British Labour left and the Third Force movement 1945–49' *Journal of Modern History* 56, 2 (1984) pp. 197–226.

Schroeder, P.W. 'Munich and the British tradition', *Historical Journal* 19, 1 (1976) 223–43.

Schwabe, K. *Woodrow Wilson, Revolutionary Germany and Peacemaking 1918–19* Chapel Hill: University of North Carolina Press, 1985.

Schweiger, C. 'British-German relations in the European Union after the war on Iraq' *German Politics* 13, 1 (2004) pp. 35–55.

Seldon, A. 'The Churchill administration 1951–55' In Hennessy, P. and Seldon, A. (eds) *Ruling Performance: British Governments from Attlee to Thatcher* Oxford: Blackwell, 1987 pp. 63–97.

——*Major: A Political Life* London: Weidenfeld and Nicolson, 1997.

Self, R.C. (ed.) *The Austen Chamberlain Diary Letters* Cambridge: Royal Historical Society Camden Series, 1995.

——*Britain, America and the War Debt Controversy: The Economic Diplomacy of an Unspecial Relationship 1917–1941* London: Routledge, 2006.

Shapiro, M. 'The European Court of Justice' In Sbragia, A.M. (ed.) *Euro-politics: Institutions and Policymaking in the "New" European Community* Washington, DC: Brookings Institution Press, 1992 pp. 123–56.

Sharp, A. 'Britain and the channel tunnel 1919–20' *Australian Journal of Politics and History* 25 (1979) pp. 210–15.

——*The Versailles Settlement: Peacemaking in Paris 1919* London: Macmillan, 1991.

Shepherd, G. *Shepherd's Watch* London: Politicos, 2000.

Sherrington, P. 'Confronting Europe: UK political parties and the EU 2000–2005' *British Journal of Politics and International Relations* 8, 1 (2006) pp. 69–78.

Shlaim, A. 'Prelude to downfall: The British offer of union to France, June 1940' *Journal of Contemporary History* 9, 3 (1974), pp. 26–63.

——*Britain and the Origins of European Unity 1940–51* Reading: University of Reading Graduate School of Contemporary European Studies, 1978.

Sked, A. and Cook, C. *Post-war Britain: A Political History* Harmondsworth: Penguin, 1990.

Smart, N. (ed.) *The Diaries of Robert Bernays, 1932–39: An Insider's Account of the House of Commons* Lampeter: Edwin Mellon Press, 1996.

Smith, J. 'A missed opportunity? New Labour's European policy 1997–2005' *International Affairs* 81, 4 (2005) pp. 703–21.

Smith, M. *British Air Strategy Between the Wars* Oxford: Clarendon Press, 1984.

Sowemimo, M. 'Conservative Party and European integration 1988–95' *Party Politics* 2, 1 (1996) pp. 77–97.

Spaak, P.H. *The Continuing Battle: Memoirs of a European 1936–1966* Trans. H. Fox, London: Weidenfeld and Nicolson, 1971.

Spence, J. 'Movements in the public mood 1961–75' In Jowell, R. and Hoinville, G. (eds) *Britain into Europe: Public Opinion and the EEC 1961–75* London: Croom Helm, 1976 pp. 18–36.

Spicer, M. *A Treaty Too Far: A New Policy for Europe* London: Fourth Estate, 1992.

Stafford, P. 'Political autobiography and the art of the plausible: R.A. Butler at the Foreign Office 1938–39' *Historical Journal* 28, 4 (1985) pp. 901–22.

Stannard Baker, R. *Woodrow Wilson and the World Settlement* Garden City NY: Doubleday, 1922.

Stephens, P. *Politics and the Pound: The Tories, the Economy and Europe* London: Macmillan, 1996.

——'The Blair government and Europe' *Political Quarterly* 72, 1 (2001) pp. 67–75.

Stirk, P.M.R. 'Introduction: Crisis and continuity in interwar Europe' In Stirk, P.M.R. (ed.) *European Unity in Context: The Interwar Period* London, Pinter, 1989 pp. 1–22.

Stoddart, K. 'Nuclear weapons in Britain's policy towards France 1960–74' *Diplomacy and Statecraft* 18, 4 (2007) pp. 719–44.

Stone, G. 'Britain, France and the Spanish problem 1936–39' In Richardson, D. and Stone, G. (eds) *Decisions and Diplomacy: Essays in Twentieth Century International History* London: Routledge, 1995, pp. 129–52.

Stuart, M. *Douglas Hurd: The Public Servant: An Authorised Biography* Edinburgh: Mainstream, 1998.

Taylor, J. *Please Stay to the Adjournment* Studley: Brewin Books, 2003.

Teasdale, A.L. 'The politics of the 1999 European elections' *Government and Opposition* 34, 4 (1999) pp. 435–55.

Tebbit, N. *Upwardly Mobile* London: Weidenfeld and Nicolson, 1988.

Templewood, Lord (Samuel Hoare) *Nine Troubled Years* London: Collins, 1954.

Thatcher, M. *Downing Street Years* London: HarperCollins, 1993.

——*Complete Public Statements of Margaret Thatcher, 1945–90* Oxford: Oxford University Press, 1998. CD-Rom.

——*Statecraft: Strategies for a Changing World* London: HarperCollins, 2003.

Thompson, D. 'The Rome Treaty and the law' *Crossbow*, July–September 1962. London: Bow Group.

Thompson, H. *The British Conservative Government and the European Exchange Rate Mechanism 1979–1994* London: Pinter, 1996.

Thorpe, A. '"In a rather emotional state" The Labour Party and British intervention in Greece 1944–45' *English Historical Review* 21, (2006) pp. 1015–1105.

Thorpe, D.R. *Alec Douglas-Home* London: Sinclair-Stevenson, 1996.

Tomlinson, J. 'Marshall Aid and the "shortage economy" in Britain in the 1940s' *Contemporary European History* 9, 1 (2000) pp. 137–55.

Toomey, J. *Harold Wilson's EEC Application* Dublin: UCD Press, 2007.

Toschi, S. 'Washington-London-Paris: An untenable triangle, 1960–63' *Journal of European Integration History* 1, 2 (1995) pp. 81–110.

Trachtenberg, M. *Reparations in World Politics: France and European Economic Diplomacy 1916–23* New York: Columbia University Press, 1980.

Tratt, J. *The Macmillan Government and Europe: A Study in the Process of Policy Development* Basingstoke: Macmillan, 1996.

Tsebelis, G. 'Thinking about the recent past and the future of the EU' *Journal of Common Market Studies* 46, 2 (2008) pp. 265–92.

Turner, J. *The Tories and Europe* Manchester: Manchester University Press, 2000.

Urban, G. *Diplomacy and Illusion in the Court of Margaret Thatcher: An Insider's View* London: I.B. Tauris, 1996.

Urwin, D.W. *The Community of Europe: A History of European Integration since 1945* Harlow: Longman, 1991 pp. 7–12.

Vanthoor, W.F.W. *A Chronological History of the European Union* Cheltenham: Edward Elgar, 1999.

Waley, D. *British Public Opinion and the Abyssinian War* London: Temple Smith, 1975.

Walker, P. *The Ascent of Britain*, London: Sidgwick and Jackson, 1977.

——*Staying Power: An Autobiography* London: Bloomsbury, 1991.

Walker Smith, D. and Walker, P. *A Call to the Commonwealth: The Constructive Case* London: Methuen, 1962.

Wallace, W. *Foreign Policy Process in Britain* London: RIIA, 1975.

——'Defence: The defence of sovereignty or the defence of Germany?' In Moran, R. and Bray, C. (eds) *Partners and Rivals in Western Europe: Britain, France and Germany* Aldershot: Gower, 1986 pp. 230–32.

——'The collapse of British foreign policy' *International Affairs* 82, 1 (2005) pp. 53–68.

Watkin, K. *Britain Divided: The Effect of the Spanish Civil War on British Public Opinion* London: Nelson, 1963.

Watt, D.C. *How War Came: The Immediate Origins of the Second World War 1938–39* London: Heinemann, 1989.

Webb, P. 'The attitudinal assimilation of Europe by the Conservative parliamentary party' *British Politics* 3 (2008) pp. 427–44.

Weigall, D. and Stirk, P. (eds) *The Origins and Development of the European Community* Leicester: Leicester University Press, 1992.

Weiler, J.H.M. 'The reformation of European constitutionalism' *Journal of Common Market Studies* 35, 1 (1997) pp. 97–131.

Wendt, B.J. '"Economic appeasement" A crisis strategy' In Mommsen, W.J. and Kettenacker, L. (eds) *The Fascist Challenge and the Policy of Appeasement* London: Allen and Unwin, 1983 pp. 157–72.

Westlake, M. *Britain's Emerging Euro-Elites* Aldershot: Dartmouth, 1994.

White, R. 'The Europeanism of Coudenhove-Kalergi' In Stirk, P.M.R. (ed.) *European Unity in Context: The Interwar Period* London: Pinter, 1989 pp. 23–40.

——'Cordial caution: The British response to the French proposal for European federal union in 1930' In Bosco, A. (ed.) *The Federal Idea: Volume 1: The History of Federalism from the Enlightenment to 1945* London: Lothian Foundation Press, 1991 pp. 237–62.

Whiteley, P., Stewart, P., Sanders, M. and Clarke, H. 'The issue agenda and voting in 2005' In Norris, P. and Wlezien, C. (eds) *Britain Votes 2005* Oxford: Oxford University Press, 2005, pp. 146–61.

Williams, A. 'Sir John Bradbury and the Reparations Commission 1920–25' *Diplomacy and Statecraft* 13, 3 (2002) pp. 81–102.

Wilson, G. *Special Interests and Policy Making: Agricultural Politics and Politics in Britain and the United States of America* London: Wiley, 1977.

Wilson, H. *The Labour Government 1964–70: A Personal Record* London: Weidenfeld and Nicolson, 1971.

Wilson, K. *Channel Tunnel Visions, 1850–1945: Dreams and Nightmares* London: Hambledon, 1994.

Wincott, D. 'A community of law? "European" law and judicial politics: The Court of Justice and beyond' *Government and Opposition* 35, 1 (2000) pp. 3–26.

Windrich, E. *British Labour's Foreign Policy* Palo Alto, CA: Stanford University Press, 1952.

Woodward, E.L. and Butler, R. (eds) *Documents on British Foreign Policy*, 2nd series, vol. 1, London: HMSO, 1949.

——*Documents on British Foreign Policy*, 3rd Series, vol. 1, London: HMSO, 1949.

Wright, J. *Gustav Stresemann: Weimar's Greatest Statesman* Oxford: Oxford University Press, 2002.

Young, H. *One of Us: Life of Margaret Thatcher* London: Pan, 1990.

——*This Blessed Plot: Britain and Europe from Churchill to Blair* London: Macmillan, 1998.

Young, J.W. 'Churchill's "no" to Europe: The "rejection" of European Union by Churchill's post-war government' *Historical Journal* 28, 4 (1985) pp. 923–37.

——'German rearmament and the European Defence Community' In Young, J.W. (ed.) *The Foreign Policy of Churchill's Peacetime Administration 1951–55* Leicester: Leicester University Press, 1988 pp. 81–108.

——'The Schuman plan and the British Association' In Young, J.W. (ed.) *The Foreign Policy of Churchill's Peacetime Administration* Leicester: Leicester University Press, 1988 pp. 109–34.

——*Britain and European Unity 1945–1999*, 2nd edn, Basingstoke: Macmillan, 2000.

Young, J.W. (ed.) *The Foreign Policy of Churchill's Peacetime Administration 1951–55* Leicester: Leicester University Press, 1988.

Zeigler, P. *Harold Wilson: The Authorized Life* London: Weidenfeld and Nicolson, 1993.

Zurcher, A.J. *The Struggle to Unite Europe 1940–58* New York: New York University Press, 1958.

Websites

BBC News On-line www.news.bbc.co.uk
Cabinet Office www.cabinetoffice.gov.uk
Conservative Party www.conservatives.com
Coverbrowser www.coverbrowser.com
Daily Telegraph www.telegraph.co.uk

Eurobarometer www.europa.eu/public_opinion
House of Commons Publications www.publications.parliament.uk
I Want a Referendum Campaign www.iwantareferendum.com
Political Parties' Election Manifestos www.psr.keele.ac.uk
Prime Minister's Office: Number 10 Downing Street www.number10.gov.uk
Sun Headlines www.sunheadlines.blogspot.com
Thatcher Foundation and Archive www.margaretthatcher.org

Archival collections cited

Archives of the British Conservative Party Harvester Press microfiche
Archives of the British Labour Party Harvester Press microfiche
Lord Boyle Mss Brotherton Library, Leeds University
Brooks, Collin Mss Private possession
Cabinet, Prime Minister's Office and miscellaneous governmental papers National Archives, Kew
Chamberlain, Neville Mss Birmingham University Library
Conservative Party Archive Bodleian Library, Oxford
Dodds-Parker, Douglas Mss Magdalen College, Oxford
Eden, Anthony [Avon] Mss Birmingham University Library
Headlam, Cutherbert Durham Record Office
Lord Hinchingbrooke Mss Dorset Record Office
Macmillan Cabinet Papers 1957–63 on-line Adam Matthew Publishing
Macmillan, Harold (personal and ministerial) Bodleian Library, Oxford
Makins, Ernest Bodleian Library, Oxford
Marten, Neill Mss Bodleian Library, Oxford
Lord Selborne [Wolmer] Mss Bodleian Library, Oxford
Thatcher, Margaret Mss Thatcher Foundation www.margaretthatcher.org
Lord Winterton Mss Bodleian Library, Oxford
Lord Woolton, Mss Bodleian Library, Oxford

Index